Surviving Amid Chaos

Weapons of Mass Destruction

Series Editors: Joseph M. Siracusa and Aiden Warren

The series focuses on weapons of mass destruction (WMDs), discussing all issues surrounding nuclear, chemical, radiological, and biological weapons. The volumes aim to present varying historical, contemporary, state, non-state, traditional, and non-traditional approaches from emerging scholars, established academics, and those involved in the foreign and security policy domains.

In the context of the nuclear section of the WMD series, it is evident that despite there being fewer nuclear weapons today than during the Cold War era, the threat remains paramount. More states in more unstable regions have attained such weapons, terrorists may pursue them, and the command and control systems in even the most sophisticated nuclear-armed states remain susceptible not only to system and human error but, increasingly, to cyber-attacks. The failure of armed states to disarm, the inability to prevent new states and non-state actors from gaining access to WMDs, and the expansion of nuclear energy plants present a real security danger today. As such, the series is timely and necessary.

Joseph M. Siracusa is professor of Human Security and International Diplomacy and Deputy Dean of Global and Language Studies at the Royal Melbourne Institute of Technology University, Australia.

Aiden Warren is senior lecturer in the School of Global, Urban and Social Studies at the Royal Melbourne Institute of Technology University in Melbourne, Australia.

Titles in the Series

A History of U.S. Nuclear Testing and Its Influence on Nuclear Thought, 1945–1963
Joseph Siracusa and David M. Blades (2014)
The Challenges of Nuclear Non-Proliferation, Richard D. Burns and Philip Coyle (2015)
Nuclear Iran: Accord and Détente since the Geneva Agreement of 2013
Nader Entessar and Kaveh Afrasiabi (2015)
Weapons of Mass Destruction: An Introduction to Today's Security Dilemma
Richard D. Burns, Joseph Siracusa, and Aiden Warren (2016)
India-Pakistan Nuclear Diplomacy: Constructivism and the Prospects for Nuclear Arms Control and Disarmament in South Asia, Mario Carranza (2016)

Surviving Amid Chaos

Israel's Nuclear Strategy

Louis René Beres

ROWMAN & LITTLEFIELD
Lanham • Boulder • New York • London

Published by Rowman & Littlefield
A wholly owned subsidiary of The Rowman & Littlefield Publishing Group, Inc.
4501 Forbes Boulevard, Suite 200, Lanham, Maryland 20706
www.rowman.com

Unit A, Whitacre Mews, 26-34 Stannary Street, London SE11 4AB

British Library Cataloguing in Publication Information Available

Library of Congress Cataloging-in-Publication Data

Names: Beres, Louis René
Title: Surviving amid chaos : Israel's nuclear strategy / Louis René Beres.
Description: Lanham : Rowman & Littlefield, [2016] | Series: Weapons of mass destruction series | Includes index.
Identifiers: LCCN 2015050840 (print) | LCCN 2016000178 (ebook) | ISBN 9781442253254 (cloth : alk. paper) | ISBN 9781442253261 (Electronic)
Subjects: LCSH: Nuclear weapons—Israel. | Nuclear weapons—Government policy—Israel. | Israel—Military policy.
Classification: LCC U264.5.I75 B47 2016 (print) | LCC U264.5.I75 (ebook) | DDC 355.02/17095694—dc23 LC record available at http://lccn.loc.gov/2015050840

∞ ™ The paper used in this publication meets the minimum requirements of American National Standard for Information Sciences Permanence of Paper for Printed Library Materials, ANSI/NISO Z39.48-1992.

Printed in the United States of America

In loving memory of my parents, Sigmund and Margaret Beres, who upon fleeing Nazi-occupied Vienna on their wedding night in July 1938, learned a still-earlier meaning of Jewish survival amid chaos.

Contents

Acknowledgments

Over many years of working on variously difficult analytic elements of Israeli nuclear strategy, I have been the beneficiary of some genuinely wise counsel, in the United States and also in Israel. For readily understandable reasons, it is probably best not to thank my intellectually supportive Israeli friends and colleagues too precisely in such a book. Nonetheless, as two of these "wise men" were conspicuously towering figures in Israel's military and defense communities and are no longer alive, I do think it proper to mention them here.

First, I gratefully acknowledge Aharon Yariv, a onetime head of IDF Military Intelligence. I knew Major General Yariv only years later, when he had become director of the Jaffee Center for Strategic Studies and invited me on several occasions to lecture at his institute. I learned a great deal about my "opaque" subject on those visits to Tel Aviv in the 1980s and came to understand almost immediately why "Ahrele" had earlier emerged as such a gifted intelligence chief, especially during the Six Day War.

Second, Yuval Ne'eman, a recognizably world-class physicist and later, president of Tel Aviv University, became an early supporter of my lectures and writings and until the end had engaged me in an almost continual strategic dialogue. On at least a few occasions, Professor Ne'eman carried out these illuminating conversations with me over fig ice cream (always his favorite flavor) at the TAU faculty club. During his own remarkable tenure in Military Intelligence and Planning, including work as chief scientist at the Ministry of Defense, Yuval, who had been educated at Imperial College, London, and was later dispatched to the War College in Paris, was appropriately credited with bringing computers and similarly "new technologies" to Israel's MI. From Ne'eman, as well as from Yariv, I learned many things about crafting a prudentially useful strategic nuclear doctrine for Israel, a country smaller than America's Lake Michigan.

More recently, I have benefited from the close support of two very distinguished American flag officers, General John T. "Jack" Chain (USAF/ret.), and Admiral Leon "Bud" Edney (USN/ret.). Both Jack and Bud have been my many-times coauthors on a substantial number of published commentaries on Israeli security matters, and each has been willing to enrich my "nuclear work" with his own unique combination of intellect, courage, and integrity. As to any special acquaintance with pertinent military matters in this book, it is certainly worth mentioning that General Chain is a former Commander in Chief, US Strategic Air Command (CINCSAC), and Admiral Edney served as NATO Supreme Allied Commander, Atlantic.

I remain greatly privileged by their special friendship and counsel.

It is perhaps also reasonable for me to mention my own *Project Daniel*, which, apropos of tackling so plainly a delicate security issue, had been tasked back in 2003 with more systematically identifying Israel's principal nuclear challenges and opportunities. In addition to the other five members of this unique project, I wish to thank Hon. Zalman Shoval, Israel's two-time ambassador to the United States, for his valuable assistance and good offices. Initially, of course, *Project Daniel*'s principal concern had been with managing the already unhidden nuclear danger from Iran, but today, although this specific danger remains front and center in any convincing hierarchy of perils, there simultaneously exist assorted other worrisome landscapes of Israeli nuclear concern. These sometimes intersecting or possibly even "synergistic" threats, as this book shall soon reveal, now loom more or less menacingly on Jerusalem's strategic horizon.

Reciprocally, these particular threats will require a distinctly feasible configuration of apt Israeli responses. It is my sincere hope that this book can become part of remediating such prospectively existential hazards and, correspondingly, suggesting certain still-needed national nuclear policy refinements.

To this pleasing record of acknowledgments, I now also wish to thank Marie-Claire Antoine, my editor, for encouraging a newly retired professor to delay his once-calming plans for a life of leisure, and Valerie, my dear wife of almost fifty years, for encouraging me to seize on a reassuringly tranquil "next chapter." In this complementary combination of influences, at least with reference to an ancient philosopher's insightful "unity of opposites," Heraclitus was substantially correct.

Finally, much as I might wish it were otherwise, I alone must bear responsibility for what has been written in this complex little book, including any still-remaining errors and infelicities, which I must now also claim as my very own.

Louis René Beres
West Lafayette, Indiana
December, 2015

Introduction

Intellectual Antecedents and Scientific Imperatives

"I tell you, ye have still chaos in you."

—Friedrich Nietzsche, *Thus Spake Zarathustra*

For many years, I have been studying a subject that does not really seem to exist but is nonetheless of obvious significance. Even now, with the Middle East in the grip of an evidently expanding chaos, Israel's nuclear strategy appears notably speculative and conjectural. In any discernibly precise forms, at least, Israel's "bomb" is still carefully closeted in the tiny country's "basement." To date, it has never been *meaningfully* acknowledged.[1]

Still, anyone who examines the wider region's prospects for war and peace will readily appreciate the utterly core importance of Israel's nuclear doctrine and, of course, its presumed nuclear weapons.

This is a book about this vital doctrine and those corresponding weapons. It is *not* an investigative effort designed to ascertain or identify what is actually being fashioned in Jerusalem and Tel Aviv. It is surely not just another exposé intended to elicit ad hominem judgments and gossipy controversies; rather, it offers a more appropriately analytic assessment of what Israel's nuclear strategy actually *ought to be*. In this regard, it represents a conscientious and purposefully scientific assessment, one that is expressly oriented toward further enhancing a beleaguered mini-state's national security.

Philosophically and epistemologically, I need offer no excuses for expressing any open concern for Israel's survival. After all, there is nothing about such concern that should in any way undermine proper science. Indeed, there is a distinctly central moral imperative to enlist science on behalf of human rights at every amenable level of world affairs.[2] This is an imperative that I accept, seriously and unapologetically.

Born in Switzerland at the end of World War II as the only child of Austrian Jewish refugees, my own life has been shaped in considerable measure by Israel's indispensable existential struggle. In 1967, shortly after arriving at Princeton to begin my doctoral studies, I quickly discovered the university's historic and special place in the development of *American* nuclear weapons and policy. From that discovery, which included such towering Princeton figures as Albert Einstein and J. Robert

Oppenheimer, it was easy to fathom that certain of these same geostrategic insights could be effectively applied to other countries. Unsurprisingly, it had then occurred to me, as it had occurred much earlier to David Ben-Gurion, Israel's first prime minister, that the pertinent list should *especially* include Israel.

In 1971, by the time I had become a professor at Purdue University in the American Midwest, I began to lecture in Israel and Europe about various critical elements of Israel's strategic doctrine, including venues at leading Israeli centers for strategic studies and the country's IDF National Security College.[3] In 1986, I edited one of the very first books on this subject, gathering together assorted original essays on these complex issues, written by Israel's leading nuclear strategists and also by a few Americans of equal stature. The collection *Security or Armageddon: Israel's Nuclear Strategy*,[4] contained twelve never-before published chapters on Israel's nuclear options. These chapters, nuanced and comprehensive, ran the gamut of constituent concepts and issues, including deliberate ambiguity, regional proliferation, implications for superpower strategic policies, and prospects for nuclear terrorism.[5]

Then, as now, the announced task was for creating systematic and scientific analyses. Then, as now, it was an inherently problematic plan. By definition, the subject lacked any regional empirical content, and many needed judgments were unavoidably based on extrapolations from what one prominent American scholar had called the protracted US-Soviet nuclear standoff—that is, a "delicate balance of terror."[6] Naturally, even the selected universe of "cases" pertaining to what American atomic physicist J. Robert Oppenheimer had identified metaphorically as "two scorpions in a bottle"[7] was conspicuously small and therefore of distinctly limited analytical import. After all (fortunately, of course), there had never been any genuine nuclear war.

Ultimately, the source of all proper science, whatever the particular investigator's underlying values, must be a determined will to truth, not a self-serving will to power.[8] In applying this apt source to particular matters of Israel's nuclear strategy, a number of limitations generic to this rarefied analytic genre should now be pointed out. Most importantly perhaps, laypersons and professional strategists alike will need to understand the basically subjective nature of relevant probability and risk calculations. Despite the fashionably mathematical language found in many contemporary "expert" assessments, such analytic estimates of probability are ordinarily little other than more or less judicious expressions of personal belief. Similarly, national policy-guiding expectations of risk have typically been extrapolated directly from these intrinsically subjective probability calculations.[9]

There are useful examples. Over a number of years, however clandestinely, both Israeli and American strategists have sought to assign a meaningful numerical value to the probability of an eventual Iranian nuclear attack. But any truly accurate nuclear attack probability estimates would need to be based on the recorded frequency of past events. So just how many nuclear attacks are there for us to actually study?

The answer, of course, is none.

The only two examples of atomic weapons being used in war (Hiroshima and Nagasaki in August 1945) refer to a nonnuclear adversary with which the attacking country (the United States) was already engaged in purely conventional warfare. For analytical purposes, those circumstances cannot be correctly construed as an example of a true nuclear war.

In essence, nuclear strategy is a "game" that certain sane national leaders have to play—for them, there is no real alternative—but it is also irremediably a contest that will never fully account for Carl von Clausewitz's (1780–1831) "fog of war" or his idea of "friction."[10] When life insurance actuaries compile biographic and demographic statistics to determine the expected morbidity of their clients, they encounter no dearth of relevant data. But when strategists seek to determine the likelihood of a catastrophic Iranian response to an American and/or Israeli preemption targeting that Islamic country's nuclear assets and infrastructures, there are no usable data.

This doesn't mean that Israel's nuclear strategy can never be defended as a useful or cost-effective activity—quite the contrary—but rather that any such strategy must always be contingent on very selective or partial knowledge. This cautionary caveat becomes even more compelling in those particular cases where a nuclear or prospectively nuclear adversary might still be judged "irrational."[11]

Presently, the well-publicized case of Iran should come most urgently to mind.

Unavoidably, going forward, Israeli nuclear risk assessment will be largely subjective, but it will still need to be accurate. This observation is not necessarily distinctive to the atomic age. Much earlier, in the second century of the Common Era, a grave strategic mistake was made in ancient Israel.

In the year 132 CE, the Bar Kokhba Rebellion pushed the Jewish people to the outer margins of history. In his important book on that event, Yehoshafat Harkabi, a former head of Israeli Military Intelligence (AMAN), speaks of the dangers that lurk in unrealistic assessments of risk. By choosing rebelliousness detached from responsibility, argues Harkabi, Israel behaved suicidally.[12]

Harkabi maintains that risk taking for Israel is "occasionally necessary" but "the national existence is never to be jeopardized." In principle, this appears to be abundantly sound advice; yet in the nuclear age, not taking certain very great risks (e.g., preemption against a still nonnuclear Iran) could sometimes entail even greater risks (e.g., in the future, Iranian nuclear attack). How, therefore, acknowledging the fixed limits of scientific examination, shall Jerusalem best weigh these and other interrelated risks?[13]

In good measure, the answer to this question must involve judgments based on preferences (Sigmund Freud would call them "wish fulfillment") rather than on consciously dispassionate appraisals. "Men as a rule willingly believe what they want to believe," says Julius Caesar in chapter 18 of his *Gallic War*. For Israel, the enduring impact of Caesar's insight should already have become evident on October 6, 1973, with the unexpected start of the Yom Kippur War. Until then, the country had been committed to an idea known generally as "the concept," or the *kontzeptziya*—the self-deceiving notion that the Arabs were somehow unwilling or incapable of renewing their hostilities against the Jewish State.

AMAN's overall assessment of enemy designs, which had lasted until October 5, 1973, was that war was "highly improbable" or "improbable." It was precisely this blatantly unwarranted assumption that created a more modern (than Bar Kokhba) and monumental intelligence blunder—the *mechdal* in postwar Hebrew parlance. To be sure, this is a blunder that could be repeated at much greater cost in the future.

Ultimately, of course, the Israeli strategists' overriding objective must be avoidance of a nuclear war. Even a "limited" nuclear exchange would create an unprecedented catastrophe. The immediate effects of the explosions—thermal and nuclear radiation and blast damages—would generate large and potentially intolerable swaths of devastation.

In substantial numbers, victims would suffer flash and flame burns. Retinal burns could occur in the eyes of persons as distant as several hundred miles beyond the actual explosions. Persons would be crushed by collapsing buildings or torn apart by flying glass. Others would fall victim to raging firestorms. Expectedly, fallout injuries would include whole-body radiation injury, more evidently superficial radiation burns occasioned by soft radiation, and assorted injuries caused by the deposit of radioactive substances within each affected human body.

Even with only the Hiroshima and Nagasaki events as tangible empirical evidence, we can still know reliably that ordinary medical facilities would be taxed far beyond their capacities and that essential water supplies would quickly become unusable. Almost certainly, housing and shelter would no longer be available to the survivors. Alarmingly, transportation and communication could break down to near prehistoric levels. Overwhelming food shortages, too, would likely become the new norm.

There is more. As Israel and its nuclear adversary would have entered into a nuclear exchange as modern industrial economies, their prior networks of interlocking and interdependent exchange systems would now lie in tatters. Virtually everyone in the impacted states would be deprived of any manageable means to earn a livelihood. Emergency services would effectively disappear altogether. Before anything could be born from such a Dantesque calamity, a heroic gravedigger would have to wield the forceps.

As this book will soon clarify, Israel must always do everything possible to avoid any actual nuclear exchange. Always, its nuclear weapons must be oriented toward deterrence *ex ante*, not revenge *ex post*. In the end, as is likely already understood even by laypersons, there can never be any meaningful idea of victory in a nuclear war.[14]

ANALYTIC MEANINGS OF CHAOS

Israel's nuclear strategy, as the book title suggests, can never be assessed or fashioned in a world-historical vacuum. Inevitably, it will be impacted by the degree and quality of prevailing international order. More precisely, ongoing and heightening turmoil in the Middle East signals potentially catastrophic regional transformations. For Israel, attentive to strategic "synergies" between area wars, insurgencies, and revolutions, the greatest dangers could now stem from the numbingly growing prospect of *chaos*.

For the most part, the world system has been "merely" *anarchic* since the Peace of Westphalia, in 1648,[15] but anarchy is not the same as chaos. The differences here can be germane to Israel's nuclear strategy.

Anarchy means "only" the absence of government. In world politics, the prevailing structure of power and authority remains anarchic because, quite literally, there exists no designated center of control above the separate nation-states. Chaos is really much "more" than anarchy. In virtually any "form," it can play havoc with the best laid plans of nations. It represents a constantly changing or protean condition, one that can readily impair "normal," and possibly indispensable, security preparations.

This condition is markedly different from the more "normal" chaos that has been associated, conceptually and historically, with Clausewitz's "fog of war." Authentic chaos describes a genuinely deep and wholly systemic unraveling that can rapidly create unprecedented and primal forms of conflict. Even in an improved world system that was no longer anarchic, chaos could still promptly smother any new hopes for national or global survival.

In world politics, strategic truth can be counterintuitive. In world politics, which is not geometry, the whole can sometimes be greater than the sum of its parts. For Israel, the most obvious chaos-based perils concern the currently expanding violence in Iraq and Syria and the near-simultaneous developments of Iranian nuclearization and Palestinian statehood.

In facing these variously intersecting perils, Jerusalem is already keenly aware that the Hashemite monarchy in Jordan is vulnerable to Islamic radicalism and the current al-Sisi military regime in Cairo may not be able to control the reaspiring Muslim Brotherhood indefinitely.

Pakistan is another critical source of wider area transformation, from mere anarchy to genuine chaos. In this connection, if the country's already nuclear regime should fall to Jihadists, all other regional sources of chaotic disintegration could rapidly pale into relative insignificance. It may be significant that Pakistan is currently reorienting its own nuclear strategy toward a greater reliance on tactical or "war-fighting" nuclear weapons. Although the regime's rationale here is plainly to enhance national nuclear deterrence vis-à-vis India, it could also create foreseeably great hazards if there should ever be a successful coup d'état in Islamabad.

In a presumptively worst case scenario for Israel, Jihadists would take interpenetrating and simultaneous control in several of the more unstable Arab and North African governments. Ultimately, these "martyrdom-driven" leaders could get their hands on certain formidable weapons of mass destruction. This conceivable prospect, even if the acquired weapons were all to remain nonnuclear, could still bring to mind the more or less plausible scenario of a *suicide bomber in macrocosm.*

This is a prospect that is already being taken seriously in specific reference to coup-vulnerable Pakistan and a nearly nuclear Iran.

With the advance of chaos, Israel might have to face certain nuclear and ideologically Islamist enemies on both Iranian and Arab fronts. Moreover, even in the absence of old enemies with new nuclear arms, nuclear and biological materials could still find their way to Hezbollah in Lebanon and/or to Hamas. All along the way, both Jerusalem and Washington could find themselves in a problematic position of having to take sides with one set of enemies against another.

The English philosopher Thomas Hobbes had already recognized that although international relations must exist in a "state of nature," a condition of anarchy (not of chaos), these relations are nonetheless more tolerable than the condition of individual human beings who must live in anarchy.[16] This is so, argued Hobbes back in the seventeenth century, because nations lack the capacity of individuals to completely destroy one another.

Not any more.

Now, proliferation of nuclear weapons, especially in the Middle East, could reduce the usual anarchy of international relations to an authentically Hobbesian chaos of "nature." Then, as more and more nations come to share what Hobbes had called a "dreadful equality," an increasingly symmetrical capacity to render mortal destruction, the portent of regional nuclear calamity could expectedly become more likely.

For Israel, expanding chaos portends a very unusual and even paradoxical kind of fragility. As a relentlessly beleaguered microstate, Israel could become the principal victim of rampant international disorder. Indeed, in view of the exceptionally far-reaching interrelatedness of all world politics, this could transpire even if the actual precipitating events of *war* and *terror* would occur elsewhere—that is, in another distant region of our planet.

Oddly, perhaps, global chaos may still reveal both sense and form. Generated by explosions of mega-war and mega-terror, disintegrations of world authority could assume a discernible shape. How, precisely, should this shape, this peculiar "geometry" of chaos, be deciphered and understood by Israel? As a corollary and vital question, Israel's leaders must also inquire: "How exactly should we deal with potentially *irrational* nuclear adversaries in both state and terrorist groups?"[17]

The world, like the individual nation-states that comprise it, is best understood as a *system*. What happens in any one part of this system always affects what happens in some or all of the other parts. When global deterioration is marked and begins to spread from one country to another, the effects could undermine international stability in general. When deterioration is sudden and catastrophic, as it would be following the onset of unconventional war and/or unconventional terrorism, the unraveling effects could be immediate and overwhelming.

The State of Israel, a system of interdependent and interpenetrating parts like every other state, exists precariously in a larger world system. Aware that an incremental collapse of world authority structures will, in one way or another, impact its (*few*) friends as well as its (*many*) enemies, leaders of the Jewish State must now advance informed expectations of collapse (social scientists would call these expectations "plausible scenarios") in order to prepare suitable forms of response. Finally, recognizing that rapid and far-reaching global collapse could spawn a more or less complete return to "everyone for himself" in world politics, what philosopher Thomas Hobbes called a "war of all against all,"[18] Israel's leaders must now consider how they should respond to any future life in a global "state of nature."[19]

Such eleventh-hour considerations will be all the more critical to the extent that the triggering mechanism of collapse would likely originate within the Middle East from massive chemical and biological and, in the future, even nuclear attacks against Israel.

Chaotic disintegration of the world system, whether slow and incremental or sudden and catastrophic, will dramatically impact the Israeli system. In the clearest manifestation of this impact, Israel will have to orient its military planning and doctrine to a variety of worst case possibilities, focusing much more on the whole range of self-help security options than on any traditional forms of cooperative diplomacy and alliance guarantees.[20] Within the country, any diplomatic processes still premised on outdated assumptions of reason and rationality would have to be curtailed in recognition of now fully apparent regional "insults" to civilization.

Israel's always-wavering judgments about a two-state solution with Palestinians will soon need to be made, at least in part, in consideration of anticipated world-system changes. Such a problematic reorientation of planning, from expectations of largely separate and unrelated threats to informed presumptions of fully interrelated dangers, could provide an essential framework for facing the increasingly uncertain strategic future. The conceptual or philosophic origin of this framework would be a prior Israeli government willingness to extract usable policy implications from an emerging *geometry of chaos*.

There is also an important "feedback loop" here. Israel's particular reactions, as a system within a system, to growing expressions of worldwide chaos will themselves impact these expressions. Should Israel's leaders respond to seemingly unstoppable regional disorder by hardening their commitment to all still-relevant forms of self-reliance, including appropriate and lawful resorts to preemptive military force, Israel's enemies would surely respond, individually or collectively, in similarly "self-reliant" ways.

What are these ways? How exactly should Israel respond to such responses? These are primary dialectical questions that should now be raised by Israel's strategic planners, questions which we shall consider in the coming chapters. It is already time for all concerned with Israel's nuclear strategy to consider the feedback implications of *creation in reverse*.

By likening both the world as a whole and their own mini-state in particular to the biological concept of "system," Israel's leadership could learn, before it is too late, that states "die" not only because of a direct, mortal blow, but also in reaction to a series of distinctly less than mortal blows. This is because, after a time, even multiple "minor" insults to an organism can produce a breakdown of immunities that pave the way for life-endangering pathogens. Taken by itself, any one such insult (e.g., a local infection, an injury, an impediment to vision or hearing or memory) will not cause death. But cumulatively over time, these attacks can become fatal by affecting the organism's overall will to live and/or making it possible for a "major" insult to take place without allowing any adequate defense.

Taken by themselves, Israel's intermittent and possibly still-planned surrenders of land for empty promises, continuing reluctance to accept certain preemption options, and one-sided adherence to so-called peace agreements may not bring about sudden national disappearance. Taken *together*, however, these insults, occurring as they do within a far broader worldwide pattern of escalating chaos, could have a decisively weakening impact.

Chaos is not anarchy. It is *more* than anarchy. For Israel in particular, chaos should now be taken as a distinctly realistic outcome of certain ongoing and still-impending regional conflicts. As such, it must become an expressly considered element of Israel's nuclear strategy.

THINKING OUTSIDE THE BOX

Israel's nuclear strategy, like all strategic theory, is essentially a "net." In the interpenetrating worlds of war and peace, only those who cast will catch.[21] This net must be constantly rewoven and refined. More generally, without a carefully derived and markedly innovative system of theory, the IDF would be unable to conform its critical *order of battle* to the constantly changing *correlation of forces*.[22] This increasingly lethal correlation is already mustering on the regional battlefield.

Not all pertinent IDF planning problems are purely theoretical or conceptual. Even where nuclear strategic thinking *does* proceed on a sound intellectual foundation—for example, one that would involve appropriately dialectical reasoning—it would still need to remain sheltered from potentially unsound *political* judgments. But that's a warning for a very different book.

What actually needs to be done now?

First, Israel's strategic planners must look directly, unhesitatingly, and relentlessly at their country's *existential* threats, both conspicuous and inconspicuous, and then proceed to identify these threats as the primary object and rationale of their subsequent inquiries. They must in this task (1) maintain an unambiguous hierarchy of what is most important to safeguard and secure, and (2) display corollary obeisance to the precise rank orderings of this foundational hierarchy.

Second, Israeli planners must understand conceptually that (a) Israel is a *system*, (b) existential threats confronting Israel are themselves interrelated or systemic, and (c) the complex effects of these systemic threats on Israel must be examined *together*.

Third, Israeli nuclear planners must never overlook that the *entire world arena* is best understood as a *system*[23] and that any disintegration of power and authority structures within this wider macrosystem will impact, with more or less enormous and at least partially foreseeable consequences, the Israeli microsystem.

Fourth, Israeli planners must sometimes agree to turn away from too much "prudence"—that is, from too mainstream kinds of strategic analyses. A likely assumption of historic and current Israeli strategic planning is the orthodox assumption of *rationality* in enemy calculations. Because the functioning of nuclear deterrence necessarily depends on this core assumption, Israeli strategists may turn away from those residual or unexpected circumstances in which rationality would not be expected to operate. A plausibly dangerous result of such distraction could be that Israeli strategic planners accomplish too little to prepare the political leadership in Jerusalem for (increasingly probable) confrontations with *irrational* enemy states or with equally irrational substate proxies. Nowadays, one need only watch the news about ISIS, Hezbollah, and so on to recognize the growing danger of irrationality from terrorist group adversaries.

Fifth, Israeli planners may need to recognize certain advantages of private as opposed to collective thought. Here, they should be reminded of Aristotle's early view on these advantages—a view likely held today by only a tiny handful of military intelligence guidance operations: *Deception occurs to a greater extent when we are investigating with others than by ourselves, for an investigation with someone else is carried on quite as much by means of the thing itself.* There is a suitably correct time for collaborative or team investigations, but in matters concerning Israeli national security, we could sometimes discover still greater conceptual value in the private musings of talented single individuals than in the combined efforts of entire academic centers of strategic studies.

At first hearing, such advice may sound altogether counterintuitive or even "crazy." Still, certain very rarely gifted individuals are sometimes able to make optimal intellectual contributions by drawing on the irreducible core of their own private intellectual powers. In this specific connection, I can recall my own earlier acquaintance with two onetime leaders of AMAN, Major General Aharon Yariv and Professor Yuval Ne'eman. Over the years of our acquaintance, it became thoroughly clear to me that both Yariv's and Ne'eman's main contributions to Israeli security policy were the product of sustained *private and independent* intellectual thought. Ultimately, of course, the wisdom of Aristotle's dictum is always contingent on the actual availability of "rarely gifted individuals."

Sixth, Israeli nuclear strategists will need to continually widen their considerations of nuclear weapons and national strategy. This widening should be conducted, naturally, in consonance with all of the other above-listed strategic planning requirements. Key issues here will be those concerning nuclear targeting doctrine, deliberate nuclear ambiguity,[24] and ballistic missile defense. Related concerns should center on informed investigations of "rationality of pretended irrationality" postures and on more or less explicit intimations of a refined "Samson" doctrine.[25]

Seventh, Israeli nuclear strategists should pay special attention to the compelling requirements of intellectual *audacity*, of seeking to sometimes steer clear of seeking safety in a comfortably theoretic middle ground. This means that the country's nuclear planners will occasionally need to take risks, both personal and professional, in seeking serious policy answers to vital questions about Israeli nuclear strategy. In the end of course, those individuals charged with responsibility for fashioning this strategy must be guided only by the overriding obligation to enhance Israel's safety and security from existential and potentially existential aggressions.[26]

THE NEED FOR AVANT-GARDE THINKING

Normally, when we think of "avant-garde," we think of the cutting edge of artistic or poetic innovation. But the term's actual origin lies in specifically military parlance. It is a term that could now be applied with potentially considerable benefit to the exploration and development of Israel's nuclear strategy.

Whether cultural or strategic, the raison d'être of any avant-garde movement must be a purposeful and imaginative disruption of the status quo. By its very nature, the term is also *activist,* meaning that it signifies a *marching toward.* Today, those who are responsible for Israel's nuclear strategy should be mindful of significantly close connections between the way they approach their subject and the ultimate utility of their recommendations.

To begin cultivating such mindfulness, they should be attentive to the idea of "paradigm" in science.

The concept of paradigm is most famously expressed in an important work of contemporary epistemology by Thomas S. Kuhn. In *The Structure of Scientific Revolutions,* Princeton professor Kuhn refers to certain examples of scientific practice that can provide theoretical models for further inquiry—Ptolemaic or Copernican astronomy, Aristotelian dynamics, Newtonian mechanics, and so on. At any given moment, we are taught that the prevailing model or paradigm within a discipline lays out the basic parameters for all further examinations.

For scholars and planners, the transformations of these paradigms represent "scientific revolutions." What does this observation have to do with imperative reformations and reformulations of Israeli nuclear strategy? The answer lies in antecedent attention to avant-garde modes of thinking. Reciprocally, the absence of any such marching-toward thinking could wrongfully direct Israeli military planners to static and unproductive models of nuclear strategy.

This advice does not come in a historical vacuum. It need not be assessed *ex nihilo.* There is ample precedent for what is required.

For evidence of the transition in dominant paradigms, from war histories to war studies, we need only consider the seminal works of Maurice de Saxe, Chevalier de Folard, Guibert, Count Raimondo Montecuccoli, Henry Lloyd, and even Frederick the Great. Strategic planners may also recall reactions to those principles contained in Thucydides and later in such manuals on warfare as Maurice's *Strategicon,* Leo VI's *Tactica,* and Machiavelli's *Art of War.* From Helmuth von Moltke to Giulio Douhet's

Command of the Air, the beneficial influence of a strategic avant-garde is plainly evident.

Just as evident, after World War II, a good deal of orthodox military thinking was appropriately challenged by the very first generation of expressly "nuclear thinkers," primarily Albert Wohlstetter, Herman Kahn, Bernard Brodie, Anatol Rapoport, and Thomas Schelling. Without necessarily supplanting a conventional wisdom that had ranged from Sun Tzu[27] to Clausewitz and beyond, they nonetheless recognized that nuclear strategy would, in many ways, now have to be regarded as *sui generis*. With this timely recognition, they quickly became a recognizable avant-garde.

What still newer ideas should be brought forward in the making of Israel's nuclear strategy? One idea already mentioned here is the obligation to challenge long-held assumptions about human rationality in strategic calculations. Because the functioning of nuclear deterrence has been deemed contingent on this core assumption, strategic thinkers have tended to ignore or look away from ever even launching such a challenge.

But how should Israel protect itself against prospectively irrational adversaries armed with nuclear weapons? This is not a question that can ever be ignored by those who must shape Israel's nuclear strategy.[28] Instead, as Prime Minister Benjamin Netanyahu has himself made perfectly clear, it deserves an absolute pride of place in the Jewish State's required hierarchy of existential concerns.

Another avant-garde initiative concerns the widely alleged immutability of human nature. Historically, by regarding behavioral factors as irremediably fixed, strategists and planners may have focused much too narrowly on tactical manipulations of force structure, power balances,[29] and government policies. In contrast, an aspiring avant-garde thinker could make new sense of the excruciatingly important observation once uttered by Immanuel Kant. "Out of timber so crooked as that from which man is made," said the late-eighteenth-century German philosopher, "nothing entirely straight can be built."[30]

Yet another paradigm shift to be considered in avant-garde approaches to Israel's nuclear strategy would concern a "strategic dialectic."[31] With such an orientation, Israeli planners could get far beyond largely reportorial or narrative comparisons of force structures and weapon system inventories. Here, these planners would need an avant-garde to advance a distinctly dialectical series of nuclear strategic issues, one wherein each advanced thought presents a complication that then moves inquiry forward to the next pertinent thought.[32] Contained in this illuminating strategic dialectic would be a relentless obligation to keep on thinking, an obligation that can never be fulfilled altogether (because of what the philosophers correctly call an "infinite regress problem") but must be ventured nonetheless.

Intellectual creativity represents yet another quality that could bring avant-garde benefits to the making of Israel's nuclear strategy. Such creativity could be made manifest at any stage of the scientific investigation, including the initial formation of underlying concepts and the fashioning of subsequent hypotheses. Significantly, in the history of science, the greatest breakthroughs were accomplished not by merely workmanlike accumulations of facts and figures but by thoroughly remarkable intuitions. Moreover, the most successful applications of a strategic avant-garde to Israeli nuclear planning will not be made by those who seek the most exhaustive or comprehensive compilations of relevant factors but rather by those who can successfully abstract the smallest possible useful number of independent or explanatory variables. These will be the parsimonious planners who are able to say the most, with the least.

In the final analysis, it is somewhere in the dialectical opposition between analytic orthodoxy and developing avant-garde orientations that Israeli planners should now shape the contours of Israel's nuclear strategy.

It is to most precisely locate this crucial "somewhere" that the following book chapters are encouragingly dedicated.

"We are often asked," said the late Italian Jewish writer and Holocaust survivor, Primo Levi, in *The Drowned and the Saved*, "as if our past conferred a prophetic ability upon us, whether Auschwitz will return." Before we attempt to answer such a terrible question, it is first necessary to understand that an "Auschwitz return" need not take the same form as the original Nazi kingdom of death. In fact as well as in law, war and genocide need not be mutually exclusive,[33] and soon certain of Israel's enemies could at least contemplate effectively genocidal attacks on the Jewish State. It follows that Israel's nuclear strategy could ultimately represent nothing less than the final bulwark against another Auschwitz.

It should go without saying that to correctly shape this complex strategy presents an incomparably heavy burden of both responsibility and opportunity.

NOTES

1. There are two prominently recorded incidents in which an explicit reference was made to Israel's bomb by a prime minister, but neither of these events went beyond a purely vague and general commentary. On December 22, 1995, then Prime Minister Shimon Peres declared to the Israeli press that Israel would be willing "to give up the atom" in exchange for peace. Years later, on December 11, 2006, Prime Minister Ehud Olmert uttered a very similar remark.

2. In his very important *The Advancement of Learning*, Francis Bacon—who had already distanced himself from the earlier Greek philosophers who had eschewed tangible facts—urged that science work consciously and hand in hand with the indispensable alleviation of human suffering. Here, scientists were cautioned by Bacon never to lose sight of an underlying set of distinctly ethical obligations. In my own

book, now before the reader, this particular set is made very explicit. It concerns ensuring Israel's physical survival amid unambiguously genocidal enemies.

3. See, for example, Louis René Beres, "Overview of Threats Facing Israel," lecture presentation at National Security College (IDF), Israel, March 6, 1994 (Major General Yossi Ben Hanan, Officer Commanding [OC]).

4. See Louis René Beres, *Security or Armageddon: Israel's Nuclear Strategy* (Lexington, MA: Lexington Books, 1986), 242 pp. An earlier book by this author had also dealt intensively with Middle Eastern nuclear issues. See Louis René Beres, *Apocalypse: Nuclear Catastrophe in World Politics* (Chicago and London: The University of Chicago Press, 1980), 315 pp.

5. Seven years earlier, I had authored *Terrorism and Global Security: The Nuclear Threat* (Boulder, CO: Westview Press, 1979), 161 pp.

6. See Albert Wohlstetter, "The Delicate Balance of Terror," *Foreign Affairs*, Vol. 37, No. 2 (January 1959), pp. 211–234.

7. See Louis René Beres, "Like Two Scorpions in a Bottle: Could Israel and a Nuclear Iran Coexist in the Middle East?" *The Israel Journal of Foreign Affairs*, Vol. 8, No. 1, 2014, pp. 23–32.

8. See, on this fundamental point, Karl Jaspers, *Reason and Anti-Reason in Our Time* (Hamden, CT: Archon Books, 1971), 96 pp.

9. For an early look at these limitations, see Anatol Rapoport, *Strategy and Conscience* (New York: Schocken Books, 1964), 323 pp.

10. See Carl von Clausewitz, *On War*, tr. Peter Paret and Michael Howard (Princeton, NJ: Princeton University Press, 1976); and also Barry D. Watts, *Clausewitzian Friction and Future War*, Institute for National Strategic Studies, National Defense University, McNair Paper 52, October 1996, Washington, DC.

11. In studies of world politics, rationality and irrationality have taken on very specific meanings. More precisely, an actor (state or substate) is determinedly rational to the extent that its leadership always values collective survival more highly than any other conceivable preference or combination of preferences. Conversely, an irrational actor might not always display such a determinable preference ordering. Apropos of the scientific limitations already discussed above, however, ascertaining where such an adversary (e.g., Iran) would actually be rational or irrational can represent a very imprecise undertaking.

12. See Yehoshafat Harkabi, *The Bar Kokhba Syndrome: Risk and Realism in International Politics* (Chappaqua, NY: Rossel Books, 1983), 206 pp.

13. Regarding Iran, see Louis René Beres and John T. Chain (General/USAF/ret.), "Could Israel Safely Deter a Nuclear Iran?" *The Atlantic*, August 2012; and also Professor Louis René Beres and General Chain, "Israel and Iran at the Eleventh Hour," *Oxford University Press* (OUP Blog), February 23, 2012. General Chain was commander-in-chief, US Strategic Air Command (CINCSAC).

14. On these core points, see *Israel's Strategic Future: The Final Report of Project Daniel*, The Project Daniel Group (Louis René Beres, Chair), Ariel Center for Policy Research, ACPR Policy Paper No. 155, Israel, May 2004. This special report was delivered by hand to Prime Minister Ariel Sharon on January 16, 2003. The Group's six members were Professor Louis René Beres (Chair); Naaman Belkind, former Assistant to the Israeli Deputy Minister of Defense for Special Means; Major General/Professor Isaac Ben-Israel (IDF/ret.); Dr. Rand Fishbein; Dr. Adir Pridor, Lt. Colonel (ret.), Israel Air Force, and Head of Military Analyses, RAFAEL, Israel; and Colonel (ret.), Israel Air Force and Member of Knesset, Yoash Tsiddon-Chatto.

15. From an expressly international law perspective, our still-anarchic international system originated with the Peace of Westphalia. See Treaty of Peace of Munster, Oct. 1648, 1 Consol. T.S. 271; and Treaty of Peace of Osnabruck, Oct. 1648, 1, Consol. T.S. 119.

16. See Thomas Hobbes, *Leviathan*, Chapter XIII, "Of the Naturall Condition of Mankind, as concerning their Felicity, and Misery" (1651).

17. Even if Israeli nuclear planners could assume that specified enemy leaderships were expectedly rational, this would say nothing about the accuracy of the information used by these leaderships in making their rational calculations. Rationality always refers only to the *intention* of maximizing certain values or preferences (e.g., national survival). It does not tell observers anything about whether the information actually being used by the enemy is correct or incorrect. Hence, fully rational enemy leaderships may still make errors in calculation that would lead them to nuclear war. More generally, there are several related command and control issues here that could impel a perfectly rational adversary, or combination of adversaries, toward certain risky nuclear behaviors. For an excellent assessment of particular factors that could influence the C3 (command, control, and communications) paradigms of nuclear weapons in the Middle East, see Shmuel Bar and Oded Brosh, *Culture of Command and Control of Nuclear Weapons in the Middle East*, Herzliya Working Paper, IDC Herzliya, February 6–9, 2011, 11 pp.

18. See Thomas Hobbes, *Leviathan*, Chapter XIII, "Of the Naturall Condition of Mankind, as concerning their Felicity, and Misery" (1651).

19. Ibid.

20. See Thomas Hobbes, *Leviathan*, Chapter XVII, "Of the Causes, Generation, and Definition of a Common-Wealth" (1651).

21. The metaphor is usually attributed to the German poet Novalis, cited by Karl Popper as epigraph to his *The Logic of Scientific Discovery* (New York: Harper & Row, 1959). The poet's exact words, according to Popper, are "[t]heories are nets; only he who casts, will catch."

22. See Louis René Beres, "Understanding the 'Correlation of Forces' in the Middle East: Israel's Urgent Strategic Imperative," *Israel Journal of Foreign Affairs*, Vol. IV, No. 1, 2010, pp. 77–88.

23. For interesting philosophical background here, see Pierre Teilhard de Chardin, *The Phenomenon of Man* (New York: Harper & Row, 1959).

24. See Louis René Beres, *Looking Ahead: Revising Israel's Nuclear Ambiguity in the Middle East*, Herzliya Conference Policy Paper, Herzliya Conference, March 11–14, 2013 (IDC Herzliya, Israel).

25. See Louis René Beres, "Israel and Samson: Biblical Lessons for Israel's Strategy in the Nuclear Age," *Israel Affairs*, Vol. 1, No. 3, July 2005, pp. 491–503.

26. For the crime of aggression under international law, see Resolution on the Definition of Aggression, adopted by the UN General Assembly, Dec. 14, 1974, UNGA Res. 3314 (xxix), 29 UN GAOR, Supp. (No. 31), 142, UN Doc. A/9631 (1975), reprinted in 13 ILM, 710 (1974).

27. See Louis René Beres, "Lessons for Israel from Ancient Chinese Military Thought: Facing Iranian Nuclearization with Sun-Tzu," *Harvard National Security Journal*, Harvard Law School, October 24, 2013.

28. The Israeli nuclear strategist could benefit here from Basque philosopher Miguel de Unamuno's instructive remark about the German philosopher Hegel: "Hegel made famous his aphorism that all the rational is real, and all the real is rational; but there are many of us who, unconvinced by Hegel, continue to believe that the real, the really real, is *irrational*—that reason builds upon *irrationalities* [emphasis in original]."

29. Historically, the idea of a *balance of power*—an idea of which the nuclear-age *balance of terror* is a current variant—has never been more than a facile metaphor. In fact, it has never had anything to do with true equilibrium. Because such a balance is always a matter of individual and more or less subjective perceptions, adversary states may never be sufficiently confident that strategic circumstances are suitably "balanced" in their favor. In consequence, as each side perpetually fears that it will be left behind, the search for balance inevitably produces wider insecurity and further disequilibrium.

30. For those who might be interested in the original German, it is "*Aus so krummem Holze, als woraus der Mensch gemacht ist, kann nichts ganz Gerades gezimmert werden.*"

31. The base term "dialectic" originates from the Greek expression for the art of conversation. A common contemporary meaning is a method of seeking truth by correct reasoning. From the standpoint of shaping Israel's nuclear strategy, the following representative operations could be regarded as essential but nonexclusive components: (1) a method of refutation conducted by examining logical consequences, (2) a method of division or repeated logical analysis of genera into species, (3) logical reasoning using premises that are probable or generally accepted, (4) formal logic, and (5) the logical development of thought through thesis and antithesis to fruitful synthesis of these opposites.

32. Dialectical thinking seemingly originated in fifth-century BCE Athens, as Zeno, author of the *Paradoxes*, had been acknowledged by Aristotle as its inventor. Further, in the middle dialogues of Plato, dialectic emerges as the supreme form of philosophic/analytic method. The dialectician, says Plato, is the special one who knows how to ask and then answer vital questions. From the standpoint of a necessary avant-garde in Israeli strategic planning, this knowledge should never simply be taken for granted.

33. This point has been acknowledged by every single Israeli prime minister, from David Ben-Gurion, who already saw the need for a national nuclear deterrent, to Benjamin Netanyahu, whose ongoing warnings against a nuclear Iran are plainly animated by the need to prevent another Auschwitz. On June 7, 1981, when Israel preemptively destroyed the Osiraq nuclear reactor outside of Baghdad to thwart a nuclear-armed Saddam Hussein, then Israeli Prime Minister Menachem Begin very explicitly justified the self-defense attack as necessary to "prevent another Holocaust."

ONE

The Core Requirement of Nuclear Weapons

"The safety of the People Shall be the highest law."

—Cicero, *De Legibus*

To succeed in their several interrelated purposes, Israel's nuclear weapons will need to be guided by antecedent doctrine. Such doctrine, moreover, must contain, implicitly or explicitly, a primary and detailed explanation of what these particular weapons are expected to accomplish. Oddly enough, although most observers of Middle East geopolitics already have some idea that Israel's nuclear forces are either useful or useless—or at least fall somewhere in between these two polar descriptions on a proper continuum of calculable possibilities—little has been done to systematically answer the underlying question: *Why does Israel actually need nuclear weapons?*

What follows represents a comprehensive and fact-based response.[1] Only when this utterly core question has finally been addressed can we meaningfully progress to any wider descriptions and assessments of Israel's nuclear strategy.

To suitably begin this essential response, one may recall that for many years, the states in world politics—sometimes alleged "friends" as well as expressed enemies—have generally called on Israel to denuclearize. On December 2, 2014, for a recent example, the UN General Assembly approved a long-familiar Arab-initiated resolution, one calling on Israel to turn away from nuclear weapons. This resolution, adopted in a 161–5 vote, took special care to note that Israel remains the only Middle Eastern state that is not party to the Treaty on the Non-Proliferation of Nuclear Weapons of 1968 (NPT). More precisely, it insisted that Israel "accede to that Treaty without delay, not to develop, produce, test, or otherwise acquire nuclear weapons, and to renounce possession of nuclear weapons."

Also demanded was that Israel put all its pertinent nuclear facilities under close monitoring control of the UN's International Atomic Energy Agency.

What, if anything, was wrong with this seemingly benign demand?

A great deal, especially from the dual standpoints of fairness and stability. Among other things, including the inherent right of all sovereign states not to join the NPT, or any other treaty for that matter, the UN resolution simply chose to ignore that Israel's nuclear weapons and infrastructures remain purposefully unthreatening. Even more fundamentally, for a country that is more conspicuously imperiled than any other—and one facing existential perils from both state and substate adversaries—the nuclear "equalizer" is necessary to ensure its basic physical survival.

Historically, this overriding need had already been recognized at the very beginnings of the Jewish State by David Ben-Gurion, Israel's first and enviably prescient prime minister.

Even in complex geostrategic realms, some matters are perfectly clear. One may consider, in this regard, that if all of Israel's state enemies were somehow to abide by the legally codified expectations of nonproliferation, their cumulative advantage in mass could still be substantial enough to create intolerable threats and genocidal harms. In other words, even if these states were all willing to remain nonnuclear (today, an almost inconceivable scenario, especially as the Sunni Arabs worry increasingly about a nearly nuclear Shiite Iran), the combined attack danger to Israel could still be more or less overwhelming.

It's not a difficult extrapolation to make. Even thoroughly NPT-compliant Arab and Iranian enemies could endanger a newly nonnuclear Israel. This potentially existential peril could be generated by either certain individual enemy states or by a varied assortment of conceivable alliance collaborations.

The actual levels of danger posed to Israel could be exacerbated, in portentous increments, by instances of enemy state cooperation with various terror groups, especially if the cooperating nonstate organizations, whether Sunni or Shia, were energetically Jihadist.

But why exactly does Israel need specifically *nuclear* weapons? Despite the significant number of books and articles that conveniently skirt around this core question, very little of substance has been offered in the way of providing a helpfully *conceptual* answer.[2] What follows, therefore, in this chapter, is an informed attempt to remedy this major analytic deficiency, and to accomplish this essential remediation within the disciplining parameters of a competent "strategic dialectic."

1. Israel needs nuclear weapons to *deter* large conventional attacks by enemy states. The effectiveness of any such Israeli nuclear deterrence will depend on, among other things, (a) perceived vulnerability of Israeli nuclear forces, (b) perceived destructiveness of Israeli nuclear forces, (c) perceived willingness of Israeli leadership to follow through on nuclear threats, (d) perceived capacities of prospective attackers' active defenses, (e) perceptions of Israeli targeting doctrine (countervalue vs. counterforce),[3] (f) perceptions of Israel's probable retaliatory response when there is an expectation of nonnuclear but chemical and/or biological[4] counterretaliations, (g) disclosure or continued nondisclosure of Israel's nuclear arsenal, and (h) creation or noncreation of a Palestinian state.[5] For all of the above, "perceived" refers to *enemy views* of Israel.

2. Israel needs nuclear weapons to *deter* all levels of unconventional (chemical, biological, and nuclear [CBN]) attacks. The effectiveness of these forms of Israeli nuclear deterrence will also depend on (a) to (h) above. In this connection, Israel's nuclear weapons are needed to deter enemy *escalation* of conventional warfare to unconventional warfare, and of one form of unconventional warfare to another (i.e., escalation of chemical warfare to biological warfare, biological warfare to chemical warfare, or biological/chemical warfare to nuclear warfare).

3. Israel needs nuclear weapons to *preempt* enemy nuclear attacks. This does not mean that Israeli preemptions of such attacks would *necessarily* be nuclear (more than likely, they would always be nonnuclear) but only that they *could* be nuclear.[6] Of course, should Israel ever need to use its nuclear forces for such a purpose, it would inevitably signify the failure of these forces as a *deterrent* (as per number 2 above). Such failure is increasingly plausible because of the problematic nature of nuclear deterrence in general, and in the particular circumstances of the Middle East.[7]

4. Israel needs its nuclear weapons to support conventional preemptions against enemy nuclear assets. With such weapons, Israel can maintain, explicitly or implicitly, a threat of nuclear counterretaliation.[8] Without such weapons, Israel, having to rely entirely on nonnuclear forces, might not be able to deter enemy retaliations for the Israeli preemptive attack.

5. Israel needs nuclear weapons to support conventional preemptions against enemy nonnuclear (CBN) assets. With such weapons, Israel can maintain, explicitly or implicitly, a threat of nuclear counterretaliation. Without such weapons, Israel, having to rely entirely on nonnuclear forces, might not be able to deter enemy retaliations for the Israeli preemptive attack.

6. Israel needs nuclear weapons for nuclear war fighting.[9] Although, in the best of all possible worlds, this need will never have to arise, and although Israel should absolutely avoid nuclear war fighting whenever still possible, it cannot be wished away or discounted altogether. Rather, even as the most utterly unwelcome strategic option, it must still be taken seriously by Israeli planners and decision makers. Among the probable paths to nuclear war fighting are the following: enemy nuclear first strikes against Israel, enemy nonnuclear first strikes against Israel that elicit Israeli nuclear reprisals either immediately or via incremental escalation processes, Israeli nuclear preemptions against enemy states with nuclear assets, and Israeli nonnuclear preemptions against enemy states with nuclear assets that elicit enemy nuclear reprisals either immediately or via incremental escalation processes. Other pertinent paths to nuclear war fighting could include accidental/unintentional/inadvertent nuclear attacks among Israel and regional enemy states and even the escalatory consequences of nuclear terrorism against the Jewish State.[10] As long as it can be assumed that Israel is altogether determined to endure, there *are* conditions where Jerusalem could resort to nuclear war fighting. This holds true if (a) enemy first strikes against Israel would not destroy Israel's second-strike nuclear capability, (b) enemy retaliations for an Israeli conventional preemption would not destroy Israel's nuclear counterretaliatory capability, (c) Israeli preemptive strikes involving nuclear weapons would not destroy enemy second-strike nuclear capabilities, and (d) Israeli retaliation for enemy conventional first strikes would not destroy enemy nuclear counterretaliatory capabilities. It follows, from the standpoint of Israel's nuclear requirements, that Jerusalem should prepare to do whatever is needed to ensure the likelihood of (a) and (b) above, and the unlikelihood of (c) and (d).

7. Israel needs nuclear weapons for the "Samson Option." Although any such use of nuclear weapons by definition would be profoundly catastrophic, Israel apparently plans that it would be better to "die with the Philistines" than to die alone. This understanding is much more than a doctrinal matter of Jewish honor and a refutation of the "Masada complex" (suicide without punishment[11] of the aggressor). It *could* (depending on awareness by enemy states) also represent an integral and indispensable element of Israel's nuclear deterrent. The biblical analogy is somewhat misleading. Samson chose suicide by pushing apart the temple pillars, whereas Israel, using nuclear weapons as a last resort, would not be *choosing* "suicide" or even necessarily committing suicide. For states, the criteria of "life" and "death" are hardly as clear cut as they are for individual persons. Finally, it is essential that Israel's leaders, in

considering possible uses of nuclear weapon,s regard the Samson Option as one to be precluded by prior, correct resort to all other nuclear options. Stated differently, a resort to the Samson Option by Israel would imply the complete failure of all other options and the subsequent failure of its nuclear weapons to provide essential national security.

DETERRENCE OPTIONS

Israel needs nuclear weapons, among other purposes, to deter certain large conventional attacks and all levels of unconventional attack. Still, the effectiveness of nuclear weapons in meeting these needs is somewhat limited and exceedingly problematic. Even if Jerusalem should move toward partial or full disclosure of its nuclear weapons,[12] it cannot reasonably rely entirely on nuclear deterrence for survival.[13]

Aware of these core limitations, Israel must nonetheless seek to strengthen nuclear deterrence such that an enemy state will always calculate that a first strike on the Jewish State would be irrational. This means taking appropriate steps to convince the enemy state that the probable costs of such a strike will always exceed the benefits. To accomplish this important objective, Israel must convince prospective attackers that it maintains both the *willingness* and the *capacity* to retaliate with nuclear weapons.

Where an enemy state considering an attack on Israel would be unconvinced about either one, or both, of these essential components of nuclear deterrence, it might sometimes choose to strike first, depending on the particular value or utility it places on the expected consequence of such an attack.

Regarding willingness, even if Jerusalem were prepared to respond to certain attacks with nuclear reprisals, an enemy failure to recognize such preparedness could still provoke an attack on Israel. Misperception and/or errors in information could immobilize nuclear deterrence. It is also conceivable that Jerusalem could, in fact, lack willingness to retaliate, and that this lack would be *correctly* perceived by enemy decision makers.

In this case, Israeli nuclear deterrence would be immobilized, not because of any "confused signals" but rather because of signals that had not been purposefully distorted.

Regarding capacity, even if Jerusalem maintains a substantial arsenal of nuclear weapons, it is essential that enemy states believe these weapons to be distinctly usable. This means, among other things, that if a first-strike attack were believed capable of destroying Israel's arsenal, the Jewish State's nuclear deterrent could be immobilized. Moreover, even if Israel's nuclear weapons were configured such that they could not be destroyed by an enemy first strike, enemy misperceptions or misjudgments about Israeli vulnerability could still occasion the catastrophic failure of nuclear deterrence.

A further complication concerns enemy state deployment of antitactical ballistic missile defenses, which might sometimes contribute to an affirmative attack decision against Israel by lowering the attacker's expected costs.[14]

The importance of "usable" nuclear weapons must also be examined from the standpoint of probable harms. Should all of Israel's nuclear weapons be perceived by a would-be attacker as very high-yield, indiscriminate, "city-busting" (countervalue) weapons, rather than minimal-yield, war-fighting (counterforce) weapons, they might not deter. Contrary to the uninformed conventional wisdom on the subject, successful nuclear deterrence, to the extent possible, may sometimes vary *inversely* with perceived destructiveness. It follows that Israeli nuclear deterrence requires not only visibly secure second-strike forces, but also forces that could recognizably be used productively in war or in singular reprisals.

No examination of Israeli nuclear deterrence options would be complete without consideration of the "disclosure" issue.[15] From the beginning, Israel's bomb has been stored in the "basement." For the future, however, it is by no means certain that an undeclared nuclear deterrent will be capable of meeting Jerusalem's long-term security goals, or that it will even be equal in effectiveness to an openly declared nuclear deterrent.

At first glance, the disclosure issue may appear inconsequential. Everyone, after all, *knows* that Israel has the bomb. What, then, would be the purpose of belaboring the obvious? Indeed, might not such unnecessary saber rattling actually prove too provocative, thus occasioning Arab and/or Iranian first strikes that might not otherwise even have been contemplated?

To answer these difficult questions, we must first understand that disclosure would not be intended to reveal the obvious (i.e., merely that Israel *has* the bomb), but instead to heighten enemy perceptions of Jerusalem's capable nuclear forces and/or its willingness to use these forces in reprisal for certain first-strike attacks. What, exactly, are the plausible connections between an openly declared nuclear weapons capacity and enemy perceptions of Israeli nuclear deterrence? One such connection concerns the relation between disclosure and the perceived vulnerability of Israel's nuclear forces to preemptive destruction. Another such connection concerns the relationship between disclosure and perceived capacity of Jerusalem's nuclear forces to penetrate the attacking state's active defenses.[16]

To the extent that removing the bomb from the basement, or disclosure, would encourage enemy views of an Israeli force that is sufficiently invulnerable to first-strike attacks and/or is capable of piercing enemy active defense systems, disclosure could then represent a rational and prudent option for Israel. Here, the operational benefits of disclosure would derive from certain deliberate flows of information about dispersion, multiplication, hardening, speed, and evasiveness of nuclear weapons systems, and some other pertinent technical features of nuclear weapons. Most importantly, such flows, which could also refer to C3I (command, control, communications, intelligence) invulnerability and possible predelegations of launch authority, would serve to remove lingering enemy doubts about Israel's nuclear force capabilities. These doubts, should they be left unchallenged, could lethally undermine Israeli nuclear deterrence.

Removing the bomb from Israel's basement could also heighten enemy perceptions of Jerusalem's willingness to make good on its retaliatory threats. For example, by releasing information about its nuclear forces that identifies distinctly usable weapons, Israel might correspondingly remove any doubts about Jerusalem's nuclear resolve. Here, a prospective attacker, newly aware that Israel could conceivably retaliate without generating intolerably high levels of civilian harms (possibly because of enhanced radiation and/or subkiloton weapons) could be more likely, because of Jerusalem's disclosure, to actually believe Israel's nuclear threats.

All this brings to mind the connections between disclosure, doctrine, and deterrence. To the extent that Israel's strategic doctrine actually identifies nuanced and graduated forms of reprisal—forms calibrating Israeli retaliations to particular levels of provocation—any disclosure of such doctrine (at least in its broadest and most unspecific contours) could contribute more or less mightily to Israel's nuclear deterrence. Without such disclosure, Israel's enemies would be kept guessing about Jerusalem's probable responses, a condition of protracted uncertainty that might be able to serve Israel's security for a while longer but, at one time or another, could fail altogether.

The plausible importance of a "graduated deterrent" was recognized early on in the nuclear age by Raymond Aron. Commenting in his classic text, *On War*, Aron remarked:

> The thermonuclear weapon, especially now that both sides have it, is destined to prevent war. But can one prevent a minor aggression by threatening excessive reprisals? Should one not adjust the threat to the aggression, in other words, graduate the threat? [17]

Although Aron was referring to a condition of mutual nuclear deterrence, a condition that does not yet obtain in the fragmenting Middle East, his awareness of the need for graduation—what in American doctrine later came to be called "flexible response" [18] —was prescient and astute. Should Israel continue to keep its bomb in the basement, any deterrent benefits that might subsequently accrue from a doctrine of graduated nuclear reprisals would likely be lost. It follows that measured disclosure could substantially enhance these benefits of Israeli doctrine, and should be considered with expanding seriousness as enemy unconventional threats become expectedly more ominous.

In looking over nuclear weapons and nuclear deterrence, Israeli planners must also pay close attention to the assumption of *rationality*. Assessments of Israeli nuclear deterrence always assume a rational state enemy. But this assumption of rationality is becoming increasingly problematic.

There is, in essence, no compelling reason to assume that prospective attackers of the Jewish State will always choose deliberately among all possible options, and then according to assiduously fashioned comparisons of expected costs and benefits. As long as such enemies are increasingly capable of WMD missile attacks on Israel, and so long as Jerusalem is unable to intercept these attacks with near-perfect or possibly even perfect reliability,[19] this means that Israeli dependence on standard visions of nuclear deterrence could at some time yield unacceptable consequences.

Quo vadis? Where does Israel go from here? Barring the now nearly inconceivable prospect of a successful peace process—that is, one that does not produce a Palestinian state together with a corollary dismembering of Israel—Jerusalem must still seek security beyond those particular protections afforded by nuclear deterrence.

Israel, without in any way diminishing its essential effort to confront enemy states with nuclear weapons capacity and resolve, must also prepare appropriately for certain preemptive[20] attacks against pertinent hard targets.[21] Most important among these prospective hard targets would be certain unconventional missile capabilities and associated infrastructures.

PREEMPTION OPTIONS

Israel needs its nuclear weapons to undertake and/or to support various possible forms of preemption. In making its preemption decisions, Israel will need to determine whether any such essential defensive strikes, known jurisprudentially as expressions of anticipatory self-defense,[22] would be tactically cost effective. This, in turn, would depend on a number of critical variables including (a) expected probability of enemy first strikes, (b) expected disutility of enemy first strikes (itself dependent on the nature of enemy weaponry, projected enemy targeting doctrine, and multiplication/dispersion/hardening of Israeli nuclear forces), (c) expected schedule of enemy unconventional weapons deployment, (d) expected efficiency of enemy active defenses over time (antitactical ballistic missile developments), (e) expected efficiency of Israeli active defenses over time, (f) expected efficiency of Israeli hard-target counterforce operations over time, (g) expected reactions of unaffected regional enemies, and (h) expected US and world community reactions to Israeli preemptions.

Regarding preemption options, Israel's overall question must present as follows: Because Jerusalem must plan for such forms of anticipatory self-defense, against which particular configurations of hard targets should they then be directed, and precisely when should they be mounted? If it is assumed that pertinent enemy states will only add to their CBN arsenals and these incremental additions would make effective Israeli preemptions more and more difficult, any rational Israeli strategy would seem to compel Jerusalem to strike defensively as soon as possible.

If, however, it should be assumed that there will be no significant enlargement/deployment of enemy unconventional weapons over time, this may suggest instead a diminished rationale for Israel to strike first.

Critical considerations here would include assorted Israeli assumptions about enemy rationality, expectations about tangible costs to Israel of enemy aggression in the near term, comparisons of the costs to Israel of enemy near-term aggression with those of enemy reprisals to Israeli preemptive attacks, and projected efficacy, over time, of Israeli and enemy advanced tactical ballistic missile (ATBM) operations.

Israel's inclinations to strike preemptively in certain circumstances could be affected in part by the steps taken by prospective target states to guard against any Israeli preemption. Should Israel refrain too long from striking first, enemy states could then implement protective measures that would pose additional hazards to Israel. These inhibiting measures could include the attachment of "hair trigger" launch mechanisms to nuclear weapon systems and/or the adoption of "launch-on-warning" policies,[23] possibly coupled in some fashion with predelegations of launch authority.

Optimally, Israel would do everything possible to prevent any such measures from being installed in the first place, especially because of the expanded risks of accidental or unauthorized attacks against its armaments and population centers.[24] But if such measures should become a fait accompli, Jerusalem might then still calculate that a preemptive strike would be cost effective. This is because an expected enemy retaliation, however damaging, might appear *less unacceptable* than the expected consequences of enemy first strikes, strikes likely occasioned by the failure of critical "antipreemption" measures.

Perhaps the single most important factor in Israeli judgments on the preemption option will be the *expected rationality* of enemy decision makers. If these leaders could be expected to strike at Israel with unconventional forces, irrespective of anticipated Israeli counterstrikes, deterrence would not work. This means that enemy strikes could be expected even if enemy leaders understood that Israel had successfully deployed its own nuclear weapons in survivable modes, Israel's weapons were entirely capable of penetrating enemy active defenses, and Israel's leaders were determinably willing to retaliate.

If faced with an irrational enemy seemingly bent on launching unconventional aggression, Israel could have no effective choice but to abandon reliance on the traditional modes of nuclear deterrence. Here, preemption/prevention could become obligatory; the only real policy questions would then center on specific matters of timing, targeting, and ordnance.

Initial judgments concerning enemy definitions of "unacceptable damage" would have to be made with very great care. Indeed, there could be essentially no room for error on this core Israeli judgment.

Even if it is not faced with an irrational enemy, Israel will have to plan carefully for preemption options, planning that must ultimately take into account Jerusalem's nuclear weapons. In the course of any such planning, it would become important to recognize that enemy capabilities and intentions are not separate or discrete, but more or less interpenetrating, interdependent, and *interactive.* This means (1) capabilities could affect intentions and vice versa and (2) the combined effects of capabilities and intentions could be *synergistic,* producing policy outcomes that are accelerated and/or exceed the simple sum of these discrete effects.

Most urgently, Israel must consider the particular dangers from Iran.[25] Those who might still downplay the Iranian threat to Israel would likely argue that Tehran's cumulative unconventional capabilities will remain problematic, and/or its actual willingness to attack Israel—fundamentalist Shiite ideologies notwithstanding—is reassuringly low. Yet over the next several years, despite the July 2015 Vienna Agreement on Iran, that country's progress on nuclear weapons will almost certainly be dramatic and could even create the conditions whereby a first strike against Israel would at some time be construed as rational.

Whether correct or incorrect in its particular calculations, any Iranian leadership that *believed* it could strike Israel with impunity or near impunity, or at least without incurring *what it would define* as unacceptable costs, could plausibly decide to undertake such a strike.

Any such motivation could be heightened further, to the extent that Iran might remain uncertain about Israel's own preemption plans. With such dialectics, Iranian capabilities could affect, and then possibly even determine, Iranian intentions.

The Iranian threat to Israel might originate from a different direction. In this alternate scenario, Iran's intentions toward the Jewish State, irremediably hostile and perhaps even genocidal,[26] could continually animate Tehran's enthusiastic development of unconventional military capabilities. Now representing far-reaching hatreds rather than just narrowly propagandistic bravado, Iranian diatribes against Israel could effectively ensure the production/deployment of forces, weapons, and postures to more meaningfully threaten the Jewish State.

Such circumstances now warrant careful attention in Jerusalem.[27]

Always, the most complex relationships between enemy capabilities and intentions would concern *synergy*. The issue here is not whether or to what extent one threat component affects the other, but instead how various combinations might (a) produce an ongoing series of interactions that move relentlessly through their own unstoppable, dialectical momentum toward war, or (b) produce a wholly new effect, one of which either capability or intention is individually inadequate. An example of (a) would be an enemy (Iranian) "bolt from the blue" attack against Israel that is launched only because of the particularly interactive way in which capabilities and intentions feed on each other. An example of (b) would be any enemy (Iranian) attack against Israel—bolt from the blue or product of escalation, conventional or unconventional—that would not otherwise have taken place.

An intervening variable in this discussion of intentions, capabilities, and preemption options is the rapidly disappearing peace process. To be sure, conventional wisdom has always been quick to suggest that the *Roadmap*, by demonstrating and codifying Israel's commitment to peaceful settlement of disputes, would diminish the enemy (Iranian) nuclear threat. After all, queries this bit of wisdom, wouldn't world public opinion uniformly condemn Iran for any acts of aggression directed against a presumptively peacemaking Israel?

Amid an alleged search for peace, wouldn't Iranian aggressive intentions be reduced, or even removed, a fortuitous change that could then correspondingly slow down Tehran's pertinent unconventional militarization and consequently the overall danger to Israel issuing from that enemy state?

Probably not. The conventional wisdom here is likely unwise. At best, it is merely partial.

Following the Oslo Accords,[28] Israel's inclination to preempt enemy (Iranian) aggression had likely been diminished. Plainly, the entire global community would have frowned on any such preemption launched in the midst of an ongoing and incremental search for peace in the region.

If Iran should recognize these effective inhibitions on Israeli preemption options as ongoing, its leaders could then calculate as follows: "As our (Iranian) militarization will be less threatened by an Israeli preemptive attack during a peace process, we (Iran) should *increase* our capabilities—especially our unconventional weapons capabilities—as quickly as practicable." Such a calculation could enlarge Iranian intentions to attack Israel, and even render cost effective certain hostile actions by Iran that might not otherwise have been seriously considered.

Because the peace process might produce a Palestinian state,[29] the effects on enemy capabilities and intentions and therefore on Israeli preemption options could become significant. Immediately, Israel's substantial loss of strategic depth would be recognized by enemy states as a significant military liability for Jerusalem.[30] Such recognition in turn could heat up enemy intentions against Israel, occasioning an accelerated search for new capabilities and also an incrementally heightened risk of major war.

Israel could foresee such enemy calculations and also seek to compensate for its loss of territories in different ways. For one, Jerusalem could decide that it was high time to take its bomb out of the basement as a deterrence-enhancing measure, but this still might not be enough of a productive strategy. For another it could, at least in principle, also accept a greater willingness to launch preemptive strikes against enemy hard targets, strikes ultimately backed up by Israeli nuclear weapons and doctrine.

Made aware of such Israeli intentions, intentions that would derive from Israel's newly generated territorial vulnerabilities, enemy states could then respond in a more or less parallel fashion, preparing more openly and quickly for nuclearization and/or various first-strike attacks against the Jewish State.

In this particular scenario, the pertinent relationships between capabilities, intentions, and preemption options would be made manifest not only within Israel and certain enemy states, but also between Israel and these states. These relationships, too, could sometimes become authentically synergistic, thereby generating certain ominous cycles of escalation, some perhaps with unintended and potentially catastrophic consequences.

Even if considered by itself, in isolation, a Palestinian state would affect the capabilities and intentions of both Israel and its enemies. But if such a state were created at the same time that Israel had reduced or abandoned its nuclear weapons capabilities, the impact could then become far more substantial. This particular narrative, moreover, should not be dismissed out of hand.

What would happen if Israel were ever willing to relinquish its nuclear options by acceding to the NPT as a nonnuclear weapon state and to simultaneously accept a Palestinian state?[31] Under such concessionary circumstances,[32] Israel would not only be more vulnerable to enemy first strikes; it would also be deprived of its essential preemption options. This is the case because Israeli counterretaliatory deterrence would have been immobilized by the reduction or removal of its nuclear weapons potential, and Israeli preemptions could not possibly be one hundred percent effective against enemy unconventional forces.

A less than one hundred percent level of effectiveness could be tolerable if Israel had a perfect, or even near-perfect, ATBM capability, but such a capability is not yet possible.

How might enemy states respond to Israel's weakened capabilities and also to its correspondingly diminished preemption options? An informed observer might expect certain of these states, especially Iran, to move more purposefully and ambitiously toward full-fledged nuclear status, a move that would likely encourage first-strike intentions against Israel. There, is then, an important intranational (within Israel) interaction between NPT expectations for Israel and the creation of a Palestinian state, and an important international interaction (Israel and its enemies) between reduced Israeli capabilities/intentions and enlarged enemy capabilities/intentions.

These synergies, in turn, could impair regional or even world security, affecting the capabilities and intentions of other pertinent states, and revealing, in effect, a more or less corrosive "synergy of synergies" or "cascade of synergies."

Finally, regarding Israeli nuclear weapons and Israeli preemption options, it is vital for Israeli strategic planners to further explore the questions of counterforce versus countervalue strategies.[33] Should Israel opt primarily for the former, which might appear more reasonable, enemy first strikes could also become more likely. Recognizing this, Israel could then become more likely to strike first itself.

Should Israel alternatively opt primarily for a recognizably countervalue nuclear strategy, the preemption option could then become less compelling, but the consequences to Israel if nuclear deterrence were somehow to fail would likely be worse. This is because any largely countervalue strategy by definition would carry a tangibly diminished damage limitation capability.

NUCLEAR WAR-FIGHTING OPTIONS

In principle, at least, Israel needs nuclear weapons for possible nuclear war fighting. Should its nuclear deterrence options and/or preemption options fail, Israel's hard-target counterforce capabilities could become more or less critical to national survival. These capabilities would depend in part on holding appropriate nuclear weapons.[34]

What exactly would be "appropriate"? Instead of Armageddon-type weapons (see discussion below on the Samson Option), Israel could require precision, low-yield nuclear warheads, weapons that could reduce collateral damage to acceptable levels, and hypervelocity nuclear warheads, which could help overcome enemy active defenses. Israel would also benefit from certain radio-frequency weapons. These are nuclear warheads that are tailored to produce as much electromagnetic pulse as possible, destroying electronics and communications over wide areas.

Regarding the nuclear weapons needed by Israel for nuclear war fighting, Jerusalem could sometimes require an intermediate option between capitulation on the one hand and resorting to inappropriately large nuclear weapons on the other.

Naturally, all such discussion will be objectionable to people of feeling and sensitivity. In the best of all possible worlds, it would be far better to speak auspiciously of nuclear nonproliferation and nuclear arms control, or even sustainable nuclear deterrence,[35] than of nuclear war fighting. Yet the Middle East remains a particularly dangerous neighborhood, and, paradoxically, failures to confront the most terrible possibilities could produce the most terrible harms.

THE SAMSON OPTION

Israel needs nuclear weapons, additional to the other essential rationales already discussed, for certain last-resort purposes. Although, contrary to popular view, this is the least important need—by definition any actual resort to a Samson Option would reveal the failure and collapse of all other essential security functions—it is not altogether unimportant. This is because Israeli *preparations* for last-resort operations could still play a productive role in enhancing Israeli nuclear deterrence, preemption, and war-fighting options.

Regarding prospective contributions to Israeli nuclear deterrence, preparations for a Samson Option could help convince would-be attackers that any planned aggressions would not prove gainful. This is especially the case if pertinent Israeli preparations were coupled with some level of *disclosure*, if Israel's "Samson" weapons appeared sufficiently invulnerable to enemy first strikes, and if these weapons were identifiably *countervalue* in mission function.[36] In view of what strategists sometimes call the "rationality of pretended irrationality," Samson could also assist Israeli nuclear deterrence by demonstrating a determined willingness to take existential risks, but this would hold true only if Israel's last-resort options were not tied definitionally to expectations of *certain* destruction.

To some extent at least, the nuclear deterrence benefits of pretended irrationality would depend on an enemy awareness of Israel's countervalue targeting.

Regarding prospective contributions to preemption options, preparations for a Samson Option could convince *Israel* that essential defensive first strikes might be undertaken with diminished expectations of unacceptably destructive enemy retaliations. This would depend, of course, on antecedent Israeli decisions on disclosure, Israeli perceptions of the effects of disclosure on enemy retaliatory prospects, Israeli judgments about enemy perceptions of Samson weapons vulnerability, and an enemy awareness of Samson's countervalue force posture. As in the case of Samson and Israeli nuclear deterrence (above), certain last-resort preparations could assist Israeli preemption options by displaying a willingness to take existential risks.

But Israeli planners must remain mindful here of pretended irrationality as a double-edged sword. Brandished too "irrationally," Israeli preparations for a Samson Option could unwittingly encourage certain enemy state preemptions.

Regarding prospective contributions to Israel's nuclear war-fighting options, preparations for a Samson Option could convince enemy states that a clear victory would be impossible to achieve (i.e., that even after overwhelming the Jewish State and its military forces, these states would face their own destruction). But here it would be important for Israel to communicate to potential aggressors the following understanding: Israel's countervalue-targeted (Samson) weapons are *additional to,* not at the expense of, its counterforce-targeted (war-fighting) weapons. In the absence of any such communication, preparations for a Samson Option could effectively impair, rather than reinforce, Israel's very limited nuclear war-fighting options.

FROM PERICLES TO THE PRESENT

UN General Assembly resolutions on nonproliferation notwithstanding, Israel needs its nuclear weapons. These weapons are required to fulfill essential deterrence options, preemption options, the Samson Option, and even (at least residually) limited war-fighting options. It follows that Israel's nuclear weapons should never be negotiated away in any presumed compliance with nonproliferation treaty or nuclear weapon free zone expectations, especially in the midst of a so-called peace process and its attendant creation of Palestine.

Optimally, Israel's particular nuclear weapons choices should be made in cumulative conformance with the seven pertinent needs that have been discussed above, and more broadly with the ever-changing geostrategic context of regional and world power configurations. In the final analysis, regrettable as it may appear, the ultimate structure of Israeli security must be built largely on the tangible foundations of national nuclear weapons and posture, not on nonproliferation, nuclear weapon free zones, security regimes, or confidence-building measures. It is now up to scholars who seek a real peace for Israel, and not those who are deceived by a persistently chimerical diplomacy, to effectively construct these potentially more solid foundations.

For Israel's leaders, the time has arrived to more fully understand the core nature of enemy state intentions and capabilities. To make such an understanding possible, these leaders must first strive to recognize all pertinent connections between power and survival. Once it is learned that enemy state definitions of the former are contingent on Israel's loss of the latter, these Israeli decision-makers will finally be positioned to take appropriately remedial actions.

The UN cannot replace natural law. Correspondingly, it can never require any of its members to forfeit the Charter's "inherent right" to survival and self-defense. As a fully sovereign state, Israel maintains not only the privilege but also the obligation to ward off existential harms. In short, for a beleaguered state that is literally smaller than America's Lake Michigan, a secure and credible nuclear deterrent remains indispensable and nonnegotiable.

When Pericles delivered his *Funeral Oration* during the Peloponnesian War (431–404 BCE), he expressed confidence in an ultimate victory for Athens but also a grave concern for any self-imposed strategic errors that might be committed along the way. "What I fear more than the strategies of our enemies," warned the cautious Athenian statesman, "is our own mistakes." Although Pericles had exaggerated the separateness of enemy strategies and Athenian mistakes, there is still an enduring lesson here for present-day Israel: *In observing myriad enemy preparations for war, do not forget that the ultimate effectiveness of these preparations will depend on Israel's own considered responses.*

Whatever the unique particularities of such responses, Jerusalem must never willfully place in jeopardy its foundational nuclear infrastructures and strategies.

International law is never a suicide pact. *"The safety of the People,"* noted Cicero, *"shall be the highest law."*

NOTES

1. There is a well-known passage in Francis Bacon's *The Advancement of Learning* wherein the early philosopher of science says that the scholastics were like spiders, weaving webs out of their own heads without any consideration of surrounding facts. To be sure, these webs were admirable on account of their workmanship and fineness of thread, but they were nonetheless lacking in any true explanatory substance (I, iv, 5). Presently, in explaining Israel's nuclear weapons and corollary need for nuclear doctrine, it is important to construct upon suitably fact-based foundations, not on the diaphanous constructions of modern-day scholastics.

2. There does exist a professional and popular literature on specific and tangible security threats to Israel, especially the continuing problem of Iranian nuclear weapons, and certain related issues of conceivably reciprocal Arab nuclear proliferation. See by this author, Louis René Beres, "Like Two Scorpions in a Bottle: Could Israel and a Nuclear Iran Coexist in the Middle East?" *The Israel Journal of Foreign Affairs*, Vol. 8. No. 1, 2014, pp. 23–32; Louis René Beres and (General/USAF/ret.) John T. Chain, "Could Israel Safely Deter a Nuclear Iran?" *The Atlantic*, August 9, 2012; and Louis René Beres and General Chain, "Living With Iran," BESA Center for Strategic Studies, Israel, May 2014.

3. Counterforce strategies target an enemy's strategic military facilities and supporting infrastructures. Such strategies may be dangerous not only because of the collateral damage they might produce but also because they could heighten the likelihood of first-strike attacks.

4. Biological weapons may be of less immediate concern for Israel than chemical weapons. Although a growing number of countries have or are currently developing capabilities to employ living organisms (such as anthrax, Lassa fever, or typhus, as

opposed to inert toxins), such capabilities have limited military value. This is because their dispersal mechanisms are difficult to manage (a change of wind can make them as lethal to the attacker as to the intended victim) and it is difficult to sustain the living organisms in biological weapons in hot climates for long periods. At the same time, precisely because biological weapons are better suited for mass destruction than for use as dedicated military instruments, they could hold out greater appeal to Israel's more or less discernibly *irrational* enemies.

5. Some current Israeli supporters of a Palestinian state argue that its prospective harms to Israel could be reduced or even eliminated by ensuring that state's immediate demilitarization. For informed reasoning against this naive argument, see Louis René Beres and (Ambassador) Zalman Shoval, "Why a Demilitarized Palestinian State Would Not Remain Demilitarized: A View Under International Law," *Temple International and Comparative Law Journal*, Winter 1998, pp. 347–363; and Louis René Beres and Ambassador Shoval, "On Demilitarizing a Palestinian 'Entity' and the Golan Heights: An International Law Perspective," *Vanderbilt Journal of Transnational Law*, Vol. 28, No. 5, November 1995, pp. 959–972.

6. Both Israeli nuclear and nonnuclear preemptions of enemy unconventional attacks could lead to nuclear exchanges. This would depend in part on the effectiveness and breadth of Israeli targeting, the surviving number of enemy nuclear weapons, and the willingness of enemy leaders to risk an Israeli nuclear counterretaliation.

7. Regarding the particular context of Israeli deterrence, a *rational* state enemy of the Jewish State will accept or reject a first-strike option by comparing the costs and benefits of each alternative. Where the expected costs of striking first are taken to exceed expected gains, this enemy will be deterred. But where these expected costs are believed to be *exceeded by* expected gains, deterrence will fail.

8. Israel's nuclear counterretaliatory threat could conceivably be diminished by certain enemy threats of unacceptably damaging counter counterretaliations. There is an infinite regress process at work here, one that is confusing and bothersome to consider. Nonetheless, its annoying complexity in escalatory dynamics does not in any way rule out its relevance.

9. For generic assessments of the probable consequences of nuclear war fighting by this author, see, for example, Louis René Beres, *Apocalypse: Nuclear Catastrophe in World Politics* (Chicago: University of Chicago Press, 1980); Louis René Beres, *Mimicking Sisyphus: America's Countervailing Nuclear Strategy* (Lexington, MA: Lexington Books, 1983); Louis René Beres, *Reason and Realpolitik: U.S. Foreign Policy and World Order* (Lexington, MA: Lexington Books, 1984); and Louis René Beres, ed., *Security or Armageddon: Israel's Nuclear Strategy* (Lexington, MA: Lexington Books, 1986).

10. Regarding very early writings by this author on nuclear terrorism, see Louis René Beres, *Security Threats and Effective Remedies: Israel's Strategic, Tactical and Legal Options*, Ariel Center for Policy Research (Israel), Policy Paper #102, April 2000, 110 pp.; Louis René Beres, *Terrorism and Global Security: The Nuclear Threat*, second ed. (Boulder and London: Westview Press, 1987); and Louis René Beres, "Confronting Nuclear Terrorism," *The Hastings International and Comparative Law Review*, Vol. 14, No. 1, Fall 1990, pp. 129–154; Summer 1994.

11. Punishment of aggression is a firm and longstanding expectation of international criminal law. The peremptory principle of *nullum crimen sine poena* (no crime without a punishment) has its origins in the Code of Hammurabi (c. 1728–1686 BCE); the Laws of Eshnunna (c. 2000 BCE); the even earlier Code of Ur-Nammu (c. 2100 BCE), and the law of exact retaliation, or *lex talionis*, presented in three separate passages of the Torah.

12. See most recently by this writer, Louis René Beres, "Israel's Strategic Doctrine: Updating Intelligence Community Responsibilities," *International Journal of Intelligence and Counterintelligence*, 2015, 28:1, pp. 89–104; Louis René Beres, "Changing Direction? Updating Israel's Nuclear Doctrine," *Strategic Assessment*, The Institute for National Security Studies, Tel Aviv University, Vol. 17, No. 3, October 2014, pp. 93–106; Louis René Beres, "Facing Myriad Enemies: Core Elements of Israeli Nuclear Deterrence,"

The Brown Journal of World Affairs, Fall/Winter 2013, Vol. XX, Issue 1, pp. 17–30; and Louis René Beres, "Looking Ahead: Revising Israel's Nuclear Ambiguity in the Middle East," Herzliya Conference, Policy Paper, Herzliya Conference, March 11–14, 2013 (IDC Herzliya, Israel).

13. Nor can Israel rely on nuclear protections offered by the United States as "extended deterrence." Indeed, implausible and unreliable during the Cold War, extended deterrence in the current world order is even more problematic. With the effective disappearance of Israel as a "strategic asset," the United States would almost certainly not regard any conceivable nuclear retaliation on behalf of Israel to be cost effective. Moreover, in the event of a "Cold War II," Israel could even find itself lined up more closely on certain issues with Moscow than with Washington. See on this prospect, Louis René Beres, "Staying Strong: Enhancing Israel's Essential Strategic Options," *Harvard National Security Journal*, Harvard Law School, June 13, 2014.

14. The flip side of this calculation is the effect of Israel's own active defense system. Should a would-be attacker believe Israel's *Hetz* (or related/integrated systems) would display an appropriately high degree of effectiveness, such belief could then discourage an attack decision against Israel by lowering the attacker's expected benefits.

15. Analytically, disclosure should not be treated dichotomously (i.e., only two options: disclosure or nondisclosure) but *continuously*. This would allow Israeli planners to identify multiple disclosure options along a broad continuum of possibilities and to choose that particular *level* of released information that is presumed maximally gainful to Israeli nuclear deterrence.

16. For now, Israeli nuclear forces could surely penetrate the active defenses of *any* enemy attacker after the Jewish State had itself absorbed a first-strike attack. This could change in the future if there were substantial enemy progress on appropriate forms of antitactical ballistic missile (ATBM) defenses and/or an enemy state or states were allowed to achieve a devastating first-strike capability (i.e., one would effectively preclude an Israeli reprisal).

17. See Aron's *On War*, Terence Kilmartin, tr. (New York: Doubleday Anchor, 1959), p. 81.

18. In the United States, "flexible response" ultimately evolved into doctrine known as the "countervailing nuclear strategy." Codified in Presidential Directive #59, which was signed on July 25, 1980, and later reaffirmed by President Ronald Reagan, this strategy represented the latest retreat from the doctrine of "massive retaliation" (a doctrine authoritatively defined by John Foster Dulles on January 13, 1954). The countervailing strategy envisioned a broad array of nuclear retaliatory options within a carefully defined spectrum of deterrence.

19. With particular reference to Arrow/*Hetz*, an Israeli ATBM deployment could sometimes become little more than a refashioned Bar-Lev line, perhaps encouraging false reassurances and providing little real soft-target protection. In the case of possible space-based defense against ballistic missiles, this refashioned Bar-Lev line could even display "orbiting" characteristics. On Israel and Arrow, see Louis René Beres and Major General (IDF/ret.) Isaac Ben-Israel, "Think Anticipatory Self-Defense," *The Jerusalem Post*, October 22, 2007; Professor Beres and Major General Ben-Israel, "The Limits of Deterrence," *Washington Times*, November 21, 2007; Professor Beres and MG Ben-Israel, "Deterring Iran," *Washington Times*, June 10, 2007; and Professor Beres and MG Ben-Israel, "Deterring Iranian Nuclear Attack," *Washington Times*, January 27, 2009.

20. Jurisprudentially, there is an important distinction between preemptive attacks and preventive attacks. Preemption is a military strategy of striking an enemy first in the expectation that the only recognizable alternative is to be struck first oneself. A preemptive attack is launched by a state that believes enemy forces are about to attack. A preventive attack, however, is launched not out of concern for imminent hostilities but for fear of a longer-term deterioration in the presumptive vital military balance.

21. Contrary to conventional wisdom, both nuclear deterrence and associated forms of nuclear strategy, including preemption, can fully support the authoritative expectations of international law. The adequacy of international law in preventing nuclear

war in the Middle East will depend on far more than certain formal treaties, customs, and general principles. It will depend especially on the success or failure of particular country strategies in the region. If Israel's nuclear strategy should reduce the threat of nuclear war because of either successful forms of nuclear deterrence or essential preemptive strikes, this strategy could then be considered as an authentic component of international law enforcement.

22. For early scholarly examinations of anticipatory self-defense by this author and with particular reference to Israel, see Louis René Beres, "Preserving the Third Temple: Israel's Right of Anticipatory Self-Defense Under International Law," *Vanderbilt Journal of Transnational Law*, Vol. 26, No. 1, April 1993, pp. 111–148; Louis René Beres, "After the Gulf War: Israel, Preemption and Anticipatory Self-Defense," *Houston Journal of International Law*, Vol. 13, No. 2, Spring 1991, pp. 259–280; and Louis René Beres, "Striking 'First': Israel's Post Gulf War Options Under International Law," *Loyola of Los Angeles International and Comparative Law Journal*, Vol. 14, Nov. 1991, pp. 1–24.

23. "Launch on warning" describes a strategic doctrine that calls for the retaliatory launch of bombers and/or missiles on receipt of warning that a missile attack is under way. This doctrine, which requires launch before the attacking warheads reach their intended targets, is sometimes called "launch on positive or confirmed notification of attack," to distinguish between the possible and actual attack.

24. Other risks to Israel of such measures could be associated with the compressed time available to enemy decision makers under prompt launch options, and Jerusalem's uncertainty about thresholds of attack above which enemy decision makers would opt for a prompt launch. Even if well-defined thresholds were known to Israeli leaders (this assumes, of course, the antecedent premise that enemy decision makers had actually advanced such authoritative definitions), they could still be low enough to become destabilizing.

25. On July 23, 2014, Iran's Supreme Leader, Ali Khamenei, called openly for the annihilation of Israel. See Y. Mansharof, E. Kharrazi, Y. Lahat, and A. Savyon, "Quds Day in Iran: Calls for Annihilation of Israel and Arming the West Bank," MEMRI, July 25, 2014, *Inquiry and Analysis Series Report*, No. 1107.

26. War and genocide need not be mutually exclusive. War might well be the means whereby genocide is undertaken. According to Articles II and III of the Genocide Convention, which entered into force on January 12, 1951, genocide includes any of several listed acts "committed with intent to destroy, in whole or in part, a national, ethnical, racial or religious group as such." See Convention on the Prevention and Punishment of the Crime of Genocide, done at New York, Dec. 9, 1948. Entered into force, Jan. 12, 1951. 78 UNTS 277.

27. A portion of the Islamic world's genocidal intentions against "Jewish occupiers" predates the creation of Israel in 1948. On November 28, 1941, Haj Amin, the Grand Mufti of Jerusalem, met in Berlin with Adolph Hitler. The acknowledged subject of their meeting was "The Jewish Question."

28. From the start, the Oslo Accords were arguably null and void according to authoritative international law. All states are obligated by international law to seek out and prosecute the perpetrators of crimes of war, crimes against peace, crimes against humanity, and crimes of terrorism. See, among others, *Draft Code of Offenses Against the Peace and Security of Mankind*, GAOR, No. 9, A/2693. Derived from the norm of *nullum crimen sine poena* (no crime without a punishment), this peremptory obligation was plainly violated by Israel's volitional agreement with a known terrorist organization.

29. See Louis René Beres, "Implications of a Palestinian State for Israeli Security and Nuclear War: A Jurisprudential Assessment," *Dickinson Journal of International Law*, Vol. 17, No. 2, pp. 229–286.

30. A great deal, of course, has been written on the question of strategic depth. The heart of the issue was addressed as early as June 29, 1967, when a US Joint Chiefs of Staff memorandum specified that returning Israel to pre-1967 boundaries would drastically increase its vulnerability. The then Chairman of the JCS, General Earl Wheeler,

concluded that for *minimal* deterrence and defense, Israel must retain Sharm el-Sheikh and Wadi El Girali in the Sinai; the entire Gaza Strip; the high ground and plateaus of the mountains in Judea and Samaria; and the Golan Heights, east of Quneitra.

31. This question was examined fully by this author, many years back. See Louis René Beres, "The Nonproliferation Treaty and the Loss of Israel's Strategic Assets: The Looming Threat," *Nativ*, Vol. 6, No. 6, November 1993, pp. 15–18.

32. Similar circumstances might be occasioned by Israeli adherence to a *nuclear weapons free zone* arrangement for the Middle East. For Israel, such a zonal agreement could leave the Jewish State more vulnerable to certain devastating enemy attacks. Deprived of its ultimate form of deterrence and war fighting, Israel, at best, could be subject to massive conventional and/or chemical and biological first strikes. At worst, an enemy state or states would continue clandestinely to acquire nuclear weapons, leaving Israel to face the choice of extinction or capitulation. Nonetheless, it should still be noted here that nuclear war fighting could never be an optimal option for Israel. This point was in fact a major conclusion of *Israel's Strategic Future: The Final Report of Project Daniel*, ACPR Policy Paper No. 155, ACPR, Israel, May 2004, 64 pp. See also Louis René Beres, "Facing Iran's Ongoing Nuclearization: A Retrospective on Project Daniel," *International Journal of Intelligence and Counterintelligence*, Vol. 22, Issue 3, June 2009, pp. 491–514. Professor Beres served as chair of Project Daniel.

33. In considering this question, Israeli planners should undertake antecedent investigations of enemy inclinations to strike first and associated enemy intentions to strike all at once or in stages.

34. A contrary position was offered by Yehoshafat Harkabi, a former head of Aman (IDF Military Intelligence). Writing in *The Bar Kokhba Syndrome*, Harkabi argues that while "it is not absurd for the nuclear powers to plan for nuclear warfare," nuclear war itself *is* "absurd." See *The Bar Kokhba Syndrome: Risk and Realism in International Politics* (Chappaqua, NY: Rossel Books, 1983).

35. It should be recalled that Israeli preparations for nuclear war fighting could be conceived not as distinct *alternatives* to nuclear deterrence, but as essential and even integral *components* of nuclear deterrence. Some years ago, Colin Gray, reasoning about US-Soviet nuclear relations, argued that a vital connection exists between "likely net prowess in war and the quality of pre-war deterrent effect." (See Colin Gray, "National Style in Strategy: The American Example," *International Security*, 6, No. 2, fall 1981, p. 35.) Elsewhere, in a published debate with this writer, Gray said essentially the same thing: "Fortunately, there is every reason to believe that probable high proficiency in war-waging yields optimum deterrent effect." (See Gray, "Presidential Directive 59: Flawed But Useful," *Parameters*, 11, No. 1, March 1981, p. 34. Gray was responding directly to Louis René Beres, "Presidential Directive 59: A Critical Assessment," *Parameters*, March 1981, pp. 19–28.)

36. By definition, the Samson Option would be executed with countervalue-targeted nuclear weapons. Reasonably, Israeli last-resort operations could come into play only after all Israeli counterforce options had already been exhausted.

TWO

Refining Strategic Choices

"The primary point of Israel's nuclear forces must always be deterrence *ex ante*, not revenge *ex post*."
—*Israel's Strategic Future: The Final Report of Project Daniel* (Israel, 2004)

Sometimes strategic truth may emerge through paradox. We have just seen that Israel needs nuclear weapons not only to survive but also to best serve this existential objective through purposeful nonuse.[1] Above all, this means that nuclear weapons should operate as an effective deterrent and not as an instrument of actual war fighting.[2]

To be sure, pragmatically, at least, Israel must remain prepared for any conceivable nuclear exchange. Simultaneously, any such fearful contingency should be regarded with maximum sobriety—that is, as an absolutely residual or distinctly last resort option.

CONFRONTING CORE THREATS WITH DOCTRINE-BASED RESPONSES

For Israel, a beleaguered mini-state always beset by multiple and overlapping axes of conflict, profoundly new existential challenges are rapidly emerging. Some of these challenges are many sided and interpenetrating. Most obvious, of course, is the steady nuclearization of Iran and the exacerbating risks of a Jihadist Palestinian State. Although seemingly unrelated and discrete, these core challenges could quickly become palpably interactive, thereby creating a potentially lethal "forcer multiplier" that would function on behalf of Israel's enemies. To endure, therefore, Israel must now consciously locate and interpret these linked hazards within a coherent and suitably comprehensive context of codified *nuclear doctrine*.

For Israel's strategic future, such doctrine represents an indispensable "net." Only those who *cast*, therefore, can be expected to *catch*.

There is more. Strategic understanding can be counterintuitive. For Israel to survive, nothing will be more practical than a doctrine rooted in *good theory.* Indeed, on absolutely all matters of human preservation and national survival, good theory represents an essential tool to fashion purposeful policy and, as corollary, to prescribe pertinent orientations.

To optimize this critical work, Israeli nuclear strategists will need to begin at the beginning, acknowledging above all that regional anarchy, a debilitating inheritance of many centuries in the making, is not just a distressing or idiosyncratic function of the global moment. Rather, as these strategists shall certainly need to recognize, such disorder is embedded in the very formalized and customary structures of modern world politics.

Today, as we have already seen, these legal and geopolitical structures point unerringly to chaotic regional disintegration. Yet even in chaos, *which is never the same as anarchy,* there may also be some discernible regularities, a sort of more or less ascertainable "geometry." This discoverable *geometry of chaos* should be properly identified and then studied. Out of the melee of what is now unraveling in Syria, Libya, Egypt, Tunisia, Yemen, Iraq, Bahrain, Jordan, Lebanon, and elsewhere, Israel's strategic thinkers could still discover a usable tableau of their country's most plausible survival scenarios, but only if they can first cast fully suitable "nets."

ANARCHY, CHAOS, AND ISRAEL'S PROSPECT OF CATASTROPHIC ENEMY INTERACTIONS

Both world and regional politics remain unalterably complex. There is no good argument for examining principal threats to Israel's survival (e.g., Iran's nuclear program, Egypt's Muslim Brotherhood, Hezbollah activities in Lebanon and Syria, Hamas operations in Gaza, ISIS advances in Sinai and Syria, etc.) as if they were somehow singular and unrelated. On the contrary, there are distinctly *foreseeable interactions* between these seemingly separate catastrophic harms. And these so-called *synergies* could make the potentially existential risks[3] to Israel of anarchy and chaos even more pressing.

The dangers to Israel of chaotic regional disintegration are particular and unique. Facing not only a still-growing nuclear threat from Iran but also the more or less simultaneous appearance of Palestine, the Jewish State could quickly find itself engulfed in assorted incidents of mass-casualty terrorism and/or unconventional war. These hazards, moreover, are apt to be expanded as ISIS moves closer to seeking territorial gains across Jordan, all the way to the West Bank (Judea/Samaria)—a movement that could mean subsequent "displacements" of Hamas and Fatah by the ISIS death cult in "Palestine."

Should this happen, it would represent an unanticipated irony—that is, that the greatest threat to Palestinian statehood did not turn out to be the Jewish State, but rather another Sunni Arab terrorist organization. For Israel, moreover, an ISIS-dominated state of Palestine would likely prove far worse than one more expressly faithful to Fatah and/or Hamas.

Credo quia absurdum (I believe because it is absurd). This is an ancient adage (Tertullian) that Israeli nuclear strategists should promptly place as a revealing "frontlet" between their eyes.

A growing threat to Israel will assuredly be the suicide bomber in macrocosm. The probability of genuine Middle East chaos could be massively enlarged by assorted instances of *enemy irrationality*. If, for example, Israel should begin to face a Jihadist adversary that would value certain presumed religious expectations more highly than its own physical survival, Israel's deterrent could be weakened or immobilized. Such a paralysis of Israeli power could, at some point, imply a heightened threat of nuclear and/or biological war.

"The blood-dimmed tide is loosed," wrote the great Irish poet W. B. Yeats, "and everywhere the ceremony of innocence is drowned." Now assembled in almost two hundred armed tribal camps still quite benignly called *nation-states*, all peoples, not exclusively Israelis and their neighbors, coexist very insecurely on a determinedly fractured planet.[4]

In one worst case scenario, there will be no safety in arms, no rescues from political authority, and no reassuring answers from science. Then new wars will rage until every flower of culture is trampled and until all things human are leveled in a conspicuously primal disorder. "The worst," once remarked Friedrich Durrenmatt, "does sometimes happen."

Durrenmatt, a prescient Swiss playwright, was not mistaken. Lamentably, in history and world politics, the "worst" is actually a very old story. So, too, is anarchy. Chaos, however, is not. There *is* a meaningful analytic difference here, especially for Israel.

Aware that even an incremental collapse of remaining world authority structures will impact its friends as well as its enemies, Israel's leaders will need to heed Durrenmatt's incontestable observation about the "worst." This means they will need to advance certain precise and compelling premonitions of collapse in order to chart durable paths to survival. Such a dual awareness is likely not yet in place. Instead, the principal paths under serious diplomatic consideration in Jerusalem still seem to concern certain enemy-specific "sanctions" against Iran and the badly twisted cartographies of a two-state solution.

Once again, especially if they should pay attention to the viscerally disingenuous suggestions of prominent pundits and politicos, Israel's leaders could waste more precious time with noisily ritualistic and clichéd considerations of American peace plans. Instead, they should begin to consider immediately how Israel ought to respond to international life in a global *state of nature*. In this connection, the specific triggering mechanism of our disassembling world's incremental descent into chaos could originate from a variety of different mass-casualty assaults against Israel and/or from similar and possibly simultaneous assaults against other Western democracies.

Even the traditionally powerful United States, now facing huge economic and infrastructure dislocations, would not be immune to this starkly remorseless vulnerability.

Any chaotic disintegration of the world system would fundamentally transform the Israeli system. Again, recalling the Swiss playwright, such a transformation could ultimately involve total or near-total destruction. In anticipation, Israel will have to orient its strategic planning to an assortment of dire-case prospects, thus focusing much more deliberately, albeit reluctantly, on a wide range of primarily *self-help* security options.

Durrenmatt's *State of Nations* remains the *State of Nature.* For Israel, certain prominent but time-dishonored processes of peacemaking, processes that are conveniently, but erroneously, premised on allegedly "scientific" assumptions of *reason* and *rationality,* may finally have to be renounced.

Israel's periodically considered surrender of territories, egregiously one-sided prisoner swaps, short-sighted reluctance to accept certain critical and once-viable preemption options (although recently, Israeli preemptions may have taken the new and nonexplosive forms of *cyber defense* and *cyber warfare*), and even its prior releases of live terrorists in exchange for slain Jews may never bring about direct and total defeat. Taken together, however, these synergistic policy errors will have a *cumulatively* weakening and possibly "mortal" effect on Israel. Whether the principal effect here will be one that "merely" impairs the Jewish State's commitment to endure or one that also opens it up operationally to a devastating missile attack and/or to major acts of terror is evidently not yet clear. Nonetheless, still-possible and meaningful clarifications do rest on patient and capable examinations of the prevailing *geometry of chaos.*

For Israel, the fragmenting situations in North Africa and the Middle East are just the beginning. Wider patterns of anarchy, chaos, and disorder are also likely. What might still be avoided, however, is wholesale mega-destruction.

This avoidance will require a primary and antecedent awareness in Jerusalem/Tel Aviv that in current world politics, as in any other primordial *state of nature,* survival demands resolute courage, an openly intellectual imagination, and a thoroughly determined conviction that even huge short-term national losses are preferable to long-term national disappearance. This means that any rational calculations of exercising the preemption option must take account of, among other things, ongoing enemy preparations for chemical, biological, and nuclear (CBN) war.

Where it is assumed that enemy states will be adding to their unconventional arsenals, and that these additions would make effective Israeli preemptions increasingly difficult, rationality would compel Israel to act definitively as soon as possible. If, however, it should be assumed that there will be no significant enlargement/deployment of enemy unconventional weapons over time, this may suggest a diminished rationale for Israel to strike first in anticipatory self-defense. Critical decisional considerations here would include assumptions about enemy rationality, expectations concerning costs to Israel of an enemy aggression in the near term, comparisons of costs to Israel of enemy near-term aggression with those of enemy reprisals to an Israeli preemption, and projected efficacy over time of Israeli and enemy ATBM (antitactical ballistic missile) operations.

In all matters involving active defenses in the nuclear age, an especially complicated strategic dialectic will need to be fashioned and contemplated. Sometimes this many-sided dialectic could produce substantially counterintuitive conclusions. For example, seemingly efficient enemy active defenses could pose not just the prospect of unstable deterrence but also a psychological threat to Israeli security. This is because certain enemy perceptions of such efficiency could then prod first-strike attacks against Israel.

On the other hand, it is also conceivable that such perceptions could generate enemy feelings of greater security from Israeli first strikes. These feelings, in turn, could plausibly reduce enemy incentives toward striking first. Moreover, depending on Israel's own more objective assessments of enemy active defenses and enemy perceptions of this efficiency, Israel may or may not decide to preempt.

Flipped over, so to speak, these intersecting arguments suggest that efficient Israeli active defenses (e.g., Arrow) could sometimes be, at least partially and/or potentially, injurious to Israel. This is because any Israeli perceptions of such advanced efficiency could prod preemptive attacks against certain enemy states. On the other hand, once again, these perceptions could occasion feelings of greater security from enemy first strikes, thereby effectively reducing Israel's incentive to strike first itself. Should these security expectations prove false, Israel may then have forgone an indispensable opportunity for self-defense. Should these expectations prove correct, Israel will have likely avoided a needlessly destructive and very corrosive military engagement.

Depending on certain enemy states' own objective assessments of Israel's active defenses and Israel's particular perceptions of these defenses, these foes may or may not decide to strike first themselves.

There are still other relevant factors in all such complex calculations. Any Israeli decision on preemption should take into close account the relative vulnerability and size of its own and enemy nuclear weapons/associated command and control systems over time. Significantly, all nuclear powers would not be the same. There will be meaningful differences between such powers, based not only on usual measures of yield and destructiveness but also on assessments of size, durability, survivability, and penetration capability.

Recalling Leo Szilard's classic phrase about nuclear powers equipped with only "the sting of the bee"[5] (the bee dies after it has stung, at least in this illustrative metaphor), Israel's inclination to strike first should be greatest where its enemies are relegated to a "bee sting" nuclear capacity but smallest where Israel itself is not so limited.

All of this means, *inter alia,* that an enemy's preemption option could appear most compelling where Israel displays bee sting capacity only and where the enemy is not similarly constrained. This implies, further, that Israel must now do whatever it can to ensure that (a) pertinent enemy states are prevented from ever achieving anything more than a bee sting nuclear capacity, and (b) Israel itself is prevented from ever being reduced to a bee sting nuclear status.

Nonetheless, it is still possible that Israel could find itself with only a bee sting capacity themselves and then discover that certain of its enemies had progressed beyond such limitations. Here, the residual rationality of any Israeli preemption could not automatically be ruled out in spite of Israel's recognizably marked nuclear inferiority—especially if an enemy first strike might be expected with a calculably high degree of probability. Although the expected costs of any such Israeli preemption would (by definition) be overwhelming, they might still be less overwhelming than the expected costs of not preempting.

Similarly, if an enemy should find itself with only a bee sting capacity and recognize that Israel is not similarly constrained, it might then perhaps decide, quite rationally, to strike first itself. Expecting an Israeli preemption under such conditions of relative inferiority, an enemy state would likely anticipate extraordinary harms but arguably less extraordinary than the cumulatively expected harms of not striking first. It follows that Israel should do whatever is possible to (a) convince enemy states that it is not preparing for any preemption and (b) always prepare for launching a preemptive strike. From the standpoint of national self-interest and international law, such a patently Machiavellian stance would be entirely sensible.

What is Israel to do amid all such bewilderingly complicated dialectics and synergies? The options, which are not necessarily mutually exclusive, are at least readily identifiable. No single available option or combination of options is fully attractive or foolproof. Hence, in the final analysis, Israel faces having to choose the least unattractive option or configuration of options.

IRAN, PALESTINE, AND THE REGIONAL CORRELATION OF FORCES

In the currently visible hierarchy of catastrophic threats to Israel, Iranian nuclearization looms largest, and certainly most conspicuously. But there are also other critical hazards on the strategic horizon and several with distinctly synergistic qualities. Oddly, because it is still unrecognized by so many well-meaning Israelis, the most serious such hazard is the parallel or coincident creation of a Palestinian State. This is the case whether Palestine is ultimately fashioned by formal voting at the UN, or in some other manner that is more or less consistent with the criteria of statehood authoritatively identified at the Convention on Rights and Duties of States (Montevideo Convention, 1934).

With Palestine, Prime Minister Netanyahu's stated requirements for demilitarization notwithstanding, the "worst" *would* happen. Israel's senior operational planners, therefore, must look very closely at all of the country's interpenetrating and interwoven security challenges. Keeping especially Iran and Palestine in mind, particular attention will need to be directed toward what military thinkers have sometimes identified as the *correlation of forces*, but now with a substantially improved orientation to both (a) the *prevailing* correlation and (b) the *preferred* correlation.

Since the Second Lebanon War (2006),[6] IDF strategists and tacticians have likely begun to use this operational planning concept in creative and nontraditional ways. Historically, a correlation of forces approach has generally been applied as a tangible *measure* of competitive armed forces, ranging from quantitative considerations at the subunit level and extending all the way up to assessments of major formations. It has also been used to compare resources and capabilities at both the operational levels of day-to-day strategy and the much higher levels of *grand strategy*. At times, this particular application has been related to the similar, but less comprehensive, military notion of *force ratios*.

Presently, facing an even broader and more ominous variety of existential security threats than before, perils originating from both state and substate adversaries, Israel must undertake broader and more complex correlation of forces assessments. In this new and wider search, IDF strategists should seek more than a traditionally *objective* yardstick for the appropriate measurement of opposing forces. Although defense strategists in Tel Aviv already routinely compare all available data concerning both the numerical and qualitative characteristics of relevant units, including, among other things, personnel, weaponry, and equipment, IDF commanders will now also need to cultivate some newly *subjective*, or "phenomenological," kinds of understanding.

This unorthodox recommendation may appear to fly in the face of more usual military emphases on "facts," but—in war, as well as in peace—facts are often the result of very personal and very particular *interpretations.* In the final analysis, as is well-known to serious scholars of epistemology and methodology, *all* facts are essentially interpreted facts.

In exploiting a suitably improved concept of a correlation of forces, Israel's senior nuclear planners will seemingly have to reject a basic axiom of geometry. They will need to recognize, in this apparent rejection, that some critical force measurements must not only remain inherently imprecise, but that the unavoidable imprecision may itself include important forms of military understanding. For example, a particular enemy's consuming dedication to certain presumed religious expectations, his utterly uncompromising strength of will, may resist more traditional sorts of measurement, but may still be determinative. Where this would turn out to be the case, moreover, it could reflect the very highest form of power in world politics—that is, *power over death.*

In certain military assessments, as in human psychology, there are ascertainable variables that are stubbornly refractory to measurement but, critically, perhaps, may still be of very considerable importance.

Several emerging hazards to Israeli national security will be shaped by a distinctively Westphalian *geometry of chaos.* In this delicately unbalanced and largely unprecedented set of imprecise calculations, the whole, paradoxically, may turn out to be more (or less) than the calculable sum of its parts. It follows that Israeli planners will need to bring a still more nuanced and intellectually unorthodox approach to their multidisciplinary work. This means, especially, a counterintuitive awareness that proper planning could sometimes presume enemy *irrationality,* and that such planning must also be able to distinguish between *authentic* enemy irrationality and *pretended* enemy irrationality. With this approach, in principle at least, increasingly indispensable efforts to understand the nearly nuclear Iranian enemy could be optimized.

How can IDF nuclear planners reliably recognize the difference between real and contrived irrationality? This is a genuinely urgent question. It cannot be answered by offering any standard references to a more traditional correlation of forces mode of analysis. There will be no available textbook to consult.

These same issues of rational decision making will have to be looked at from the standpoint of enhancing Israel's own capacity to project certain purposeful images of military import. Reciprocally, therefore, IDF nuclear strategists will have to decide when Israel would be better served in both its deterrence and war-fighting capabilities by the deliberate projection of an image of *limited* or *partial irrationality*. Earlier, these strategists should recall, Moshe Dayan had displayed a viscerally useful idea of this posture when he warned: "Israel must be seen as a mad dog, too dangerous to bother."

But Israeli planners must also be mindful here of pretended irrationality as a double-edged sword. Brandished too provocatively, any recognizable preparations for a so-called Samson Option could unexpectedly *encourage* certain enemy preemptions. Significantly, there is no historically based playbook from which Israeli planners could meaningfully extrapolate here.

By its improved use of correlation of forces thinking, Israel will need to seize every available operational initiative, including certain appropriate intelligence and counterintelligence functions. This would be its best way to influence and control each pertinent enemy's particular matrix of expectations. Naturally, this is a tall policy order, especially as these multiple enemies will include both state and substate adversaries, often with substantial and subtle interactions between them. Moreover, in an age of chemical, biological, and nuclear weapons, the consequences of certain IDF planning failures could become *literally* intolerable.

FROM GENERAL TO PARTICULAR: OPERATIONALIZING THE IDF CORRELATION OF FORCES

Now, in greater detail, with new and particular uncertainties in the Middle East and North Africa, what should be the more *holistic* IDF nuclear strategist's concept of correlation of forces?

First, this concept must take careful account of all enemy leaders' *intentions* as well as *capabilities*. Such an accounting, oriented to both extant and prospective leaders, is necessarily more subjective than any more traditional assessments of personnel, weapons, and basic logistical data. But such an accounting, despite relying less on tangible scientific modeling, would also need to be aptly thoughtful and nuanced.

It will not be enough for IDF nuclear strategists to judiciously gather and examine relevant data from all of the usual sources. It will also be important to put Israeli planners directly into the "shoes" of each actual and prospective enemy leader, president, king, or terrorist, thus determining, among other things, what relevant Israeli capacities and vulnerabilities may look like *to them*.

Second, expanding more precisely what has just been discussed, any properly refined IDF correlation of forces concept must take a very close measure of enemy leaders' *rationality*. Any adversary that does not conform to the presumed rules of rational behavior in world politics, as we already know, might not be deterred by any Israeli threats, military or otherwise. This is the case even where Israel would actually possess both the *capacity* and the *resolve* to make good on expressed deterrent threats.

Where an enemy state or substate would not value its own continued survival more highly than any other preference or combination of preferences, the standard logic of deterrence could be immobilized.

This sobering point now refers especially to prospective nuclear security threats from a potentially unstable Iran. In this widely recognized theater of possible future war, especially if the Islamic country's president and his clerical handlers should subscribe to certain faith-based expectations of a Shiite apocalypse, Israel could find itself confronting a *suicide bomber in macrocosm*. Of course, this radically unfavorable scenario would be necessarily contingent on a prior willingness by both Jerusalem/Tel Aviv and Washington to forgo any still-remaining preemption options.

Insofar as assassination/targeted killing may be considered as a specific form of preemption (*anticipatory self-defense*, under international law), it is plausible that the United States and Israel could both abandon any operational plans for the more standard and recognizable military forms of a defensive first strike, but still remain more or less willing to selectively kill Iranian leaders and/or Iranian nuclear scientists. In essence, viewed from the standpoint of an expanded and improved IDF correlation of forces orientation, this could mean the more *formal* inclusion of assassination and sabotage within the country's strategic doctrine.[7]

Third, IDF planning assessments will need to consider the organization of constantly changing enemy state units and their training standards, morale, reconnaissance capabilities, battle experience, and suitability and adaptability to the prospective battlefield. Traditionally, these sorts of assessment are quite routine and not exceedingly difficult to make or innovate, at least on an individual or piecemeal basis. But now, creative IDF nuclear strategists will be those who are able to conceptualize such ordinarily diverse factors *together, in their entirety*. Recalling Sun Tzu's *The Art of War*, one vital purpose of this new strategic holism should be to avoid protracted warfare.[8] Indeed, the ancient Chinese strategist's observation that "[n]o country has ever profited from protracted warfare" is *always* especially meaningful to Israel and has always been an integral part of IDF doctrine.[9]

Fourth, and closely related to number 3 (above), IDF nuclear assessments must consider the cumulative *capabilities* and *intentions* of Israel's *nonstate* enemies—that is, the entire configuration of anti-Israel terrorist groups. In the future, such assessments must offer more than a simple group-by-group consideration. Rather, the groups in question should also be appraised in their *entirety*, collectively, as they may effectively interrelate with one another vis-à-vis Israel. These several hostile groups will also need to be examined in their uniquely interactive relationships with identifiably core enemy states. This last point might best be characterized as an essential IDF correlation of forces search for vital *synergies* that obtain between its state and substate adversaries.

There is nothing really new about the concept of "asymmetric warfare," but today, especially in the Middle East, the really crucial asymmetry lies not in particular force structures or ratios but rather in *determination* and *strength of will*. In a similar vein, Clausewitz, in his *Principles of War* (1812), had spoken of the need for "audacity." This intangible quality represents yet another crucial variable for IDF strategic nuclear planners; inevitably, it must elude any kind of reassuringly precise measurement.

Fifth, and once again recalling Sun Tzu—this time his spatial injunction that "[i]f there is no place to go, it is fatal terrain"—IDF *strategic* planning judgments should take suitable note of the still-ongoing metamorphosis of a fragmented nonstate adversary (Fatah/Hamas) into an aspiring sovereign state adversary (Palestine). As has been well known since 1967, with such a significantly injurious metamorphosis, Israel's strategic depth would shrink to decisively less manageable levels. Further, any expanding enemy momentum to fold Israel itself *into* the new Arab state would be energized. There can be little reasonable doubt about Palestinian irredentist ambitions. After all, the official maps of Palestine drawn by both the Palestine Authority and Hamas already include *all of Israel.* Cartographically, throughout the Arab/Islamic world, Israel has already been eliminated.

If, however, because of insistent peace pressures coming from various directions Palestinian statehood cannot be avoided, could Israel still live with Palestine?

In one respect, at least, any codified institutionalization of disparate Arab enemies into Palestine could possibly offer some geostrategic benefit to Israel. Now, for example, certain forms of Israeli reprisal and retaliation would likely be easier, and thus more purposeful. Yet there would also be a corresponding and incontestably serious loss of strategic depth through its substantial surrender of utterly vital territories. And this is to say nothing of the obvious historical, religious, and legal grounds that exist for maintaining full Israeli possession of Judea and Samaria (the West Bank).

EXPLOITING STRATEGIC OPPORTUNITIES: THE IMPORTANCE OF FORCE MULTIPLIERS

In the matter of synergies, IDF nuclear planners will also need to consider and look for critical new *force multipliers*. A force multiplier is a collection of related characteristics, other than weapons and force size, that may make any military organization more effective in combat. A force multiplier may be generalship, tactical surprise, tactical mobility, or certain command and control system enhancements. It could include such imaginative and less costly forms of preemption as assassination[10] (targeted killing)[11] and/or sabotage. It will now also include well-integrated components of cyber warfare and a reciprocal capacity to prevent and blunt any incoming cyber attacks.

For Israel, "worms" should now have their very special decompositional place.

In time, this definitionally "boring" force multiplier could prove to be even more decisive than any others. Although nonexistent in the times of Sun Tzu and Clausewitz, "cyber audacity" could already represent a key component of Israel's necessarily broadened approach to the correlation of forces.

The presence of any force multiplier may *create* synergy. Again in the matter of Israel, we must acknowledge the antecedent "geometry of chaos." Understanding this more fully, IDF fighting units—and also the sources of nuclear deterrence—could conceivably emerge more effective than the mere sum of their respective parts.

Before this can happen, however, senior nuclear planners must ensure that their analyses and consequent recommendations are detached from any sort of false hopes. Here, the ancient advice of Thucydides (416 BCE), writing on the ultimatum of the Athenians to the Melians during the Peloponnesian War, will be instructive: "But hope is by nature an expensive commodity, and those who are risking their all on one cast find out what it means only when they are already ruined."

The overriding objective of any IDF correlation of forces war planning must be to inform leadership decisions about two always complementary matters: (1) perceived vulnerabilities of Israel, and (2) perceived vulnerabilities of enemy states and nonstates. For Aman (the IDF Intelligence branch) in particular, this means gathering and assessing crucial strategic information—for example, information concerning the expected persuasiveness of the country's still-undisclosed nuclear deterrence posture. To endure well into the predictably uncertain future, such information, and not any cascading series of *unfounded hopes*, must remain at the core of Aman's carefully structured orientation to the regional correlation of forces.

All of this information, especially whatever might concern Israel's "opaque" or undeclared nuclear deterrent, must flow reliably and quickly to key "consumers" within the broader IDF sphere, and then to the country's political leadership in Jerusalem. Once it is received and digested by this leadership, including, of course, the other security services and the General Staff, selected information should also flow as needed to the national warning centers, operating force commanders, contingency operations planners, research directors, combat/training developers, and national resource allocators. Above all, IDF strategic nuclear planners performing such sensitive work must firmly resist any and all pressures that might be imposed by divergent political interests in order to support certain plainly preconceived hopes.

Conceptually, in a world of growing international anarchy,[12] this means that IDF correlation of forces planning responsibility should include (1) recognizing enemy force multipliers, (2) challenging and undermining enemy force multipliers, and (3) developing and refining Israel's own force multipliers. Regarding number (3), this means a particularly heavy IDF emphasis on air superiority, communications, intelligence, and surprise. Once again, recalling Moshe Dayan's aptly canine metaphor, it *may* also mean a heightened and calculated (and counterintuitive) awareness of the possible benefits of sometimes appearing less than completely rational to one's enemies.

It is routinely assumed that Israel's security from an enemy missile attack is reasonably well ensured by nuclear deterrence, however opaque or ambiguous. But such a strategy of dissuasion must also depend on many complex and interpenetrating conditions and perceptions. Taken by itself, Israel's mere possession of nuclear weapons, even if it should be fully or partially disclosed, can never adequately bestow meaningful safety.

By definition, a rational state enemy of Israel will always accept or reject a first-strike option by comparing the costs and benefits of each available alternative. Where the expected costs of striking first are taken to exceed expected gains, this enemy will be deterred. But where these expected costs are believed to be exceeded by expected gains, deterrence will likely fail. Here, Israel would need to achieve "escalation dominance."

In thinking about strategy, therefore, an immediate task for Israel will be to strengthen its nuclear deterrent such that any enemy state will always calculate that a first strike on Israel would be irrational. To accomplish this objective, Israel must convince prospective attackers that it maintains both the *willingness* and the *capacity* to retaliate with its nuclear weapons.

Should an enemy state considering an attack on Israel be unconvinced about either one or both of these essential components of nuclear deterrence, it might then choose to strike first, depending on the particular value or *utility* that it places on the expected outcomes of such an attack. In part, it is precisely to prevent just such an "unconvincing" nuclear deterrence posture that Israel must now consider the expected benefits of limiting, or even ending, *deliberate ambiguity*.

TAKING THE ISRAELI BOMB OUT OF THE BASEMENT

A major focus of IDF *strategic* planning will have to be the nuclear posture of deliberate ambiguity, or the so-called *bomb in the basement*. Israel's prime minister surely understands that adequate nuclear deterrence of increasingly formidable enemies could soon require *less* nuclear secrecy. What will soon need to be determined by IDF nuclear planners focused upon an improved correlation of forces will be the precise extent and subtlety with which Israel should begin to communicate tangible elements of its nuclear positions, intentions, and capabilities to these enemies.

The geostrategic rationale for any such carefully constructed forms of nuclear disclosure would not lie in exposing the obvious—that is, that Israel simply *has* the bomb. Rather, among other things, it would be to persuade prospective attackers that Israel's nuclear weapons are both *usable* and *penetration capable.*

To protect itself against certain enemy strikes, particularly those attacks that could carry intolerable costs, IDF *defense* planners will need to prepare to exploit every relevant aspect and function of Israel's own nuclear arsenal. The success of Israel's effort here will depend not only on its particular choice of targeting doctrine (*counterforce* or *countervalue*) but also on the extent to which this choice is made known in advance to certain enemy states and their assorted substate surrogates.

Before such enemies can be suitably deterred from launching first strikes against Israel, and before they can be deterred from launching retaliatory attacks following any Israeli preemptions, it would not be enough for them to know only that Israel *has* the bomb. These enemies would also need to recognize that Israeli nuclear weapons are sufficiently *invulnerable* to such attacks and pointed directly at *high-value population targets*.

Inter alia, IDF planners working on an improved *strategic* paradigm will need to understand the following: Removing the bomb from Israel's basement could enhance Israel's nuclear deterrent to the extent that it would enlarge enemy perceptions of *secure* and *capable* Israeli nuclear forces. Such a calculated end to deliberate ambiguity could also underscore Israel's *willingness* to use these nuclear forces in reprisal for certain enemy first-strike and retaliatory attacks.

From the standpoint of successful Israeli nuclear deterrence, IDF planners must always proceed on the assumption that perceived willingness is always just as important as perceived capability. This again may bring to mind the counterintuitively presumed advantages for Israel of sometimes appearing *less than fully rational.*

There are certain circumstances in which a correlation of forces paradigm will necessarily lead IDF planners to consider certain *preemption* options. This is because there will plausibly be circumstances in which the existential risks to Israel of continuing to rely on some combination of nuclear deterrence and active defenses[13] (that is, primarily the Arrow system of ballistic missile defense) will simply be too great. In these last-resort circumstances, Israeli decision makers will need to determine whether such essential defensive strikes, known jurisprudentially as expressions of *anticipatory self-defense,* would be genuinely cost-effective.[14]

IDF planners will no doubt note that Israel's rational inclinations to strike preemptively in certain circumstances will be affected by the particular steps taken by prospective target states (e.g., Iran) to guard against any Israeli preemption. Should Israel, for any reason, refrain too long from striking first defensively, Iran could then begin to implement protective measures that would pose substantial additional obstacles and hazards for Israel. These measures could include the attachment of certain automated launch mechanisms to nuclear weapons and/or the adoption of launch-on-warning policies.

IDF planners must presume that such policies might call for the retaliatory launch of bombers and/or missiles on *receipt of warning* that an Israeli attack is under way. By requiring launch before the attacking Israeli warheads actually reached their intended targets, any enemy reliance of launch on warning could carry very grave risks of error or "accidental war."

Ultimately, the single most important factor in IDF correlation of forces planning judgments on the preemption option will be the *expected rationality* of certain enemy decision makers. If, after all, these leaders were expected to strike at Israel with unconventional forces irrespective of anticipated Israeli counterstrikes, deterrence could cease to work. This means that certain enemy strikes could be expected even if the enemy leaders fully understood that Israel had successfully deployed its own nuclear weapons in completely survivable modes, if Israel's nuclear weapons were believed to be entirely capable of penetrating the enemy's active defenses, and if Israel's leaders were altogether *willing* to retaliate.

Significantly, irrationality is not the same as crazy, and an irrational enemy leadership could still have a distinct and identifiable hierarchy of preferences—even if it is a rank ordering in which national survival is not at the more usual apex. Here, analysts would say that such an irrational enemy still maintains an order of preferences that is both consistent and transitive. More than likely, the very top of any such irrational enemy hierarchy would be occupied by certain fundamental religious (Jihadist) expectations.

A crazy enemy leadership, however, would have no discernible order of preferences, and its military actions, for the most part, would be random and unpredictable. It goes without saying that having to face a crazy adversary in world politics would be worse than having to confront a merely irrational one. Although it might still be purposeful for Israel to seek to deter an irrational Iran (by identifying that country's own unique order of preferences), there would be no point to seeking deterrence against a crazy Iran. In that particular worst case scenario, Israel's only rational option would almost certainly be to preempt and/or to fashion a near-perfect system of active antimissile defenses. This last challenge, however, would ultimately be unsustainable in both fiscal and technological terms.

No system of active defense can ever be "leakproof."

SOME FINAL THOUGHTS ON ENEMY IRRATIONALITY

A significant question now needs to be raised explicitly, and with particular reference to Iran: Could a Shiite Iranian leadership elite—*any* such Iranian leadership elite—seek nuclear weapons to bring about a welcome "end of days"? Mustn't Iran's authoritative decision makers wage a religiously mandated final battle to bring back the "Hidden Imam"?

Doctrinally at least, any such core question ought not to be dismissed out of hand. According to a very complex Shiite theology, just prior to the Mahdi's reappearance on earth, the world will be in chaos. At that time, this compelling narrative continues, Christian rule will still be broadly dominant, and a Sunni Muslim leader will lead the *first fight* against this "infidel" hegemony. Ultimately, however, following expectedly destructive conflicts in Syria and Iraq, a great general named Mansour (Victorious) will arrive to slay Shia's many enemies.

Ceremoniously, in a long-predicted triumph of faith over death, he will then plant his flag of liberation atop the Al-Aqsa Mosque in Jerusalem.

What, precisely, does this particular eschatology mean for Israel and also for the United States? The army of Mansour, aided by the newly revealed Mahdi, or Twelfth Imam, is predicted, among other things, to conquer "the Jews" and "kill them." More precisely, according to a prominent Hadith, "the last hour will not come unless the Muslims will fight against the Jews, and the Muslims will kill them."

All of this of course may seem highly improbable or contrived to us in the West. Nonetheless, a great many people in Iran and elsewhere throughout the region do believe very deeply in the riveting lore of such a Shiite apocalypse. From the critical standpoints of strategy and future war, moreover, we should recall that it is their particular system of beliefs, especially when certain Islamic political leaderships are involved, that may finally matter most. In all relevant matters of strategy, reality means *perceived* reality.

Within certain leadership circles in Tehran, any prospect of hastening the Shiite apocalypse could be decidedly welcome. In the United States and Israel, on the other hand, although both Jewish and Christian theologies also contain core elements of apocalyptic thought, any *deliberate encouragement* of a final battle between good and evil is widely rejected.

Whatever scriptural expectations of end times may be embedded in Judaism and Christianity, and however seriously these expectations may be accepted among particular American and Israeli populations, any such expressly apocalyptic visions are firmly put aside in all Western capitals as realistic policy options.

This is as it should be. There likely does exist among certain major players in the Iran nuclear story a more or less acceptable element of eschatology. But this potentially tragic drama is also fashioned out of starkly polar opposites. The sort of all-consuming, apocalyptic violence that could seem plainly positive and "purifying" in Tehran must appear manifestly negative, and even grievously defiling, in both Washington and Jerusalem.

To avoid any further acquiescence in the religiously ordained "fate" that may be planned for them in Tehran, Israel and/or the United States may still have to consider some residual forms of appropriate military action. It is, however, already very late for any gainful preemption against relevant Iranian nuclear assets and infrastructures. It is also effectively inconceivable that any US president would display the political will (or garner the necessary funds) to undertake such problematic operations. This is the case even though these actions could likely be defended in law as anticipatory self-defense.

On occasion, US presidents have hinted obliquely at one supposed military option—*reprisal*—but this is a remedy that could be carried out only *ex post*. Retaliation, unlike preemption, can come only *after the fact*. It cannot, therefore, *prevent* nuclear aggression; it can merely promise, more or less persuasively, some forms of post-catastrophe *punishment*.

For Israel, these are not abstract issues of retributive justice. Rather, they are altogether concrete issues of national survival.

In the case of Iran's Shiite theology, a nuclear first strike could conceivably be selected in deference to deeply felt religious obligations. Here, acting as the individual suicide bomber in macrocosm, Iran could potentially offer itself eagerly in the spirit of Shahada, thereby ready and willing to accept a collective death for Allah.

Traditional nuclear deterrence can exist only between fully rational adversaries—that is, between enemies who share a conspicuously overriding commitment to self-preservation. For Israel, any standoff with an already nuclear Iran could thus prove very different from what had once obtained between the United States and the Soviet Union. This might not be your father's Cold War. Echoing the seventeenth-century English philosopher Thomas Hobbes, no state, wrote Thomas Jefferson, has any right of national suicide. Every state's first obligation is the *assurance of protection.*

Innocent life *must* always be preserved. Should Iranian leaders openly proclaim their belief in the Shiite apocalypse, a series of final battles presumed indispensable for transforming the profane *world of war* into the sacred *world of Islam*, very far-reaching, and possibly problematic, measures of self-defense would then need to be considered.

From the standpoint of nuclear arms, Israel is not Iran. Israel's nuclear weapons exist only to protect the Jewish State from extraordinary forms of aggression. Understandably, this includes the prevention of another Jewish genocide, and also related crimes against humanity.

Israel's nuclear deterrent force would never be used except in defensive reprisal for massive enemy first strikes. In practice, this now means, essentially, Iranian attacks involving nuclear and/or certain biological weapons. For the time being, none of Israel's enemies is nuclear, but this is apt to change.

If it should actually have to face nuclear enemies, Israel could choose to rely on its own nuclear weapons to reduce the risks of unconventional war. But such reliance would make strategic sense only insofar as the newly nuclear enemy state(s) would remain (1) rational and (2) convinced that Israel would retaliate with nuclear weapons if attacked with nuclear and/or certain expectedly devastating biological weapons.

For Israel and its substantially weakened US ally (let's not forget that American military power is now extremely stretched and economically constrained), there would be very complex problems to solve if an enemy state such as Iran were permitted to go operationally nuclear. These problems could quickly undermine the conceptually neat but decidedly unrealistic notion of any balanced nuclear deterrence in the region, a notion now gaining some popularity in both Washington and Jerusalem. Considering the more complex and multiple axes of regional conflict, the Middle East might not sustain the comforting equilibrium that had once more or less characterized US-Soviet relations. One must use the "more or less" qualification in this connection, because the 1962 Cuban Missile Crisis just barely managed to end, as we now know, without triggering a thermonuclear war.

In the future, whether for reasons of miscalculation, accident, unauthorized capacity to fire, outright irrationality, or the presumed imperatives of Jihad, an enemy state in this fevered neighborhood could opt to launch a nuclear first strike against Israel in spite of Israel's own obvious and foreseeably secure nuclear capability. Here, an earlier Cold War type of mutual assured destruction, a "balance of terror,"[15] might not be sustainable.

After absorbing *any* enemy nuclear aggression, Israel would certainly respond with a nuclear retaliatory strike. Although nothing is publicly known about Israel's precise targeting doctrine, any such reprisal would likely be launched against the aggressor's capital city and/or similarly high-value urban targets. In any case, there could be no assurances in response to this sort of aggression that Israel would necessarily limit itself to striking back against exclusively military targets. With this in mind, Israel would be well advised, as quickly as possible, to identify explicitly, or at least hint at persuasively (so long as the bomb should remain in the basement), a recognizably countervalue retaliatory option.

This critical point should not be lost on the authoritative decision makers in Tehran.

Now, what if enemy first strikes were to involve only chemical and/or minor biological weapons? In this case, Israel might still launch a presumptively proportionate nuclear reprisal, but this would depend largely on Israel's calculated expectations of follow-up aggression and also on its associated determinations of comparative damage limitation.

Should Israel absorb a massive conventional first strike, a nuclear retaliation could not be ruled out. This reasoning is plausible if (1) the aggressor were perceived to hold nuclear or other weapons of mass destruction in reserve, and/or (2) Israel's leaders were to believe that nonnuclear retaliations could not prevent national annihilation. Recognizing Israel's exceptionally small size, the calculated threshold of existential harms, in this case, could be determinably much lower than Israel's total physical devastation.

Facing imminent existential attacks, even if it had delayed too long, Israel could still decide to preempt enemy aggression with its conventional forces. The targeted state's response would then determine Israel's subsequent moves. If this response were in any way nuclear, Israel would assuredly undertake a nuclear counterretaliation.

If this enemy retaliation were to involve chemical and/or biological weapons, Israel might also plan to take a quantum escalatory initiative. Again, this sort of initiative is known in military parlance as *escalation dominance*. It could prove necessary, even indispensable, to Israel's preservation of *intrawar deterrence*. One would need to bear in mind here that deterrence does not necessarily cease functioning immediately on the commencement of hostilities. It can continue to play a different, but still more or less productive role, *during* the ensuing conflict.

If an enemy state's response to an Israeli preemption were limited to hard-target conventional strikes, it is improbable that Israel would ever resort to nuclear counterretaliation. But if the enemy state's conventional retaliation were an all-out strike directed toward Israel's civilian populations, as well as to Israeli military targets, an Israeli nuclear counterretaliation could not automatically be excluded. Such a counterretaliation could be ruled out only if the enemy state's conventional retaliations were entirely proportionate to Israel's preemption, confined entirely to Israeli military targets, circumscribed by the legal limits of military necessity, and accompanied by explicit and verifiable assurances of no further escalation.

It is *almost* inconceivable that Israel would ever decide to preempt any enemy state aggression with a nuclear defensive strike. While particular circumstances could arise where such a defensive strike would be completely rational, and also entirely lawful according to the 1996 Advisory Opinion of the International Court of Justice (which refused to prohibit certain residual resorts to nuclear weapons that were deemed essential to national survival), it is unlikely that Israel would ever permit itself to reach such all-or-nothing circumstances. Also worth mentioning is that Israel remains pledged to the "purity of arms" (*Tohar HaNeshek*), and to incomparably strict compliance with humanitarian international law, especially the considered minimization of collateral or noncombatant harms.

Overall, an Israeli nuclear preemption is *highly* improbable. In principle, it could conceivably be expected *only* if (1) Israel's enemy or enemies had unexpectedly acquired nuclear or other unconventional weapons presumed capable of destroying the Jewish State, (2) this enemy state had been forthright that its genocidal intentions paralleled its capabilities, (3) this state was reliably believed ready to begin a final countdown to launch, and (4) Israel believed that nonnuclear preemptions could not possibly achieve levels of damage limitation consistent with its own national survival.

To reject altogether this particular argument on Israeli nuclear preemption as impossible or implausible, however, would require the antecedent assumption that national self-preservation is not Israel's highest priority. *Prima facie,* any such assumption would be incorrect.

Facing the prospect of a nuclear Iran, Israel will soon need to select refined and workable options to deal with two separate but interpenetrating levels of danger. Should Iranian leaders be judged to meet the usual tests of rationality in world politics, Israel will have to focus especially on reducing its nuclear ambiguity, taking its bomb out of the basement, and operationalizing a retaliatory force that is appropriately hardened and dispersed. In design, this second-strike nuclear force, *countervalue* not *counterforce* targeted, should be recognizably ready to inflict assured destruction against identifiable enemy cities.

Where Israel's leaders would determine that they may have to deter an irrational enemy leadership in Tehran or elsewhere, they would also have to consider the possible strategic benefits of appearing as a "mad dog" or adopting a strategy of pretended irrationality. Together with any such consideration, both Jerusalem and Tel Aviv, civilian leadership and military, will need to determine what, exactly, is valued most highly by Israel's pertinent enemies, and then prepare to issue fully credible threats designed to obstruct these ascertainably core enemy preferences.

Whether Iran's leadership is expected to be rational or irrational, Israel will need to continue with its steadily expanding programs for cyber defense and cyber war. Moreover, there exist particular circumstances wherein it could be purposeful for Israel to adopt a strategy of pretended irrationality vis-à-vis a presumably *rational* Iranian adversary.

There are additional and interpenetrating strategic challenges facing Israel. Now, confronting new forms of chaotic regional disintegration, Israel should prepare to go beyond its already expanded paradigm of numerical military assessments to additional and "softer" considerations. Within this wider and more self-consciously qualitative strategic paradigm, IDF planners should then focus on, among other areas, the cumulative and synergistic importance of unconventional weapons and low-intensity warfare in the region.

In certain circumstances, vital strategies and tactics will be indispensable and infeasible. For the Jewish State, this will have the apparent makings of an unbearable and irremediable dilemma. Yet as truth can sometimes emerge through paradox, a suitably improved correlation of forces focus could soon exploit unforeseen, but still fully purposeful, strategic options.

The more things change, the more they remain the same. The Middle East *is* characterized by very specific and consequential changes in power and threat dynamics, but the underlying forces of anarchy and chaos still retain a discernible and instructive form. It follows that Israel's strategic thinkers and planners should now stay focused on identifying certain recurrent patterns within this underlying geometry. They would then be able to deduce appropriately precise and promising policy recommendations from this discipline's *always unchanging* postulates or axioms.

We end this chapter with Machiavelli.[16] In *The Discourses*, the Florentine philosopher advances the principle of an "economy of violence," but here, on a more basic, interpersonal level: "For it is the man who uses violence to spoil things, not the man who uses it to mend them, that is blameworthy." Extrapolating this useful distinction to the substantially more complex level of world politics, Israel's nuclear weapons can still be structured as an effective deterrent for the prevention of large-scale war, including, of course, nuclear war. If shaped by a proper and comprehensive doctrine going forward, including an aptly nuanced and step-by-step termination of deliberate ambiguity, these weapons could serve to mend some very dangerous cleavages between Israel and its most refractory enemies.

Nuclear doctrine is a net. Only those who *cast* can expect to *catch*.

NOTES

1. Long before the nuclear age, ancient Chinese military theorist Sun Tzu counseled in *The Art of War*: "Subjugating the enemy's army without fighting is the true pinnacle of excellence" (see chapter 3, "Planning Offensives").

2. This does not mean, however, that preparations for war waging and effective deterrence are unrelated. On the contrary, Israel must continually bear in mind that preparations for war—including even nuclear war—could be indispensable to successful deterrence: *Si vis pacem, para bellum atomicum* ("If you want peace, prepare for atomic war.")

3. Risks threatening Israel's security may form an intricately interconnected network. Assessments of such risk must include a patient search for synergies and also for potential *cascades of failures* that could represent one especially serious iteration of synergy. Other risk properties that will warrant careful assessment within this genre include *contagion potential* and *persistence*.

4. More generically, of course, Thomas Hobbes had already described such circumstances in chapter 13 of *Leviathan*: "But though there had never been any time, wherein particular men were in a condition of warre one against another; yet, in all times, Kings and Persons of Soveraigne authority, because of their Independency, are in continuall jealousies, and in the state and posture of Gladiators; having their weap-

ons pointing, and their eyes fixed on one another; that is, their Forts, Garrisons, and Guns upon the Frontiers of their Kingdomes." In other words, these basic conditions of anarchy and war in world politics antedate the nuclear age.

5. See Leo Szilard, "The Sting of the Bee in 'Saturation Parity,'" *Bulletin of the Atomic Scientists*, March 1965, 8ff.

6. It is authoritatively presumed in senior US military circles that a US Air Force Effects-Based Approach to Operations (EBAO) was employed by the Israel Air Force (IAF) during the 2006 conflict.

7. From the standpoint of international law, it could sometimes be reasonable to examine assassination as a permissible form of *ordinary self-defense*—that is, as a forceful measure of self-help short of war that is undertaken *after* an armed attack occurs. Tactically, however, from a correlation of forces perspective, there are at least two serious problems with such a position: (1) In view of the ongoing proliferation of extraordinarily destructive weapons technologies, waiting to resort to postattack self-defense could prove unacceptably dangerous or even fatal; and (2) assassination/targeted killing, while it may prove to be helpful in *preventing* an attack in the first place, is substantially less likely to be useful in mitigating further harms once an enemy attack has already been launched and absorbed.

8. The idea of Israel embedded in protracted conflict is hardly novel. Yitzhak Rabin coined the term "dormant war" in the 1960s to describe Israel's situation when not engaged in active hostilities. Amnon Rubinstein once wrote: "It is Israel's fate to live in a hostile world that refuses to accept her, and to see her as part of the Middle East reality." Moshe Arens, a former Minister of Defense, simply regarded the entire Middle East as a region of endemic war. For Ariel Sharon, any long-term peace for Israel was "nothing but a dream." And physicist Yuval Ne'eman thought of Middle Eastern wars as a product of certain historical conditions resembling those that had existed in Europe for hundreds of years. Ne'eman and others, therefore, were urging that Israel reconcile itself with a situation of permanent or protracted war—at least for the foreseeable future. On these views, see Efraim Inbar, "Attitudes Toward War in the Israeli Political Elite," *Middle East Journal*, Vol. 44, No. 3, Summer 1990, pp. 431–445.

9. See also Niccolo Machiavelli, Book Two of *The Discourses*, where the oft-cited Florentine advises the Council of Florence on "How the Romans proceeded in the Waging of War." This Roman way, he counsels, was "to make wars short and crushing." But for Israel, the task may increasingly be to avoid any forms of major warfare altogether.

10. In his *Utopia*, published in 1516, Thomas More offered a curious but clarifying juxtaposition of foreign policy stratagems and objectives. Although the Utopians are expected to be generous toward other states, they also offer rewards for the assassination of enemy leaders (Book II). This is not because More wished to be gratuitously barbarous but rather because he was a *realistic* Utopian. Sharing with St. Augustine (whose *City of God* had been the subject of his 1501 lectures) a fundamentally dark assessment of human political arrangements, More constructed a "lesser evil" philosophy that favored a distinctly pragmatic kind of morality.

11. For important conceptual and legal distinctions between assassination and targeted killing, see Amos N. Guiora, *Legitimate Target: A Criteria-Based Approach to Targeted Killing* (Oxford: Oxford University Press, 2013), 107 pp.

12. This actual condition of anarchy stands in stark contrast to the jurisprudential assumption of solidarity between all states in the presumably common struggle against aggression and terrorism. Such a *peremptory* expectation (known formally in international law as a *jus cogens* assumption) is already mentioned in Justinian, *Corpus Juris Civilis* (533 CE); Hugo Grotius, 2 *De Jure Belli Ac Pacis Libri Tres*, chapter 20 (Francis W. Kesey, tr., Clarendon Press, 1925 [1690]); and Emmerich de Vattel, 1 *Le Droit Des Gens*, chapter 19 (1758).

13. In all matters of defense, recall Carl von Clausewitz in *On War*: "Defensive warfare . . . does not consist of waiting idly for things to happen. We must wait only if

it brings us visible and decisive advantages. That calm before the storm, when the aggressor is gathering new forces for a great blow, is most dangerous for the defender." See *Principles of War*, Hans W. Gatzke, tr., New York: Dover Publications, 2003, p. 54, III, "Strategy."

14. An antecedent or corollary concern must also be the *ethical* or *humanitarian* calculus in these particular circumstances. Although an ideal world order would contain "neither victims nor executioners," such an optimal arrangement of global power and authority is not yet on the horizon. This phrase is taken from Albert Camus, *Neither Victims Nor Executioners*, Dwight McDonald, ed., 1968. Confronting what he called "our century of fear," Camus asked his readers to be "neither victims nor executioners," living not in a world in which killing has disappeared ("we are not so crazy as that"), but one wherein killing has become illegitimate.

15. As was mentioned previously, J. Robert Oppenheimer, head of the American Manhattan Project during World War II, had later referred to the nuclear superpowers as "two scorpions in a bottle." See Louis René Beres, "Like Two Scorpions in a Bottle: Could Israel and a Nuclear Iran Coexist in the Middle East?" *The Israel Journal of Foreign Affairs*, Vol. 8, No. 1, 2014, pp. 23–32. Now that Israel must extend the metaphor to a bottle containing more and more "scorpions," extrapolations for power management and national security will become correspondingly more complex and more problematic. For antecedent notions of a persistent cold war in world politics, see most interestingly, Thomas Hobbes, *Leviathan*, chapter 13: "So the nature of War, consisteth not in actuall fighting; but in the known disposition thereto, during all the time there is no assurance to the contrary."

16. Niccolo Machiavelli joined Aristotle's plan for a more scientific study of politics with certain assumptions about geopolitics, or *Realpolitik*. His best-known conclusion in this regard focuses on the stark dilemma of practicing goodness in a generally evil world: "A man who wishes to make a profession of goodness in everything, must necessarily come to grief among so many who are not good." See *The Prince*, Chapter XV. This is a cautionary view that Israel's emerging nuclear doctrine should promptly embrace.

THREE

Deciphering Enemy Intentions and Capabilities

"Men as a rule willingly believe what they want to believe."
—Julius Caesar, *The Gallic War*

Sometimes sound strategic truth can appear with a thoroughly disorienting suddenness. For Israel, the full impact of Julius Caesar's ancient Roman military insight became explosively evident on October 5, 1973, with the Arab surprise-attack start of the Yom Kippur War. Until that galvanizing moment, the country had been widely captivated by an assumption known generally as "the concept." This belief described the then-popular notion that, after the Six Day War (1967), Israel's Arab enemies were simply incapable of renewing hostilities against a now unbeatable Jewish State.

This largely self-congratulatory assumption, although plainly premature, had been "codified" by Aman (IDF Military Intelligence). In Aman's officially expressed view, up to the very last days before the Arab attacks, war was reportedly "improbable" or even "highly improbable."

This presumptuous view, of course, had tangibly calamitous consequences. It represented, in fact, the core assumption that created an unprecedented intelligence failure for Israel, known in Hebrew parlance as the *mechdal*. In the future, similar or possibly even more erroneous expectations could occasion authentically existential results, especially if they should pertain to certain overriding matters of Israel's nuclear strategy and doctrine.

Deciphering enemy intentions and capabilities must obviously remain front and center for Israeli military preparations. But once such qualities could be reliably ascertained (and this is not likely to be an easy process by any means, especially as each factor may affect the other), the IDF would need to reaffirm its most utterly central tenet on war fighting. This is the axiomatic principle that any national war must be fought and won *quickly*.

Significantly, this unassailable doctrinal imperative is not in any way Israel-specific. Rather, it reflects wider and very ancient and medieval strategic roots, including Sun Tzu's *Art of War* and later Machiavelli's *The Discourses*. In Book Two, the Florentine philosopher offers his advice to the Council of Florence on "How the Romans proceeded to the Waging of War." The Roman way, he recalls helpfully, was "to make wars short and crushing."

Nothing has changed to make this core advice any less compelling for Israel in particular, but at the same time, the corollary need for Israel to avoid war in the first place is also much greater. After all, we live in an age of uniquely destructive weaponry, and the most successful use of such weaponry going forward may well require operational *nonuse*. In this connection, IDF planners must come back conceptually to the overarching importance of deterrence, including nuclear deterrence, a "return" that must also factor in more or less informed and prior judgments about enemy *rationality*.

REASONS FOR AN ENEMY NUCLEAR FIRST STRIKE

All things considered, whether for reasons of outright irrationality, miscalculation, accident, coup d'état, or presumed obligations of Jihad, an enemy of Israel could sometime opt to launch a nuclear first strike against Israel, despite that country's plainly secure nuclear capability. In the worst case scenario, this means that even Israel's presumptive nuclear deployments at sea (Dolphin submarines) might only be useful for revenge *ex post* and not for any successful deterrence *ex ante*.

Routinely, friends of Israel now sometimes assume that Israel's essential security from enemy missile attack is reliably assured by nuclear deterrence. The problem with this too-hopeful assumption is that any such strategy of dissuasion must ultimately depend on many complex conditions and perceptions. Taken by itself, Jerusalem's possession of nuclear weapons—even if it were more fully disclosed[1]—could never automatically bestow real safety.

By definition, following an indispensable process of dialectical reasoning, any rational state enemy of Israel would accept or reject a first-strike option by comparing the costs and benefits of each available alternative. Wherever the expected costs of striking first are taken to exceed expected gains, so goes this particular strategic calculation, the enemy will be successfully deterred. But where these expected costs are believed to be exceeded by expected gains, deterrence will necessarily fail.

IDENTIFYING LIMITATIONS OF ISRAELI NUCLEAR DETERRENCE

We may begin to see certain major ironies. Israel must increasingly rely on deterrence, but there are also substantial risks of placing too much Israeli dependence on nuclear deterrence. Always it will be a delicate balance, a calculated equilibrium that must take into close account all possible strategic options and limitations.

Regarding *willingness*, even if Jerusalem were actually prepared to respond to certain attacks with nuclear reprisals, enemy failure to recognize such preparedness could still provoke an attack on Israel. Here, misperception and/or errors in information could effectively immobilize nuclear deterrence.

Israel's military planners must always consider various complex relationships between C3I (command, control, communications, intelligence) vulnerability and contemplated predelegations of launch authority. To reduce the risks of "decapitation," an objective as essential to Israeli nuclear deterrence as providing protection for the weapons themselves, Jerusalem could consider increasing the number of authoritative decision makers—that is, those designated individuals who would now have the right to launch under certain carefully specified and residual contingencies. But because the enhanced deterrence value of any such increase would require that prospective enemies first learn that Israel had actually implemented these decapitation-avoidance predelegations (without such learning, Israel's enemies would be more likely to calculate that first-strike attacks are cost effective), those adversaries might feel increasingly compelled to preempt.

Enemy preemption incentives here would stem from certain new fears of a fully intentional Israeli first strike and/or new fears of accidental, unauthorized, or unintentional nuclear strikes launched by Israel. Aware of these probable enemy reactions to its predelegations of launch authority—predelegations that could even be complemented by launch-on-warning safeguard measures—Israel reciprocally could quickly feel more compelled to strike first itself. In essence, any such action would represent a "preemption of preemptive attack" that could or could not prove genuinely gainful, and that might or might not have been avoided altogether by certain aptly antecedent resistance to expanded predelegations of launch authority.

This entire scenario could also be played in the other direction. Here, Iran, or perhaps an Arab state enemy seeking to reduce its decapitation risks, would implement certain predelegations of launch authority, thereby encouraging Israeli preemptions and, in consequence, Iranian and/or Arab state "preemptions of an Israeli preemption." While all of this may sound dreadfully complex, it is because this subject represents an inherently complicated set of dynamic and interpenetrating processes.

Like it or not, therefore, this perplexing complexity now needs to be embraced by appropriate Israeli planners. For them, it is much the same obligation that faces physicians and scientists working to better understand human cancers. For an analogous example, we may consider that the likelihood in cancer research that a single biomarker could explain a particular malignancy's behavior is extremely low. Not only do tumors require in-depth characterization, but the microenvironment and genetic background of each individual patient, or host, would best be considered as well.

Even conspicuously enhanced predelegations of launch authority might not always successfully convey an Israeli willingness to retaliate. It is also conceivable that Jerusalem could, in fact, lack the willingness to retaliate, and that this genuine lack would be perceived correctly by enemy decision makers. In this case, Israeli nuclear deterrence could be weakened or immobilized, not because of any confused signals but rather because of signals that had not been purposefully scrambled.

The distinction here would be real and meaningful.

FURTHER PROBLEMS WITH PERCEIVED ISRAELI WILLINGNESS AND CAPACITY TO RETALIATE

On occasion, such a genuine lack of willingness could stem from an asymmetry between the provocation (e.g., a "minor" conventional attack) and a threatened nuclear response. It might also stem from counterdeterrent threats made by the attacker to unleash substantial forms of counterretaliation. This second explanation would display a dynamic interaction whereby the would-be deterrer (Israel) was itself deterred.

Regarding *capacity*, even if Jerusalem maintains a recognizably substantial arsenal of nuclear weapons, it is essential that enemy states also believe these weapons to be distinctly *usable.* This means that if a first-strike attack were believed capable of destroying Israel's arsenal, the Jewish State's nuclear deterrent could then be neutralized. Moreover, even if Israel's nuclear weapons were configured such that they could not actually be destroyed by an enemy first strike, enemy misperceptions or misjudgments about Israeli vulnerability could nonetheless occasion the sudden or incremental failure of Israeli nuclear deterrence.

A further complication here concerns enemy deployment of antitactical ballistic missile defenses, which might contribute to any attack decision against Israel by lowering the attacker's expected costs.

Should Israel seek to reduce the perceived vulnerability of its nuclear deterrent forces by some intentionally detectable combination of multiplication/dispersion/hardening, enemy states could come to erroneously believe that Jerusalem was preparing for first-strike attacks. Such erroneous beliefs would be even more likely if Israel should simultaneously seek further reduced force vulnerabilities via appropriate forms of active and passive defenses. Ironically, in seeking to stabilize deterrence by signaling an enemy or enemies that its own nuclear forces were not vulnerable to disarming first strikes (i.e., that these forces were exclusively second-strike forces with assured destruction capability), Israel could unwittingly create the impression that *it* was preparing to strike first. In this case, Israel's attempts to convince enemy states that it was not preparing for preemption could backfire, effectively offering new incentives to these enemy states to preempt themselves.

Israel's Strategic Future: The Final Report of Project Daniel had urged Israel to remain deliberately ambiguous until shortly after Iran had crossed the nuclear weapons threshold. Still, such a doctrinal change could become necessary even before Iran becomes fully nuclear—now, ironically, after the misconceived P5+1 Vienna Agreement (2015), a likely fait accompli.

Why should this be the case? Here is a meticulously detailed reply.

Should Israel calculate the cost effectiveness of any still-remaining preemption options against Iran, it would first have to assess just how credibly it could then deter any unacceptably damaging Iranian retaliation. With this in mind, Jerusalem could determine that a threat of Israeli nuclear counterretaliation would be needed to prevent any too-destructive Iranian response to an Israeli preemption but that the credibility of any such threat would also be contingent on first persuading Tehran that Israel's relevant nuclear weapons were usable, survivable, and penetration capable. Of these three constituent criteria, moreover, the first may be most important—that is, Israel may require, above all else, to signal Iran that its counterretaliatory nuclear attacks following any massive Iranian conventional retaliations would involve distinctly usable (i.e., not "too large") nuclear weapons.

Ironically, this suggests that the credibility of any nuclear threat—retaliatory or counterretaliatory—could sometimes actually vary inversely with perceived destructiveness.

Any such suggestion could appear to be counterintuitive, but is nonetheless probably still persuasive.

Another interesting and crucial question arises: To what extent, if any, would Israel's removal of the bomb from the basement affect its inclination to abandon nuclear deterrence in favor of preemption? An antecedent question must also ask the following: To what extent, if any, might the ongoing transformation of territories into an independent Palestine encourage such removal? For the moment, Israel—still buffered a bit from a hot eastern border by Judea/Samaria—can possibly afford to keep its bomb in the basement. If, however, this territory should become Palestine, Israel could likely feel more compelled to move from deliberate ambiguity to disclosure, a shift that could substantially improve the Jewish State's nuclear deterrence posture but might also enlarge the actual chances of a nuclear war should this posture fail. In any such calculation, the then-attained degree of Iranian nuclearization, and also Iranian support of Palestine, would be significant and need to be most carefully ascertained.

THE NEED FOR A BETTER ANTECEDENT UNDERSTANDING OF DISCLOSURE

At first glance, the issue of more explicit Israeli nuclear disclosure—of a codified end to deliberate nuclear ambiguity—may seem small or inconsequential. Everyone already knows that Israel has the bomb. What then would be the purpose of further belaboring the obvious?

Might not such unnecessary saber rattling even be unduly provocative, occasioning Arab and/or Iranian[2] first strikes that might not otherwise have been contemplated?

Always, the point must be that any codified disclosure would expectedly heighten enemy perceptions of Israel's capable nuclear forces and/or Israel's willingness to use these forces in specific reprisals for certain first-strike attacks.

For the moment, Israeli nuclear forces could surely penetrate the active defenses of *any* enemy attacker after the Jewish State had absorbed a first strike. This could change in the future if there were substantial enemy progress on appropriate forms of antitactical ballistic missile (ATBM) defense and/or an enemy state or states were allowed to achieve a devastating first-strike capability (i.e., one that effectively precludes an Israeli reprisal). This second prospect is itself dependent in part on Israel's developing ATBM capabilities and on Israel's particular configuration of nuclear retaliatory forces.

There is, quite plausibly, an authentically synergistic relationship between Israeli/Iranian/Arab ATBM developments, one that must continually increase arms race momentum, both defensive and offensive. From the standpoint of nuclear deterrence, this interactive relation suggests perpetual instability and offers yet another reason why Israeli security must inevitably be founded on more than purely threat system dynamics.

TOWARD A BETTER UNDERSTANDING OF ISRAELI ACTIVE DEFENSES

In the nuclear age, as we first witnessed between the superpowers during the Cold War, active defenses can sometimes be offensive and provocative. In this connection, region-wide commitments to active defense measures could heat up the area arms race, possibly occasioning all sides to accelerate their offensive weapons capabilities. Theoretically, a region-wide ATBM agreement could prevent or slow down such offensive developments (by initiating a moratorium or outright cessation of active defense measures), but—as a practical matter—it would stand no meaningful chance of success. Recognizing uncertainty and distrust as irremediable givens in any Middle East strategic equations, Jerusalem now has little choice but to continue full speed with its multiple-level active defenses and its ongoing and corollary search for required hard-target kill capabilities.

During the summer of 2015, US and Israeli defense agencies began to train operators for the Magic Wand antimissile system, scheduled to go operational by the end of 2015. Also called David's Sling, it is designed to complement and augment Iron Dome, which deals with shorter-range missiles and performed very well against Hamas rockets during IDF Gaza Operation Defensive Edge. The third and most potentially vital level of Israel's active defenses will be Arrow, most notably against any long-range Iranian nuclear threat.

Together with its Iranian mentors, Hezbollah poses the most genuinely existential threat to Israel. Still thought to possess at least 100,000 rockets, many of them accurate, the Shiite militia, based in Lebanon, serves as a core constraint of any contemplated Israeli preemption against Iran and could greatly complicate IDF protections if there should ever be a joint Iranian-Hezbollah first strike or reprisal.

During the fall of 2015, the IDF security establishment was reportedly preparing for "nightmare scenarios" involving up to 4,000 Israeli prompt fatalities in the initial exchange of fire with Hezbollah Iranian surrogates, but there is good reason to believe that such estimates fall significantly short of what could actually happen.[3] One generally unrecognized reason for this is the now greater likelihood of expanding Iranian support for Syria's Assad regime and its Hezbollah client, an ironic consequence of the summer 2015 P5+1 Vienna agreement on curbing Iranian nuclear weapons. Of course, the battered regime in Damascus is already supported by Moscow, support that underscores an increasingly "tight" form of US-Russian bipolarity.

Still, there is far more to be understood here than tangible superpower relations or calculable assessments of prospective adversity.

There seemingly exists, at least among some of Israel's conspicuously frontline adversaries, a doctrinal voluptuousness of violence, a primal voluptuousness all their own, a voluptuousness of bringing harms to the Jewish State *as such.* Although intangible and not measurable, Israel's military planners must never lose sight of this potentially consequential Islamist orientation to war and terror.

Ballistic missile defenses can never simply replace Israeli nuclear deterrence.[4] The lingering search for a fully perfect interception capability derives from the sober understanding that a single incoming nuclear warhead could produce grievously unacceptable damage. But as such a perfect interception capability is essentially impossible, at least for the foreseeable future, Israel has little choice but to maintain and prepare for a tactically viable preemption option, even if only for certain desperately last-resort circumstances.

MORE ON ASSUMPTIONS OF DECISIONAL RATIONALITY

In the traditional military lexicon, strategies of deterrence must always assume enemy rationality. In the absence of rationality—that is, in those more or less residual circumstances where an enemy state could rank order certain selected values or preferences even more highly than "staying alive" as a nation—deterrence should be expected to fail. As for those inherently more serious situations involving nuclear deterrence, the palpable consequences of failure could be unprecedented. In essence, they could be starkly catastrophic.

Dealing with substate or terrorist adversaries presents a somewhat different and potentially more hazardous set of nuclear deterrence risks. By definition, these increasingly hard-line adversaries (e.g., ISIS, Hezbollah) don't have sovereign national territories to protect. Moreover, their ultimate objectives are apt to include even martyrdom, a faith-driven preference that assuredly does not bode well for successful Israeli deterrence.

Plainly, assorted beleaguered states in the Middle East are having to deal with ISIS, Hezbollah, and other apocalyptic death cults that may never conveniently conform to the ordinary notions of decisional rationality in world politics. This is, using our most *au courant* American parlance, much more than an inconvenient truth. It is a foreseeably existential truth problem.

For now, at least, nuclear deterrence should continue to be examined *vis-à-vis* national or state adversaries, and not in reference to any Jihadist or sub state terrorist actors. Somewhat reassuringly, in this connection, even irrational national enemies of Israel could conceivably display a more or less decipherable hierarchy of preferences. Therefore, such irrational enemies could—at least in principle—be rendered subject to certain alternative forms of deterrence, forms that threaten something other than "ordinary" retaliatory destruction. Of course, as was pointed out earlier, some adversaries of Israel could also emerge as genuinely "crazy" or "mad," a more perplexing condition for which there would likely be no ascertainable deterrence protection.

"Do you know what it means to find yourselves face to face with a madman?" inquires playwright Luigi Pirandello's *Henry IV*. "Madmen, lucky folk, construct without logic, or rather with a logic that flies like a feather."

What is true for individuals is sometimes also true for states. In the often-unpredictable theater of modern world politics, a drama that routinely bristles with debilitating absurdities, decisions that still rest on logic can quickly crumble before madness. Corresponding dangers can reach the most singularly portentous or existential level—that is, whenever madness and a nuclear weapons capability should come together or coincide.

Such matters of rationality and irrationality are not fanciful or contrived. They are profoundly real and current, especially in the deeply adversarial matter of Israel and Iran. Because the international community never agreed to undertake a still-timely preemptive action (anticipatory self-defense, in the formal language of law) and committed itself instead to the bitter self-parodies of futile diplomacy, Jerusalem could sometime have to face an unapologetically genocidal Iranian nuclear adversary. Such a suicidal enemy state in Iran, one that would be animated by graphically annihilationist visions of a Shiite apocalypse, cannot merely be wished away.

Israel's Prime Minister, Benjamin Netanyahu, clearly understands that Iran's extant leadership, and possibly even a successor government in Tehran, could at some point value Israel's physical destruction more highly than its own national survival. Should this happen, the play would almost certainly end very badly for all actors, including the "victorious" Iranians.

EXEUNT OMNES?

For the foreseeable future, Israel's ultimate source of national security will have to lie in some augmented pattern or other of *sustained nuclear deterrence.* Still, whether continuously ambiguous or newly disclosed, this Israeli bomb in the basement could "crumble before madness." It follows that in certain easily imaginable instances involving aberrant enemy behavior, the outcome of failed Israeli retaliatory threats could include suffering altogether irremediable harms.

Although the logic of deterrence has traditionally required an assumption of rationality, history reveals the persistent fragility of any such theoretical expectation. We already know all too well that nations can behave in ways that are consciously and conspicuously self-destructive. Does anyone remember the Third Reich?

History may trump logic and could thus deserve eventual pride of place. Mirroring the decisively unpredictable behavior of individual human beings, national leaders could sometimes assign the very highest value to preferences other than collective self-preservation, a sort of *Götterdämmerung* (Twilight of the Gods) mentality and scenario. Until now of course, we haven't witnessed such a scenario expressly involving nuclear weapons or doctrine. But let us also be candid: our tormenting species' specifically nuclear history is also very new and largely untested.

Shall we still be reassured? For the moment, no single Iranian or other Islamic national adversary of Israel would appear to be genuinely irrational or mad. Harsh enemy rhetoric notwithstanding, no such adversary actually appears ready to launch a first strike against Israel using weapons of mass destruction. For now, at least, the plausible expectation that any such aggression would elicit a devastating reprisal is seemingly sufficient to successfully prevent an attack.

Still, by their very nature, strategic calculations are enormously complicated.[5] In this connection, faulty calculations or errors in information could lead a perfectly rational enemy state to strike first, and this particular attack decision would then not be the outcome of irrationality or madness. Technically, one should recall, judgments of rationality and irrationality must always be rooted in an ascertainably prior *intent*.

UNDERSTANDING THE URGENT IMPORTANCE OF POWER OVER DEATH

In the Middle East especially, promises of power over death should come to mind and ought not be trivialized. In fact, in world politics generally, there can be no greater power. From the Egyptian pharaohs to the present-day Iranian mullahs and ISIS fighters, palpable evidence of this particular assessment is impossible to dismiss or intelligently deride.

In world politics, to be sure, all things move perpetually in the midst of death and amid corollary hopes for immortality. Certain enemy states, therefore most likely Iran, could one day decide that excising the "Jewish cancer," or more generically, the "enemies of Allah," would be worth even the most staggering human costs. In principle, from a purely military standpoint, this genocidal prospect might be reduced or even avoided should Israel be willing to undertake certain eleventh-hour hard-target preemptions. All things considered, however, any such once-reasonable expressions of anticipatory self-defense would now be very difficult to imagine or to justify.

A meaningfully successful or cost-effective preemption is now plausibly beyond Israel's cumulative military capabilities. This does not mean that Israel would be operationally incapable of destroying a required number of Iranian nuclear assets and infrastructures but only that the net costs of any such self-defense venture would very likely exceed the calculable net benefits or gains.

Virtually all critical Iranian nuclear assets have likely already been deeply hardened, widely dispersed, and substantially multiplied. For Israel, there would also be considerable political costs attached to any now residual preemption. A preemptive attack, even one that would become an operational failure, could elicit utterly overwhelming spasms of public and diplomatic condemnation. Indeed, such deafening howls of execration would be inevitable, especially if US President Barack Obama's P5+1 Vienna agreement with Iran were still being touted as a success.

For Israel, it is plausible that certain alternative forms of preemption, including targeted assassination of nuclear scientists and/or cyber defense/cyber warfare, could still be useful, or even necessary, but it is also unlikely that any such options could permanently obviate more traditionally expedient resorts to massive military force.

A bolt-from-the-blue CBN (chemical, biological, or nuclear) attack on Israel that is launched with the expectation of "city-busting" reprisals might not necessarily exhibit irrationality or madness. Within such an attacking state's particular ordering of preferences, any presumed religious obligation to annihilate the "Zionist entity" could represent the overriding value. Here, as reasoned from the pivotal standpoint of the prospective attacker's decisional calculus, the expected benefits of producing any such blessedly apocalyptic annihilation would exceed the expected costs of any expected Israeli reprisal.

Judged from this aberrant analytic standpoint—the perspective of the would-be attacker—a seemingly "mad" attack decision could still "make sense."

An enemy state with such explicitly exterminatory orientations could effectively represent the *individual suicide bomber in macrocosm*. Whether we like to acknowledge it or not, it presents a realistic and powerful image. Just as individual Jihadists (both Shiite and Sunni) are now plainly willing to achieve personal martyrdom, so too might certain *Jihadist states* become willing to sacrifice themselves collectively.

Any Iranian or Arab leaders making the fateful decision to strike massively at Israel might be willing to make martyrs of their own *people* but probably not of *themselves.* In this very asymmetrical ethical scenario, it could be judged acceptable by these particular leaders to sacrifice more or less huge portions of their respective populations but only while they, and presumably their own families, were simultaneously able to flee expeditiously to a predetermined, albeit still very much earth-bound, safe haven. These conspicuously unheroic leaders could find ample justification and comfort in the certain knowledge that the Islamic victims were authoritatively destined for a far better place.

Historically, all global strategy moves in tandem with the more or less discordant rhythms of death. Therefore, to truly understand assorted regional calculations of war, deterrence, and defense, Israeli military planners will first need a better understanding of (1) enemy orientations to death, both individual and collective, and (2) Israeli orientations to death, both individual and collective. This complex requirement is especially critical at a moment when both Jerusalem and Washington are seeking to bring ISIS under more effective operational control and to do so without strengthening Iran, Syria, and Hezbollah.

In the Middle East, only one premise is truly certain. This is that the promise of immortality remains overarching, incomparable, and in a class entirely by itself.

But successfully undermining this promise for policy purposes represents a very formidable challenge. Here, IDF planners can also learn from ancient Western and pre-Christian/pre-Islamic texts. For example, the main message of Lucretius's great poem, *On the Nature of Things*, could assist Israel's security and survival. What the young Virgil, citing Lucretius, called "fear of the doom against which no prayer avails" may still lead many Jihadists to plan to destroy "infidels and apostates." Significantly, the very last scene of Lucretius's poem is a grotesquely bloody battle that would never have taken place if the combatants had first been able to more courageously acknowledge death.

ON COUNTERING POWER OVER DEATH

With such meaningful insights in mind, what is Israel to do? It can no longer rely indefinitely on even the most creative forms of preemption/anticipatory self-defense.[6] It also can't very well choose to live indefinitely with determined theological enemies who might not always be reliably deterred by the more usual threats of retaliation and would themselves already be armed with weapons of mass destruction. Understandably, living permanently under a nuclear sword of Damocles could be much more daunting than most Israelis would actually be willing to endure.

As noted earlier, Moshe Dayan had once declared: "Israel must be seen as a mad dog; too dangerous to bother." If Israel's enemies could all still be presumed rational—that is, in the ordinary sense of valuing their physical survival more highly than any other preference or combination of preferences—Jerusalem could then soon begin, among other things, to exploit certain latent strategic benefits of *pretended irrationality*. Recognizing that in particular strategic situations, it can be rational to feign irrationality, Israel could then work systematically to create more appropriately cautionary behavior among its relevant adversaries. In such cases, the threat of an Israeli resort to a Samson Option might be adequate to dissuade an enemy first strike.

Recalling Sun Tzu, more explicit Israeli hints of Samson could communicate an impressively useful grasp of the ancient Chinese strategist's advice to diminish reliance on defense and instead to seize the unorthodox. In this connection, it should not be forgotten that even Israel's highly refined and interpenetrating systems of active defense could never achieve a one hundred percent reliability of ballistic missile interception. Although not generally understood, the Arrow and related ballistic missile defense systems could be needed, primarily to enhance Israeli nuclear deterrence (hard-point defense) and not for any large-scale soft-point defense of civilian populations.

What about Dayan's earlier advice? If Israel's relevant national adversaries, probably Iran, were presumptively irrational in the ordinary sense, there would likely be no real benefit to any assumed postures of pretended irrationality. This is the case because the more probable threat of any massive Israeli nuclear counterstrike linked in enemy calculations with irrationality would be no more compelling to Iran, or to any other enemy state, than if it were confronted by an expectedly rational State of Israel.

Pretended irrationality can work only vis-à-vis fully rational adversaries. Israel could benefit from a more nuanced and cultivated understanding of the *rationality of pretended irrationality* but only in very particular reference to expectedly rational enemy states. In those circumstances where such enemy states were presumed to be irrational, something else would be needed, something other than nuclear deterrence, preemption, and/or ballistic missile defense.

Although many commentators and scholars still believe the answer to the quandary lies in certain diplomatic or political settlements, this time-dishonored belief is born largely of frustration. Freud would correctly call such belief an example of "illusion" or of always delusionary "wish fulfillment."[7]

All along, President Barack Obama's plan for keeping Iran nonnuclear was naive, at best.

No promising political settlements can ever be worked out with enemies who openly seek Israel's "liquidation," a word that is still used commonly in many Arab and Iranian newspapers, websites, and texts. Israel's enemies are not primarily concerned about land. Their incessant and lascivious war with Israel is still largely about power over death.

It remains about promises of redemption through sacrifice.

It is still about God.

It is still about immortality.

In a recent survey of Palestinians in both the West Bank and Gaza, American pollsters were able to conclude that 73 percent of Palestinians want Jews "annihilated," per Islam's canonical Hadith, quoted in the Hamas Covenant. In other words, three-quarters of those Arabs surveyed agreed with the Covenant's direct call for a Muslim genocide of the "Jews":

> [T]he Islamic Resistance Movement aspires to realize the promise of Allah, no matter how long it takes. The Prophet, Allah's prayer and peace be upon him, says: "The hour of judgment shall not come until the Muslims fight the Jews, and kill them, so that the Jews hide behind trees and stones, and each tree and stone will say: 'Oh Muslim, oh servant of Allah, there is a Jew behind me, come and kill him.'"[8]

Going forward, Israel must fully understand such Islamic eschatology, especially that technical irrationality need not signify clinical madness. Even an irrational state leadership could have an instrumental, consistent, and transitive hierarchy of wants. The first deterrent task for Israel, therefore, must be to identify this presumed hierarchy among its several state enemies. Although these states might not be deterred from contemplated aggression by even the plausibly persuasive threat of massive Israeli retaliations, they might still be dissuaded by certain threats aimed at what they do hold to be most important.

What might be most important to Israel's prospectively irrational state enemies, potentially even more important than their own physical survival as a state? One possible answer is the avoidance of certain forms of presumed *apostasy*, *shame*, and *humiliation*. This would include avoiding the potentially unendurable charge that they had somehow defiled their most sacred Islamic religious obligations.

Another answer would be leaders' strongly preferred avoidance of their own violent deaths at the hand of Israel, deaths that could be attributable to Israeli strategies of targeted killing and/or regime targeting. In these cases, the particular Islamic leaders would not themselves have been persuaded by the usually compelling benefits of martyrdom.

This last suggestion could be problematic to the extent that, theologically, being killed by Jews for the sake of Allah ought doctrinally to be regarded as a distinct positive. Dying for the sake of Allah, as we may recall, could be regarded in these leadership contexts as a clerically blessed passport to immortality.

In world politics, there can never be any greater promise of power than power over death. By definition, such power must always be based on antecedent power over time. Accordingly, Israel could benefit from finally decoding a growing and paradoxical mindset, one that identifies suicide with eternal life. Such an effort would need to focus on a plainly primary *Islamist* idea. This idea is the unambiguously seductive notion that time need not always have a "stop."

Although almost never acknowledged, Israel's vital task is intellectual. To survive, therefore, it must first learn how to transform a widespread enemy understanding that links heroic martyrdom to the conquest of time. For now, at least in principle, some of Israel's adversaries still regard *death for Allah* as the best way to soar indispensably and ecstatically above *profane time*.

In this way, these enemies reason, believers may choose *rationally* to live forever.

In Jerusalem and Washington, key decision makers must finally realize that the Jihadist fighter sees himself or herself as a *religious sacrificer*. Each such adversary, whether Sunni or Shiite, consciously aims to escape from profane time, or time without meaning, to a time that is perpetual and consequently *sacred*. By willfully abandoning the ticking clock increments that imprison ordinary mortals and thereby condemn them to a death everlasting, the Jihadist opts to slaughter both "heathen" and "infidel" in an eternally grateful exchange of murder for *immortality*.

Israel and America both must finally understand: The Jihadist terrorist kills and dies to end the presumed sovereignty of unbelievers, a sovereignty that allegedly prevents the natural supremacy of Islam from transforming the *Dar al-Harb* into the *Dar al-Islam*.

Jihadist terror is not only sanctioned in the Quran; it is commanded: "Against them make ready your strength to the utmost of your power, including steeds of war, to strike terror into the hearts of the enemies of God and your enemies, and others besides, whom ye may not know, but whom God doth know" (Q 8:60). Or yet again, "but when the forbidden months are past, then fight and slay the pagans wherever ye find them, and seize them, beleaguer them, and lie in wait for them in every stratagem of war" (Q 9:5).

Early Muslims grasped intuitively the effect these divine injunctions would produce. Shortly after the 624 CE Battle of Badr, Muhammad launched a campaign of political assassination of Jewish poets and leaders (among them old men and nursing mothers). These killings were followed by the siege, expropriation, and expulsion of the Jewish tribes of Medina, the Banu Qaynuqa and the Banu Nadir, and by the massacre of the Jewish men of the Banu Qurayza and enslavement of their women and children. Horrified by these examples, other tribes of the Peninsula capitulated, fled, or converted to Islam. In essence, calculated, calibrated application of terror often works, and today's Jihadist terrorists know it.

Jihadist terrorists have long since adapted these lessons to the modern asymmetric warfare we must now deal with on a daily basis. As Pakistani Brigadier General S. K. Malik wrote in his classic *The Quranic Concept of War* (1979): "Terror struck into the hearts of the enemies is not only a means, it is the end in itself. Once a condition of terror into the opponent's heart is obtained, hardly anything is left to be achieved." That this most fundamental of our enemies' strategic philosophy is neither studied nor scarcely even known to exist in our national war colleges or universities is a great detriment and sometimes leads to the elevation of cross-cultural competency above understanding a basic enemy threat doctrine.

In the future, Israel will need to deal with both rational and irrational adversaries. These enemies in turn will be both state and substate actors. On occasion, Israel's leaders will also have to deal with various complex and subtle combinations of rational and irrational enemies, sometimes even simultaneously.

Ultimately, Israel must also prepare to deal with nuclear madmen, both as terrorists and as national leaders. But first it must fashion a suitable plan for dealing with nuclear adversaries who are neither mad nor irrational. With such an imperative, Israel should now do everything possible to enhance its deterrence, preemption, defense, and war-fighting capabilities. This means, among other things, enhanced and explicit preparations for certain last-resort, or "Samson," operations.

SAMSON OPTION RUDIMENTS

By definition, the Samson Option would be executed with countervalue-targeted nuclear weapons. It is more or less likely that any such last-resort operations would come into play only after all Israeli counterforce options had already been exhausted.

Concerning the previously mentioned *rationality of pretended irrationality*, Samson could enhance Israeli nuclear deterrence by demonstrating a national willingness to take existential risks.

Concerning Israel's preemption options, preparations for a Samson Option could convince Israeli leaders that their own defensive first strikes would be undertaken with reduced expectations of unacceptably destructive enemy retaliations. This sort of convincing would depend, at least in part, on prior Israeli government decisions on disclosure (that is a limitation or an end to nuclear ambiguity), Israeli perceptions of the effects of disclosure on enemy retaliatory prospects, Israeli judgments about enemy perceptions of Samson weapons vulnerability, and an enemy awareness of Samson's countervalue force posture. In any event, the optimal time to modify or end Israel's "bomb in the basement" policy and thereby replace deliberate ambiguity with appropriate forms of disclosure will soon be at hand.

Similar to Samson's impact on Israeli nuclear deterrence, recognizable last-resort preparations could enhance Israeli preemption options by displaying a clear and verifiable willingness to accept certain chances. In this scenario, however, Israeli leaders must always bear in mind that *pretended irrationality* could become a double-edged sword. Brandished too flagrantly and without sufficient nuance, any Israeli preparations for a Samson Option could effectively impair rather than reinforce Israel's residual nuclear war-fighting options.

Concerning prospective contributions to Israel's nuclear war-fighting options, preparations for a Samson Option could convince enemy states that achieving any clear victory over Israel would be impossible. With such reasoning, it would become important for Israel to communicate to potential aggressors the following, very precise understanding: *Israel's countervalue-targeted Samson weapons are additional to its counterforce-targeted war-fighting weapons.* Without such a communication, any preparations for a Samson Option could conceivably impair rather than reinforce Israel's nuclear war-fighting options.

Undoubtedly, as was concluded earlier by *Project Daniel*, nuclear war fighting, wherever possible, should be scrupulously avoided by Israel.

Again, the purpose of Israel's nuclear forces and doctrine must always be deterrence *ex ante,* not revenge *ex post.*

But there still remain some readily identifiable circumstances in which nuclear exchanges could be unavoidable, whatever Israel might actually have done to prevent them. As indicated earlier, some forms of nuclear war fighting could ensue so long as enemy state first strikes launched against Israel would not destroy Israel's second-strike nuclear capability, enemy state retaliations for an Israeli conventional preemption would not destroy Israel's nuclear counterretaliatory capability, conventional Israeli preemptive strikes would not destroy enemy state second-strike nuclear capability, and Israeli retaliations for enemy state conventional first strikes would not destroy enemy state nuclear counterretaliatory capability.

PULLING IT ALL TOGETHER: FASHIONING A PURPOSEFUL STRATEGIC DOCTRINE

Promptly, Israel will need to fashion a comprehensive and suitably calibrated *strategic doctrine,* one from which various specific policies and operations could readily be extrapolated. This focused framework would identify and correlate all available strategic options (*deterrence, preemption, active defense, strategic targeting, nuclear war fighting*) with core survival goals. It would also take close account of the possible *interactions* between these strategic options and determinable *synergies* between all conceivable enemy actions directed against Israel. Actually calculating these particular interactions and synergies will present a computational task on the very highest order of intellectual difficulty.

Nuclear deterrence is a "game" that certain sane national leaders must play, but to compete effectively, a would-be winner must always first assess (1) the *expected rationality* of each critical opponent, and (2) the probable costs and benefits of *pretending irrationality* oneself. These are undoubtedly complex, interactive, and glaringly imprecise forms of assessment, but just as doubtlessly, they constitute a needed foundation for Israel's long-term security. Doctrinally, it is already time for them to become part of Jerusalem's codified and revitalized *order of battle.*

One planning component here would be to include an element of regime targeting (i.e., an announced strategy to undermine a designated enemy state's capacity to wage war by threatening to smash its leadership as well as destroy certain of its hard military assets). Regime targeting, however, would not need to serve Israel exclusively as a component of deterrence. It could also serve Jerusalem as part of a plausible preemption strategy. For example, should Israeli planners conclude that durable deterrence cannot be expected and that the preemptive destruction of pertinent enemy hard targets is tactically infeasible, eliminating or reducing enemy leadership elites could prove to be the only still-viable option.

In all such matters, it is important from the standpoint of international law to distinguish preemptive attacks from *preventive* ones. Preemption is a military strategy of striking an enemy first, in the expectation that the only alternative is to be struck first oneself. A preemptive attack is launched by a state that believes enemy forces are about to attack. A *preventive* attack, however, is launched not out of any concern for imminent hostilities but rather for fear of a longer-term deterioration in the military balance.

In a preemptive attack, the length of time by which the enemy's action is anticipated is very short, whereas in a preventive strike the interval is considerably longer. A problem for Israel, in this regard, is not only the practical difficulty of determining "imminence" but also the fact that delaying a defensive strike until imminence is plausible could prove fatal. International law, it must always be recalled, is never a suicide pact.

Regarding Israel's vulnerability to enemy first strikes, there are important subtexts. Should the Jewish State refrain from striking first until enemy states had acquired nuclear weapons, these new nuclear powers could implement protective measures that would pose additional hazards to the Jewish State. Designed to guard against preemption either by Israel or by other regional enemies, these measures could involve the attachment of "hair trigger" launch mechanisms to nuclear weapon systems and/or the adoption of "launch-on-warning" policies, possibly coupled with predelegations of launch authority.

All of this means that Israel could be increasingly endangered by steps taken by its nuclear enemies to prevent preemption. Optimally, Israel would do everything possible to prevent such steps, especially because of the expanded risks of accidental or unauthorized attacks against its armaments and populations. Yet if such steps should somehow become a fait accompli, Jerusalem might still calculate correctly that a preemptive strike would be both legal and cost effective. This is because the expected enemy retaliation, however damaging, might still appear *more tolerable* than the expected consequences of enemy first strikes—strikes most likely occasioned by the antecedent failure of "antipreemption" steps.

In the perhaps not-too-distant future, the Islamic leadership in Tehran, unless still suitably prevented in a timely fashion, could strike at Israel with unconventional forces irrespective of anticipated Israeli counterstrikes. Immobilized by Iranian irrationality,[9] Israeli nuclear deterrence will have been unable to safeguard the Jewish Commonwealth. Notwithstanding Israel's successful deployment of nuclear weapons in survivable modes, the capacity of these weapons to penetrate Iranian active defenses, and Jerusalem's clear willingness to retaliate, Iran will still have decided to launch against "infidels."

From Tehran's point of view, any sort of peace settlement with Israel is likely seen as an intolerable affront to Islam and as a negation of Iran's Islamic identity. As for territorial compromise over Palestine, this, too, is likely out of the question. Because a Muslim land in the heart of *Dar al-Islam* (the abode of Islam) can be ruled properly only by a Muslim authority, Israel's "usurpation" of *any* Arab land must allegedly be met with jihad, or holy war. Described by the current Islamic leadership in Tehran as a "cancerous growth in the Middle East," Israel is approached as a malignancy, not because of its particular policies but merely because it exists as a Jewish state.

Israel must do absolutely whatever is needed to prevent such an Iranian nuclear aggression. Abandoning the potentially self-defeating policy of a too-total reliance on nuclear deterrence, and appropriately wary of any coerced nonnuclear membership in the nonproliferation treaty (NPT) regime, Jerusalem should always prepare expeditiously for all life-saving forms of preemption. The critical questions to be addressed here are those concerning tactics (i.e., questions of timing, targeting, and configuration of ordnance). As for the underlying legality of any such preemptive measures, they could be entirely consistent with the right of anticipatory self-defense under international law.[10]

We may recall here Samuel Pufendorf's argument in *On the Duty of Man and Citizen According to Natural Law*:

> [W]here it is quite clear that the other is already planning an attack upon me, even though he has not yet fully revealed his intentions, it will be permitted at once to begin forcible self-defense, when admonished in a friendly spirit, he may put off his hostile temper; or if such admonition be likely to injure our cause. Hence, he is to be regarded as the aggressor, who first conceived the wish to injure, and prepared himself to carry it out. But the excuse of self-defense will be his, who by quickness shall overpower his slower assailant. And for defense, it is not required that one receive the first blow, or merely avoid and parry those aimed at him.[11]

Although it cannot be ruled out that an Israeli nonnuclear preemption might still lead to nuclear exchanges (this would depend in part on the effectiveness and breadth of Israeli targeting, the surviving number of enemy nuclear weapons, and the willingness of enemy leaders to risk Israeli nuclear counterretaliations), such exchanges appear more likely if Iran is allowed to deploy ever-greater numbers of unconventional weapons without interference. Should such deployment ever take place, Israel could even confront a rationally irresistible incentive to undertake *nuclear* preemption. In the very worst case scenario for Jerusalem, where nuclear deterrence had failed to protect Israel and the Jewish State had even undertaken nuclear preemption without success (i.e., without destroying the essential number of enemy missiles), any residual survival of the state could rest on active defense.

Optimally, Israel would be able to rely on the currently fashionable notion of a "multilayered active defense,"[12] but such reliance could also reflect a potentially lethal disposition to hope too much. Hence, Israeli military planners, considering all pertinent tactical issues, should now look very closely at the core Iranian threat dimensions, including the likelihood of Iranian first strikes over time, probable harms of Iranian first strikes over time, collaborative prospects between Iran and other enemy states, plausible timetables of Iranian unconventional weapons deployments, projected efficiencies of Iranian active defenses, projected efficiencies of Israeli active defenses, projected efficiencies of Israeli hard-target counterforce operations, and, of course, probable global reactions to any Israeli resort to defensive first strikes.

Now, Israel faces a dual-preemption imperative. It must in effect preempt its own military preemption of certain Iranian mass destruction weapons assets with a far-reaching public relations campaign. Unless the second preemption action precedes the first and does so in a timely and convincing fashion, any defensive destruction of Tehran's developing nuclear capacity by Israel, however indispensable to Israel's survival, could elicit uniformly critical reactions all over the world.

Recognizing such expected reactions, an Israel that had failed to prevent them with prior public education might then allow Iranian nuclearization to proceed without necessary interference.

ATTACKS ON NUCLEAR REACTORS AND CONVENTIONAL DETERRENCE

This does *not* mean, however, that Iran's nuclear threat to Israel is entirely contingent on Iranian nuclearization. In fact, an Iranian conventional attack directed against certain Israeli nuclear reactor facilities could bring variable nuclear harms to the Jewish State. Following a conventional attack on Israeli nuclear reactors, released radioactivity could contaminate hundreds or even thousands of square miles.

Such contamination could occasion occupation restrictions that would last for decades. Should certain of Israel's reactors be clustered together, the dangers would be enlarged if the contents of more than one were discharged and/or if there were any release of the inventories of spent fuel (inventories that could be co-located at reactor sites).[13] Of course, the risks of an attack on a country's nuclear reactors and infrastructures could also fall heavily and reciprocally on Israel's enemies, here, most notably Iran.

There is also the matter of conventional deterrence. Enemy states contemplating conventional attack on Israel, especially on the severely truncated Jewish State already emerging from "a 'successful' peace process," might be dissuaded only by the threat of a strong *conventional* retaliation. Hence, inasmuch as a conventional war could quickly escalate into an unconventional war, Israel's conventional deterrent could prove indispensable in offering protection against chemical, biological, and nuclear war as well as against conventional war.

Always, a persuasive conventional deterrent is a *sine qua non* of Israel's security irrespective of the persuasiveness of Jerusalem's nuclear deterrent and/or the availability of suitable preemption options.

Reciprocally, Israel's conventional and nuclear deterrents are meaningfully interrelated. For the foreseeable future, any enemy states that would launch an exclusively conventional attack on Israel would almost surely have multiple *unconventional* weapons capabilities in reserve. This means that even if Israel could rely on conventional deterrence as a first line of protection, that line must necessarily be augmented by Israeli nuclear deterrence to prevent any intrawar escalation that might be initiated by certain enemy states.

Uncomfortable truths are not easily received by states, especially on matters of conspicuously existential import. To this point at least, friends of Israel have generally remained content with the clichéd wisdom of assorted pundits, with a meandering discourse that is almost always unhelpful. Where it is taken as evidence of more serious strategic thought, this more or less reportorial wisdom could displace what is genuinely indispensable. This references a complex and comprehensive excursion into *dialectical reasoning*.

Yet there are *no* assurances that *any* discourse will actually suffice. It is even conceivable that while Israel now needs to get beyond total reliance on nuclear deterrence, the essential requirements of preemption are beyond satisfaction. This is perhaps the true dilemma of Israeli security, the prospect that no single strategy or configuration of strategies could ever be capable of preserving the state. If this is indeed the case and such a dilemma is plausible, it is now immediately incumbent on Israel's leaders and planners to prepare for survival within all pertinent constraints.

There would be no alternative.

Ein breira.

If nuclear deterrence were to break down and Israel had somehow failed to implement timely preemptive measures, the Jewish State could face conventional attacks and/or unconventional attacks including—in the future—nuclear aggression. In either case, the net result could be one form or another of nuclear war. What might be the tangible consequences of such a war? This is plainly an important question, one that must be raised simultaneously with other considerations of Israeli nuclear deterrence and preemption.

CONSEQUENCES OF A NUCLEAR WAR AND A NEW ISRAELI STRATEGIC DIALECTIC

Perhaps the first genuinely large-scale and authoritative study of nuclear war consequences was a 1975 study titled "Long-Term Worldwide Effects of Multiple Nuclear Weapons Detonations." Prepared in the United States by a special committee of the National Research Council, National Academy of Sciences, its point of departure was nothing less than

> a horrendous calamity; a hypothetical exchange involving the detonation of many nuclear weapons. In the worst case considered, about half of all nuclear weapons in current strategic arsenals, viz, 500 to 1000 weapons of yield 10 to 20 megatons each, and 4000 to 5000 lesser (sic) weapons with yields of 1 or 2 megatons each, i.e., a total of 10,000,000,000 tons of TNT equivalent are exchanged among the participants. No report can portray the enormity, the utter horror which must befall the targeted areas and adjoining territories.[14]

Of course, the scale of this early report's assumptions is vastly greater than that concerning us here, namely a believable nuclear war scenario for Israel in the Middle East. Nevertheless, the likely kinds of physical and biological effects are still relevant to our present inquiry. Some of these effects concern temperature changes, contamination of foods by radionuclides, disease epidemics in crops and domesticated animals due to ionizing radiation, shortening of growing seasons, irreversible injuries to aquatic species, long-term carcinogenesis due to inhalation of plutonium particles, radiation-induced developmental anomalies in persons in utero at the time of detonations, increase in skin cancers, and increased incidence of genetic disease that would not be limited to the offspring of the exposed generation but would extend over many generations.

Significantly, in assessing the likely effects of a nuclear war involving Israel, it will be important to look beyond *individual* effects in isolation. This means that the interactions between individual effects could produce calamitous and still unforeseen consequences. Recognizing this some years ago, a publication of the US Arms Control and Disarmament Agency, *Worldwide Effects of Nuclear War: Some Perspectives*, concluded as follows:

> In attempting to project the after-effects of a major nuclear war, we have considered separately the various kinds of damage that could occur. It is also quite possible, however, that interactions might take place among these effects, so that one type of damage would couple with another to produce new and unexpected hazards. For example, we can assess individually the consequences of heavy worldwide radiation fallout and increased solar ultraviolet, but we do not know whether the two acting together might significantly increase human, animal or plant susceptibility to disease. We can conclude that massive dust injection into the stratosphere, even greater in scale than Krakatoa

(the volcanic eruption) is unlikely by itself to produce significant climactic and environmental change, but we cannot rule out interactions with other phenomena, such as ozone depletion, which might produce utterly unexpected results. We have come to realize that nuclear weapons can be as unpredictable as they are deadly in their effects.[15]

But what specifically would be the likely effects of a "limited" nuclear war, a war of the sort that should most concern Israeli planners? To continue to answer this question, a query first raised here in the introduction, we must first subdivide this category into at least three possibilities: (1) exclusively counterforce attacks against Israeli hard targets, (2) exclusively countervalue attacks against Israeli civilian populations, and (3) mixed counterforce/countervalue attacks. Moreover, in comparing the likelihood of these three possible nuclear attacks, it will first be necessary to (a) differentiate between objectives and capabilities of enemy states, and (b) prepare a comprehensive "strategic dialectic" in which Israel anticipates enemy state reactions to its own nuclear strategies and deployments.

How shall this dialectic be prepared? In essence, Israeli planners should approach the problem as an interrelated series of thoughts, where each thought or idea about enemy capabilities/enemy intentions presents a complication that moves inquiry onward to the next thought or idea. Contained in this strategic dialectic will be an obligation to *continue thinking*, an obligation that can never be fulfilled entirely (because of what the philosophers call an "infinite regress problem") but that must still be attempted as fully and competently as possible.

Without such a dialectic, those who work on Israeli security matters will continue to focus on discrete moments in time, on static phenomena (e.g., numbers of weapons, types of weapons, leadership personalities, etc.), rather than on appropriately dynamic and generic interactions (synergies).

The advantages of a new Israeli strategic dialectic will depend, in part, on the coherence of the overall academic enterprise. Israel does not face a random set of discrete and wholly separate military threats. Rather, there exists a general threat environment within which discrete threat components "fit."

The task for Israeli strategists is not to figure out in advance each and every specific threat component (although this *is* a task of certain government intelligence analysts) but to identify a strategy that will accommodate the understanding of a broad variety of possible threats. This means an obligation to fashion a strategic "master plan," a body of generalized and interrelated propositions from which specific policy options could be derived. Such a plan would not contain all or even most of the "answers," but it could offer a comprehensive and informed framework within which all of the most important questions might be addressed.

Such a plan would never be "completed." It would serve those who oversee Israel's security needs continually, incrementally, and directly as an ongoing and expanding set of purposeful guidelines.

Returning to our more specific discussion of a strategic dialectic for Israel, planners now need to identify in broad outline certain of the expected consequences that more or less would be common to each scenario. Medically, the most widespread and potentially problematic type of injury in a nuclear attack would be burns. On this injury, Israeli planners should consider that in the United States, at the Massachusetts General Hospital—one of the very best in the country—only fifteen beds are available at any one time for the acute care of burn victims. Just to keep one such patient alive taxes this exceptional facility to the limit. No amount of advanced preparation could provide the human and material resources required for the care of even a few such patients hospitalized simultaneously in any city of the United States. Yet we must assume that at least tens of thousands of such casualties would result in every Israeli city hit by a nuclear weapon.

Overall normal society would cease to function. The pestilence of unrestrained murder and banditry would augment the pestilence of plague and epidemics. With the passage of time, many of the survivors would expect an increased incidence of degenerative diseases and various kinds of cancer. They would also expect premature death, impairment of vision, and increased sterility. Among the survivors of Hiroshima, for example, an increased incidence of leukemia and cancer of the lung, stomach, breast, ovary, and uterine cervix has been widely documented.

Some of the most delicately balanced relationships in nature could be upset by the extensive fallout. In this connection, Israelis who would survive the nuclear exchange would likely have to deal with enlarged and voracious insect populations. According to biologist Tom Stonier:

> Mushrooming insect populations are likely to spread from the radiation-damaged areas in which they arose, and, like the locusts of biblical times, wreak havoc in previously undamaged areas. Accompanying the insect plagues would be the plant diseases transmitted by insects, particularly those diseases which attack plants that have been injured or weakened by insect or radiation damage. The combined assault of radiation, insects, disease and fire could temporarily strip off the plant cover of vast areas. If the attack is sufficiently widespread, it is conceivable that a few years later almost all the forests would have been destroyed, and most of the countryside would have become converted into marginal grasslands, if not actually stripped, leaving a naked earth to be ravaged by the ever-present forces of erosion.[16]

Herbert Abrams and William E. Von Kaenel, in the November 1981 issue of *The New England Journal of Medicine*, also present an early assessment of burgeoning insect populations that is still stark and sobering:

> Insects are generally more resistant to radiation than are human beings. This fact, along with the prevalence of corpses, waste and untreated sewage, the depletion of birds, and the destruction of insecticide stocks and production, will engender a huge increase in insect growth. Mosquitoes would multiply rapidly after an attack. . . . The fly population would explode. . . . Most domestic animals and wild creatures would be killed. Trillions of flies would breed in the dead bodies. Uncontrolled growth in the insect population . . . may sharply limit the capacity to control such diseases as typhus, malaria, dengue fever and encephalitis.[17]

Certain of the biological and ecological effects of a nuclear war could be felt by other states in the region. Radioactive fallout does not respect political boundaries. Because of the manner in which nuclear explosions behave in the atmosphere, the altitude reached by the mushroom-shaped cloud would depend on the force of the explosion.

For yields in the low-kiloton range, the cloud would remain in the lower atmosphere, and its effects would be entirely local—that is, these effects would likely not extend beyond the boundaries of the combatant states. But for yields exceeding 30 kilotons, part of the cloud of radioactive debris could "punch" into the stratosphere, affecting noncombatant states as well.[18]

Throughout the Middle East region affected by nuclear exchanges, an enormous health threat would be created by thousands of rotting, unburied corpses. In many areas radiation levels could be so high that corpses could remain untouched for weeks or even months. With transportation destroyed, survivors weakened, and myriad postwar reconstruction tasks to be performed, corpse disposal would be remarkably difficult. Eventually, to bury the dead, areas much larger than Israel's now destroyed cities could be required for the cemetery.

Such prospects notwithstanding, an enemy state might still launch a nuclear first-strike against Israel. In such an event, Jerusalem would certainly respond, to the extent possible, with a nuclear retaliatory strike. As described earlier, if the enemy state's first strikes were to involve other forms of unconventional weapons (i.e., chemical and/or biological weapons), Israel *might* launch a nuclear reprisal.

Should Israel suffer a massive conventional attack by an enemy state or states, a nuclear retaliation could not be excluded, especially if (a) the aggressor were perceived to hold nuclear or other unconventional weapons in reserve, or (b) Israel's leaders were to believe that nonnuclear retaliations could not prevent actual destruction of the state.

Israel could feel compelled to preempt enemy state aggression with conventional forces. Should it undertake such a preemptive move, the targeted state's response would largely determine Jerusalem's next steps. If this response were in any way nuclear, Israel would assuredly undertake some form of nuclear counterretaliation.

If this retaliation were to involve chemical or biological weapons, Israel might also feel compelled to take the escalatory initiative. This in turn would depend on Jerusalem's judgment of enemy intent and on its calculations of essential damage limitation.

Should nuclear weapons be introduced into a conflict between Israel and its enemies, nuclear war fighting, at one level or another, could ensue. Both Israeli nuclear and nonnuclear preemptions of enemy unconventional attacks could lead to nuclear exchanges. This would depend, in part, on the effectiveness and breadth of Israeli targeting, the surviving number of enemy nuclear weapons, and the willingness of enemy leaders to risk Israeli nuclear counterretaliations. In any event, the likelihood of nuclear exchanges would appear to be greatest where pertinent enemy states are allowed to deploy ever-greater numbers of increasingly destructive unconventional weapons without some form of *timely* Israeli preemptive interference.

Should such deployment take place, Israel could effectively forfeit the nonnuclear preemption option and be forced to choose between a no-longer-timely nuclear preemption and waiting to be struck first. It follows that the risks of Israeli nuclear preemption, nuclear exchanges with an enemy state, *and* enemy nuclear first strikes could all be reduced by timely Israeli nonnuclear preemptions—directed at critical hard targets and/or "regimes." This would contradict the conventional wisdom that associates any prospective Israeli preemptive strike with aggression and expanded harms.

Once again, what about the so-called Samson Option? Many informed students of our subject identify this concept as an essential core of Israeli nuclear strategy. Although this is certainly an error, as the primary mission of Israel's nuclear weapons must always be to preserve the Jewish State (not to wreak postapocalyptic vengeance in a purposeless spasm of last-resort violence), *preparations for* a Samson Option could nonetheless be purposeful. This is because such *observable* preparations could enhance Israel's nuclear deterrence, preemption, and war-fighting capabilities.

ENHANCED NUCLEAR DETERRENCE AND AVOIDING NUCLEAR WAR

Left to themselves, insufficiently deterred or preempted, certain of Israel's prospectively nuclear state adversaries could threaten to bring the Jewish State face-to-face with the considered torments of Dante's *Inferno*: "Into the eternal darkness, into fire, into ice." It is essential, therefore, that Israeli planners and political leaders recognize immediately the obligation to strengthen their country's nuclear deterrence posture and to take proper steps to ensure that a failure of nuclear deterrence will not occasion any forms of nuclear warfare. My insistence herein on facing the graphic consequences of a regional nuclear war has stemmed not from any ill-conceived faith in the nonproliferation regime, a now-fragile configuration of formal rules highlighted by the Treaty of the Non-Proliferation of Nuclear Weapons (1968), but from the understanding that Israel's survival still depends on purposeful *self-reliance* and that such reliance in turn requires (1) a multifaceted nuclear strategy involving deterrence, preemption, and war-fighting capabilities, and (2) a corollary conventional strategy that is similarly comprehensive and undiminished by substantial territorial losses occasioned by any so-called peace process.

In specific regard to this corollary conventional strategy, Israel must always understand that a nuclear war could arrive as a result of escalation. If, for example, enemy states were to commence conventional attacks on Israel, Jerusalem could respond sooner or later with nuclear reprisals. Or if these enemy states were to begin conventional attacks on Israel, Jerusalem's conventional reprisals could then be met with enemy nuclear counterstrikes.

A persuasive Israeli conventional deterrent, to the extent that it would prevent enemy state conventional attacks in the first place, could reduce Israel's risk of escalatory exposure to nuclear war.

But why would Israel need a conventional deterrent at all? Wouldn't enemy states desist from launching conventional attacks on Israel simply out of a well-reasoned fear of nuclear retaliation? Not necessarily.

Aware that Israel would cross the nuclear threshold only in very extraordinary circumstances, these states could be convinced (rightly or wrongly) that so long as their attacks remain fully conventional, Israel's response would also be nonnuclear. This would mean, correspondingly, that the only way for Israel to deter large-scale conventional attacks could be by maintaining *visibly* large-scale conventional capabilities. Of course, enemy states contemplating first-strike attacks using chemical and/or biological weapons are apt to take more seriously Israel's (disclosed or undisclosed) nuclear deterrent.

A strong conventional capability is needed by Israel to deter or preempt conventional attacks, strikes that could, if they were undertaken, lead quickly via escalation to various forms of unconventional war.

To a significant extent, such enhanced escalatory risks can be associated with the steady fragmentation and disintegration of Syria. Here, amid an almost indecipherable complexity of friends and foes, Israel will need to refine very basic plans for launching certain conventional attacks in the region and defending against both state and substate Islamic aggressions. Uppermost here will be Iranian and Hezbollah efforts to enlarge viable bases of anti-Israel terror from the northern Golan Heights, possibly involving selected Druze elements.

Israel too will need to take much closer account of Turkish involvement. In the Kurdish part of Syria, an area has been taken over by the PYD, the Syrian sister movement of the Turkish PKK, which cooperates with Assad and is combating ISIS in Kobani and Tall Abyad. From the standpoint of overall complexity, however, this is only the tip of the iceberg, and the IDF cannot possibly calculate every nuance of regional enemy consultation and cooperation. What must absolutely be understood, however, is the visible emergence of a "Cold War II" between Russia and the United States and the best ways this emergent polar hostility could affect Syrian disintegration and thereby Israel's conventional deterrence.[19]

This also brings to mind again the sorely misnamed "peace process." Insofar as this process involves by definition the incremental surrender of strategic depth by Israel, it makes Israel's conventional deterrent more and more problematic. Over time, in consequence, Israel's conventional capacity to ward off enemy attacks could effectively disappear.

This could mean paradoxically a strengthening of the Jewish State's nuclear deterrent if enemy states perceive Israel's own sense of expanding weakness and desperation. If, however, enemy states did not perceive such a "sense" among Israel's decision makers, these states—animated by Israel's conventional force deterioration—could be encouraged to attack. The result here, spawned by Israel's failure to maintain strong conventional deterrence, could be (1) defeat of Israel in a conventional war, (2) defeat of Israel in an unconventional (chemical/biological/nuclear) war, (3) defeat of Israel in a combined conventional/unconventional war, or (4) defeat of Israel's enemies *by* Israel in an unconventional war.

For Israel, even the successful fourth possibility could be intolerable. The consequences of a nuclear war (or even a chemical/biological war) could become unexpectedly calamitous for the victor as well as for the vanquished. In such exceptional conditions of belligerency, even the traditional notions of victory and defeat could lose all serious meaning.

Israel needs a strong nuclear deterrent, but it cannot rely entirely on this one base of national security any more than it can rely on only conventional deterrence. Rather, it must rely on complementary nuclear and conventional forces and on the continuing and associated availability of critical preemption options. Taken together, preferably with suitably observable preparations for a Samson Option, these multiple bases of security could endow the Jewish State with the essential requirements of survival into the next millennium.

Without all of these interrelated security foundations, Israel's future could be founded on vain hopes,[20] an apocalyptic future that might ultimately include the palpably nightmarish visions of a regional nuclear war.

What if critical preemption options were no longer available to Israel? After all, it is entirely plausible that this is *becoming* the case, especially with regard to Iran. Shall the nation's leaders simply say "*Yihyeh B'Seder!*" (It will be OK!)?

Israel arguably deserves better than a *Shma Israel* scenario. Although it is undeniable that any state, even with the most prescient planning, could at some time find itself facing such a scenario, the essential task for each state—including the State of Israel—is to maintain strategic control to the fullest possible extent.

What exactly should this mean for the Jewish State?

More than anything else, perhaps, the imperative to maintain control suggests that there can be no perfect security condition for Israel, and its leaders must inevitably choose from a range of imperfect options. Hence, while nuclear deterrence is problematic and residual preemption prospects may be fading, there are still more or less gainful ways to configure combinations of deterrence and preemption. In certain circumstances, preemptive strikes against enemy hard targets (the only sort of preemption here under discussion) could be expected to elicit destructive reprisals (possibly even against Israeli civilian populations), yet these reprisals could prove substantially less harmful than the expected costs to Israel of relying entirely on nuclear deterrence (i.e., the costs of declining preemption).

OTHER FORMS OF POSSIBLE PREEMPTION

In principle, at least, some forms of regime targeting or targeted killing could be construed as a suitable expression of preemption. Thomas More, writing his *Utopia* in 1516, offered a pragmatic prescription for survival. Although his Utopians are expected to be generous toward other states and sovereigns, they also offer rewards for the assassination of certain enemy leaders (Book II).

This stance is not assumed because More wished his Utopians to be gratuitously barbarous but only because he was a realistic Utopian, sharing with St. Augustine (whose *City of God* had been the subject of his famous 1501 lectures) a fundamentally dark assessment of human political arrangements. More constructed a "lesser evil" philosophy that favored a very practical kind of morality. Sir Thomas understood that the most truly tragic element of all political activity is constituted of utterly conscious choices of evil for the presumed sake of a greater good.

With particular reference to contemporary Israel's security, this suggests that assassination or political killing must not always be disagreeable in the best of all possible worlds (most conspicuously for More in the Leibnizian world famously satirized by Voltaire in *Candide*), but that they may represent an indispensable expedient in a world that must always remain distressingly imperfect.[21]

For the foreseeable future, Israel's only security choices are ranged among starkly unattractive options. To act rationally, Jerusalem must choose in each case the least unattractive option. While this is indeed a challenging state of affairs, and while in the best of all possible worlds, Israel could cheerfully fall back on durable political settlements, *this* is the starkly adversarial context within which Jerusalem *must* operate.

There is no other context. There is no better world. Political settlements would be nice, but for the moment at least, they cannot be taken seriously. On matters of urgently high politics, they simply will not work.[22]

One last word about preemption. Critics of such a policy bring up, quite reasonably, that it rests on an "infinite regress" dilemma. In other words, there is always the *next* danger, always the *next* hard target. At some point, for a combination of strategic and political reasons, therefore, preemption must become infeasible.

All of this is certainly true. But imperfect and problematic as preemption happens to be, whether as a minor or major component of Israeli defense policy, these negatives need always to be *compared* to the expected costs of all reasonable alternatives. If these costs should entail assorted existential risks of national annihilation, as well they might, the downside of Israeli preemption could sometimes seem *comparatively* minor.

The upside of preemption for Israel could include more generalized enemy perceptions of greater Israeli power, perceptions that could then "feed back" productively into Israeli nuclear deterrence and meaningfully reduce certain further risks of enemy state aggressions.

Israel must always build its security on altogether realistic assessments of danger. It should never base its policies on false hopes. Recognizing that perfect security is unattainable and no single mode of security creation can ever succeed by itself, its leaders must now promptly identify those particular configurations of nuclear deterrence, defense, and preemption that would be optimally purposeful. All such identification, of course, would have to be accomplished in a world system still drifting toward ever-greater levels of chaos—that is, with a view toward avoiding any final Dionysian abyss.[23]

In the end, Iran won't likely be Israel's last Islamic enemy to "go nuclear." This means that IDF planners will need to stay abreast of all prospective Arab/Islamic nuclearization. Some good advice in this regard was provided by the Project Daniel Group, back in 2004. In *Israel's Strategic Future,* the group identified the following phases together with expected or typical durations. Some, but not all, of these phases were judged to be plausibly simultaneous:

- Develop a laboratory nuclear fission device—ten years
- Develop a fusion device (having fission technology)—ten years
- Prepare strategic materials for a nuclear device—ten years
- Develop an air bomb weapon system—eight years
- Develop a long-range missile—twelve years

- Fit a nuclear warhead onto a missile—eight years
- Build an arsenal of one hundred bombs (after completing the first bomb)—four years
- Build an arsenal of one hundred nuclear missiles (after the first)—four years
- Build a distributed system of missile launchers—five years
- Operate a fleet of nuclear missile submarines—twelve years

This list of expected phases can offer a helpful guide to the amount of time Israel might actually have to prepare for future adversarial nuclear weapon developments. It could be needed, therefore, as an informed guide to possible future preemption imperatives but only to the extent that successful long-term Israeli nuclear deterrence would be judged improbable.

"Theories are nets," says the German poet Novalis, and "only he who casts will catch."[24] Optimally, therefore, IDF planners will be able to draw on a suitably generalized body of theory from which specific policy prescriptions could be extrapolated. In so doing, it will be important to consider such diverse factors as (1) growing chaos in world affairs generally and in the Middle East especially, (2) growing bipolarity in world affairs including even the developing prospect of "Cold War II," (3) prospect of prior nuclear weapons use on the Korean Peninsula or even Southwest Asia (India-Pakistan), (4) the growing prospect of the United States becoming a guarantor of basic security for Iran and/or "Palestine," (5) incapacity of the United States and its Western allies to bring democratic governance to the Middle East (or anywhere else, for that matter), and (6) the emergence of mega-terror attacks in the Middle East and also elsewhere.

Very close to home for Israel, as we have already noted, Jordan could quickly become vulnerable to advancing ISIS forces. Should Israel come to the aid of the Hashemite monarchy in such a fight? If so, in what specific and cost-effective operational forms?

Similar questions will need to be raised in reference to another close neighbor: Egypt. Should President Abdel Fattah al-Sisi somehow fail to hold things together, the ultimate victors could be not only the country's own Muslim Brotherhood but also in nearby Gaza, Palestinian Hamas. Already, in the fall of 2015, Hamas was being targeted by ISIS, a potentially remorseless strategy suggesting that the principal impediment to Palestinian statehood is not really Israel but rather another Sunni terrorist group. Also, it is not out of the question that ISIS's expressly Egyptian offshoot, "Sinai Province of the Islamic State," could at some point decide to cooperate openly with Hamas instead of planning to defeat it.

"Just wars," wrote Hugo Grotius, the founder of modern international law, "arise from our love of the innocent."[25] Now, in the midst of an expanding civilizational struggle, Israel must use all necessary and permissible means for self-defense and self-preservation. In some instances, although "perfidious" provocations by assorted terror groups or enemy states could elicit reprisals that would bring harms to enemy noncombatants, it is these provocations, not Jerusalem's indispensable responses, that would be in violation of international humanitarian law.

International law, Israel must again bear in mind, is never a suicide pact. The refusal by Israel's state and substate enemies to accept even the most minimal expectations of global comity will likely continue, stemming in large part from presumptive Jihadist Islamic obligations. Reciprocally, Israel, together with all other imperiled states in the world system, has an overriding basic right to stay alive. Operationally, this *jus cogens*[26] right could need to be protected by exercising some forms of preemption or anticipatory self-defense.[27] Should Israel for any reason fail to heed its overriding right to endure, it could then hasten the arrival of a future once prophesied by the Irish poet Yeats, a chaotic time wherein "[t]here is no longer a virtuous nation, and the best of us live by candle light."[28]

NOTES

1. Concerning disclosure, from 1965 to the present, Israel has adopted the cautious formula: "Israel does not have nuclear weapons and will not be the first to introduce them into the region." Presumably, however, this formula is not meant to suggest that Israel will sit idly by if its enemies "go nuclear." In this connection, Yigal Allon's comment is instructive: "Israel will not be the first to introduce nuclear weapons into the Middle East, but neither will it be second." For a careful and early consideration of the entire disclosure issue, see this writer's *Security or Armageddon: Israel's Nuclear Strategy* (Lexington, MA: Lexington Books, 1986).

2. The particular strategic dangers to Israel from Iran were already recognized by then Prime Minister Netanyahu in a July 10, 1996, address to a Joint Session of the US Congress: "The most dangerous of these [regional dictatorships] is Iran, that has wed a cruel despotism to a fanatic militancy. If this regime, or its despotic neighbor Iraq, were to acquire nuclear weapons, this could presage catastrophic consequences, not only for my country, and not only for the Middle East, but for all mankind. I believe the international community must reinvigorate its efforts to isolate these regimes, and prevent them from acquiring atomic power."

3. See Kobi Finkler, "Going Operational: US, IDF Begin Training 'Magic Wand' Operators," *Arutz Sheva*, Israel National News, June 29, 2015. Magic Wand is a joint project of the Israel Defense Ministry's Home Authority, the US Missile Defense Agency (MDA), and RAFAEL, the main contractor for Magic Wand. RAFAEL works closely with US-based Raytheon on these matters. Magic Wand's Multi-Mission Radar was developed by Elta, a subsidiary of Israel Aerospace Industries. The command and control system, *Shaked Zahav*, was developed by Elisra, which is part of Elbit Systems.

4. This position can be viewed as an expression of a broader classical and prenuclear distinction between defense and "victory." For example, in Chapter Four of his *The Art of War*, Sun Tzu instructs his readers: "One who cannot be victorious assumes a defensive posture; one who can be victorious attacks. . . . Those who excel at defense bury themselves away below the lowest depths of Earth. Those who excel at offense move from above the greatest heights of Heaven." Of course, our discussion here of

Israeli nuclear strategy contrasts an emphasis on (ballistic missile) defense not with a military attack strategy but rather with *deterrence*.

5. "Everything is very simple in war," says Clausewitz, in his well-known discussion of "friction" in *On War*, "but the simplest thing is difficult."

6. A related concern here must include the ethical or humanitarian calculus in any such prospective Israeli expressions of armed force. While the best of all possible worlds would contain "neither victims nor executioners" (this high-minded phrase is taken from Albert Camus, *Neither Victims Nor Executioners*, Dwight McDonald, ed., 1968), such an ideal arrangement of world power and authority is plainly not yet visible on the horizon. Confronting what he called "our century of fear," Camus had asked his own readers to become "neither victims nor executioners," living not in a world in which killing has disappeared ("we are not so crazy as that") but one wherein killing has at least become illegitimate. This is a fine expectation of a French philosopher but certainly not one that can also be harmonized with the real world. Deprived of the capacity to act as lawful executioners, both states and individuals within states facing aggression, terrorism, and/or genocide could be forced by Camus's reasoning to become victims. The truly core problem with the Camus argument is that the will to kill must always remain unimpressed by any others' commitment to "goodness." This means, as Florentine philosopher Machiavelli recognized long before Camus, that both within and between states executioners must still have their rightful place. Without these executioners, there could only be more victims.

7. See, especially, Sigmund Freud, *The Future of an Illusion*, *Totem and Taboo*, and *Moses and Monotheism*. At the end of Chapter VI in *The Future of an Illusion*, where he has been discussing the "psychical origin of religious ideas," Freud concludes as follows: "We shall tell ourselves that it would be very nice if there were a God who created the world, and was a benevolent Providence, and if there were a moral order in the universe, and an after-life; but it is a very striking fact that all this is exactly as we are bound to wish it to be. And it would be more remarkable still if our wretched, ignorant, and downtrodden ancestors had succeeded in solving all these difficult riddles of the universe."

8. *Sahih Muslim*, Book 41, Number 6985. See further Andrew G. Bostom, "Only 73% of Palestinians Want Jews Annihilated, as Per Islam's Canonical Hadith," *American Thinker*, September 21, 2012.

9. See, on this source of immobilization, Ayatollah Khomeini, "Program for the Establishment of an Islamic Government," 1970, in *Islam and Revolution: Writings and Declarations of Imam Khomeini*, Berkeley, 1981; see also Robert S. Wistrich, *Antisemitism: The Longest Hatred*, New York: Pantheon Books, 1991, p. 219. Perhaps the best distillation of Islamic thought concerning Israel and rationality foundations of nuclear deterrence is the following statement about Jews: "The race (sic) is corrupt at the root, full of duplicity, and the Muslims have everything to lose in seeking to deal with them; they must be *exterminated* (see Gilles Kepel, *The Prophet and Pharaoh: Muslim Extremism in Egypt*, London, 1985, p. 112).

10. For early scholarly commentary by this author on anticipatory self-defense under international law with special reference to Israel, see Louis René Beres and (Col./IDF/res.) Yoash Tsiddon-Chatto, "Reconsidering Israel's Destruction of Iraq's Osiraq Nuclear Reactor," *Temple International and Comparative Law Journal*, Vol. 9, No. 2, 1995, pp. 437–449; Louis René Beres, "Preserving the Third Temple: Israel's Right of Anticipatory Self-Defenses Under International Law," *Vanderbilt Journal of Transnational Law*, Vol. 26, No. 1, April 1993, pp. 111–148; Louis René Beres, "After the Gulf War: Israel, Preemption and Anticipatory Self-Defense," *Houston Journal of International Law*, Vol. 13, No. 2, Spring 1991, pp. 259–280; Louis René Beres, "Striking 'First': Israel's Post Gulf War Options Under International Law," *Loyola of Los Angeles International and Comparative Law Journal*, Vol. 14, Nov. 1991, No. 1, pp. 1–24; Louis René Beres, "Israel and Anticipatory Self-Defense," *Arizona Journal of International and Comparative Law*, Vol. 8, 1991, pp. 89–99; and Louis René Beres, "After the SCUD Attacks: Israel, 'Palestine,' and Anticipatory Self-Defense," *Emory International Law Review*, Vol. 6, No.

1, Spring 1992, pp. 71–104. For an examination of assassination as a permissible form of anticipatory self-defense by Israel, see Louis René Beres, "On Assassination as Anticipatory Self-Defense: The Case of Israel," *Hofstra Law Review*, Vol. 20, No. 2, Winter 1991, pp. 321–340. For more general assessments of assassination as anticipatory self-defense under international law by this author, see Louis René Beres, "The Permissibility of State-Sponsored Assassination During Peace and War," *Temple International and Comparative Law Journal*, Vol. 5, No. 2, 1991, pp. 231–249; and Louis René Beres, "Victims and Executioners: Atrocity, Assassination and International Law," *Cambridge Review of International Affairs*, Winter/Spring, 1993.

11. See Samuel Pufendorf, *On the Duty of Man and Citizen According to Natural Law*, Vol. II, tr. by Frank Gardner Moore, New York: Oceana Publications, Inc., 1964, p. 32.

12. The essential components of such a multilayered approach would include space-based surveillance, boost-phase intercept, wide-area coverage, and terminal point defense systems. Sea-based systems, primarily because of their mobility/deployability, could provide more or less effective wide-area ballistic missile defense coverage.

13. For an early and informed consideration of reactor attack effects, see Bennett Ramberg, *Destruction of Nuclear Energy Facilities in War* (Lexington, MA: Lexington Books, 1980); and Bennett Ramberg, "Attacks on Nuclear Reactors: The Implications of Israel's Strike on Osiraq," *Political Science Quarterly*, Winter 1982–1983, pp. 653–669. More recently, see Bennett Ramberg, "Should Israel Close Dimona? The Radiological Consequences of a Military Strike on Israel's Plutonium-Production Reactor," *Arms Control Today*, May 2008, pp. 6–13.

14. From letter of transmittal by Dr. Philip Handler, President of the NAS, which is contained at the beginning of the report, "Long-Term Worldwide Effects of Multiple Nuclear Weapons Detonations," National Academy of Sciences, Washington, DC, 1975.

15. See *Worldwide Effects of Nuclear War: Some Perspectives*, a report of the US Arms Control and Disarmament Agency, not dated but produced after the 1975 NAS report, pp. 23–24.

16. Ibid., p. 135.

17. See *The New England Journal of Medicine*, November 1981 issue, p. 1228.

18. See *Worldwide Effects of Nuclear War: Some Perspectives*, a report of the US Arms Control and Disarmament Agency, p. 7.

19. For the best available assessment of this disintegration and its probable implications, see Brig. General Yossi Kuperwasser (IDF/res.), "The Disintegration of Syria and Its Impact on Israel," September 3, 2015. BG Kuperwasser is Director of the Project on the Regional Implications of the Syrian Civil War, at the Jerusalem Center in Israel. He was formerly Director General of the Israeli Ministry of Strategic Affairs and head of the Research and Analysis and Production Division of IDF Military Intelligence. In essence, argues BG Kuperwasser, gains by the Assad regime, Iran, and Hezbollah around the Syria-Lebanon border are plausible and will probably intensify an Iranian and Hezbollah search for capabilities against Israel in the northern Golan. In all this deterioration in the correlation of forces, moreover, the summer 2015 nuclear deal between Iran and world powers will have a significantly injurious and corrosive impact on Israel.

20. See, in this connection, a comment by Thucydides on demands of Athenians on the Melians (the *Melian Dialogues*) during the Peloponnesian War: "But hope is by nature an expensive commodity, and those who are risking their all on one cast, find out what it means only when they are already ruined."

21. Regarding legal or jurisprudential support for such an expedient—that is, for assassination as permissible preemption or anticipatory self-defense—we may consider a classic principle of authoritative international law: *Ubi cessat remedium ordinarium, ibi decurritur ad extraordinarium* (Where the ordinary remedy fails, recourse must be had to an extraordinary one). See *Black's Law Dictionary*, 1520 (6th ed., 1990).

22. The July 2015 Iran Nuclear Agreement fashioned by the P5+1 states explicitly ignores antecedent NPT prohibitions on Iran and all other nonnuclear state parties. It also ignores peremptory obligations of the 1948 Genocide Convention—obligations that must require the United States and all other Convention signatories to identify and correct instances of Iranian "incitement to genocide." Further underscoring these binding obligations is a longstanding or *jus cogens* principle that international law is ultimately deducible from natural law. In this connection, according to Blackstone, each state and nation is always expected "to aid and enforce the law of nations, as part of the common law, by inflicting an adequate punishment upon offenses against that universal law." See William Blackstone, *Commentaries on the Laws of England*, Book 4, "Of Public Wrongs." Lest anyone ask about the significance of Blackstone, one need only point out that *Commentaries* are the original and core foundation of the laws of the United States.

23. This brings to mind the closing query of Agamemnon in *The Oresteia*, by Aeschylus: "Where will it end? When will it all be lulled back into sleep, and cease, the bloody hatreds, the destruction?"

24. At the same time, we cannot be allowed to forget that theoretical fruitfulness must be achieved at some more or less tangible cost of "dehumanization." As Goethe reminds us in *Urfaust*, the original *Faust* fragment: "All theory, dear friend, is grey, And the golden tree of life is green." Translated by the author from the German: *"Grau, theurer Freund, ist alle Theorie, Und grun des Lebens goldner Baum."*

25. See Hugo Grotius, *The Law of War and Peace* 70 (William Whewell, tr.), London: John W. Parker, 1853 [1625].

26. See Vienna Convention on the Law of Treaties, May 23, 1969, art. 53, 1155 UNTS 344; reprinted in 8 ILM 679 (1969).

27. See most recently by this author, Louis René Beres, "Defending Israel Against Iranian Nuclear Aggression: War, Genocide, and International Law," *Israel Journal of Foreign Affairs*, 2015. This article argues that longstanding customary legal rights of anticipatory self-defense must now apply to threats of genocide as well as to threats of aggression and jurisprudentially the two categories of international criminality may overlap or intersect.

28. See W. B. Yeats, *The Letters of W. B. Yeats*, 691 (Alan Wade, ed.), 1954.

FOUR

Preserving a Sensible Samson Option

"I mean to show you of my strength, yet greater;
As with amaze shall strike all who behold.
This uttered, straining all his nerves he bowed;
As with the force of winds and waters pent
When mountains tremble, these two massy pillars
With horrible convulsion to and fro
He tugged, he struck, till down they came and drew
The whole roof after them, with burst of thunder
Upon the heads of all who sat beneath."

—John Milton, *Samson Agonistes*

In a field of very great complexity and transformation, no subject remains more elusive and shrouded in confusion than the so-called Samson Option. Indeed, for a large majority of those who know little or nothing about Israel's nuclear strategy, it would seem that some variant or other of Samson represents pretty much the whole story. For this group, there exist no identifiable uses for Israel's nuclear weapons other than desperate employment as a last-resort spasm of vengeance and vitriol.

Of course, as should now already be clear from previous chapters, nothing could be further from the truth. To be sure, there are certain conceivable circumstances in which such an utterly primal conception of the Samson Option could (whether reasonably or unreasonably) actually be embraced. Still, the overarching strategic purpose of Samson for Israel must always be as a tangibly meaningful enhancement of its core deterrence strategy. Once again, as we may be reminded by *Israel's Strategic Future: The Final Report of Project Daniel* (2004): "The primary point of Israel's nuclear forces must always be deterrence *ex ante*, not revenge *ex post*."

Nonetheless, Israel's nuclear deterrent could fail, and dire circumstances of last-resort war fighting could conceivably arise. In such fearful circumstances, ones where Samson could no longer purposefully assist with "deterrence *ex ante*," the biblical model would have become inappropriate. This is because even under such end-of-the-road conditions, Israel's objective should never be to "die with the Philistines" but rather to "let the Philistines die without us."

Significantly, this succinct statement of objective is not merely strategic in nature. It is also deeply embedded in historic, religious, and cultural Judaism. As Israeli scholar and former head of Military Intelligence Yehoshafat Harkabi once argued, "In all situations other than the Holocaust, ignoring consequences is a death cult, totally alien to Judaism, and to our culture."[1]

Earlier chapters have already referenced the importance of "nuclear ambiguity," or Israel's "bomb in the basement." Conceptually and doctrinally, this issue intersects importantly with the prospective utility of a Samson Option. As these security issues can be reinforcing and force multiplying, the ambiguity versus disclosure issue will still be noted and examined here, in short, wherever it might still somehow impact Samson.

What precise answers might Israel receive concerning the prospective benefits (and costs) of better utilizing some form of the Samson Option? Most fundamentally, Israel cannot expect to receive a proper answer until it has first learned to ask the pertinent question. As in all other matters of nuclear strategic thought and planning, there can be no gainful answers to questions that are never properly asked.

THE SAMSON OPTION REFORMULATED

Ordinarily, of course, any reference to the Samson Option is more or less synonymous with the view that Israel's core security has somehow already been lost, and that Samson remedies could now serve only to wreak strategically purposeless harms on a despised, but now also victorious, aggressor. Together with this residually retributive view,[2] so goes the standard Samson argument: all may indeed be lost but not without Israel's first having been able to exact a very high price from the aggressor. With Samson, with an explicit policy refutation of Jewish mass suicide without punishing the enemy, Israel would thereby reject *Masada*. By embracing Samson, in this "classic" formulation, Israel allegedly could at least plan to "die with dignity."

This is not the pragmatic Samson Option that has been discussed and evaluated herein. Instead, as the analysis will explain in considerable depth, this generally misrepresented strategic option could now be used imaginatively and deliberately to *prevent* certain deadly onslaughts on Israel. Properly exploited *before* there is any hint of national defeat, therefore Samson could help Israel to decisively push away any otherwise required resort to "final battle." It would accomplish this by substantially enhancing the country's (1) usable military power and (2) associated military resolve.

In brief, Samson's purpose, as argued in this volume's strategic dialectic, should always be to help keep Israel alive, not to keep Israel from dying alone.

To begin, the story of Samson can provide certain productive biblical insights for Israel's current strategic nuclear posture. More precisely, Israel may learn from Samson not to "die with the Philistines" but to live in spite of its enemies and despite their relentlessly zero-sum orientations to violent conflict. The biblical Samson, blinded but not powerless, was able to destroy the Philistines only by inflicting his own death. Israel is not blind. Nor is it powerful in the starkly limited sense of a physical strength that is born exclusively of religious faith or from a more or less corresponding desperation.

So what exactly is there for Israel to learn from this particular hero of the post-Pentateuch Book of Judges? What discernible strategic messages may be extracted and exploited by Jerusalem?

NAVIGATING A GEOMETRY OF CHAOS: THE CORE LOGIC OF SAMSON

First, Israel can learn that it must *prepare* to take firm hold of the enemy's "temple pillars," not because any last-resort options are of overriding importance in themselves, but because conscientious *preparations* for such options could render any last-resort scenarios for Jerusalem *less likely*. By *seemingly* taking steps to "die with the Philistines," Israel could do far more than merely prepare for the "Apocalypse." By enhancing Israel's nuclear deterrence, preemption, and war-fighting capabilities, such steps could even make the difference between achieving complete victory and suffering total defeat. The true point of taking these steps must be, therefore, *not* to die with the Philistines but rather to use *presumed preparations* for receiving such a death as a recognizable source of diplomatic and ultimately military power.

Regarding prospective contributions to Israeli nuclear deterrence, preparations for a Samson Option could help convince would-be attackers that aggression could never prove gainful. Recalling earlier comments here about "deliberate ambiguity," or the "bomb in the basement," this is especially the case if Israeli Samson preparations were coupled with appropriate levels of nuclear *disclosure* and Israel's pertinent Samson weapons plainly appeared to be sufficiently invulnerable to enemy first strikes. In view of what strategists sometimes refer to as the "rationality of pretended irrationality," Samson could also aid Israeli nuclear deterrence by demonstrating a more credible willingness to take existential risks, but this reasoning would hold true only if the country's last-resort options were not already tied to certain plausible expectations of certain destruction. Regarding prospective contributions to preemption, preparations for a Samson Option could convince Israel that needed defensive first strikes would be undertaken with diminished expectations of unacceptably destructive enemy retaliations. This conclusion would depend, of course, on certain prior Israeli decisions on nuclear disclosure, Israeli perceptions of the effects of such disclosure on enemy retaliatory prospects, and Israeli judgments about enemy perceptions of Samson weapons vulnerability. As in the case of Samson and Israeli nuclear deterrence, last-resort preparations could also assist Israel's preemption options by displaying a credible willingness to take certain existential risks.

As for assistance to nuclear options, preparations for a Samson Option could convince enemy states that a clearly gainful victory would be impossible.

Once again, Israeli planners must be mindful here of pretended irrationality as a high-risk posture. In certain situations, if brandished too "irrationally," Israeli preparations for a Samson Option could encourage rather than discourage enemy preemptions. Regrettably, there is no textbook to which Jerusalem could turn, and determining the optimal levels of pretended irrationality could ultimately prove to be as much of an art as a science.

Whether Samson is evaluated from the standpoint of enhancing Israel's deterrence, preemption, or nuclear war-fighting options—or from any particular combination of these basic options—special attention will need to be paid to the attendant risks of nuclear proliferation. This means that in making its pertinent strategic assessments, Israeli planners should never base their final conclusions on commonsense models of singular or discrete enemy threats. Whatever the level of hostility and peril within a prominent dyad of prospective conflict (e.g., Israel vs. Iran, Israel vs. Syria, etc.), the true threat to Israel will also have to account for assorted corollary and intersecting risks of nuclear proliferation.

To adapt J. Robert Oppenheimer's early metaphor about nuclear weapons spread, the question will then become: *What happens when there is an expanding number of "scorpions in the bottle"?*

SAMSON INTERSECTIONS AND SYNERGIES

For Israel, the matter of intersection or possible synergy between attendant risks is especially important. A subsidiary concern here must be intersections or synergies between Iranian strategic policy decisions and Israeli reactions, or vice versa. In other words, throughout the increasingly complex theatrics of regional nuclear strategy, each side will inevitably base its pertinent judgments not only on wholly abstract or objective considerations of enemy threat but also on its particular subjective perceptions of that enemy's own expected options and policies.

For the analyst, the possibly plausible narratives and scenarios here could quickly become overwhelming and bewildering, but they will need to be dealt with nonetheless. In geostrategic terms, as in life generally, "what is, is."

For Israel, there is no sensible alternative.

Let us examine some of the relevant geostrategic landscapes. For the moment, it would appear, Egypt is no longer a strategic threat to Israel. But this comforting assessment is based not only on General al-Sisi's apparent capacity to effectively contain Islamic radicalism, but also on Cairo's presumptive determination to remain nonnuclear.

During 2015, Sunni Egypt, plainly worried about a still-nuclearizing Shiite Iran, had been in talks with Russia about building Egypt its own military nuclear capacity. The eventual outcome of these talks could well impact the future of Israel-Egypt relations, as well as Egypt's much wider relations in the region and the world.

Historically and philosophically, the anarchic state of nations has been described as more tolerable and less insecure than the condition of individual human beings in nature. This is the case, so goes the classical argument of Thomas Hobbes, because among individuals having to coexist in anarchy, "the weakest has strength enough to kill the strongest, either by secret machination, or by confederacy with others, that are in the same danger with himselfe."[3] Now, however, the most utterly corrosive conditions of individual Man in nature could be replicated in the much wider realms of world politics. In other words, with the spread of nuclear weapons, even tiny states without significant military forces could still become able to "kill" a more or less substantial number of other states. Moreover, as has already been described in this volume, the longstanding structural anarchy of world politics is rapidly becoming a disintegrating context of much more far-reaching dissolution. It is, in essence, rapidly devolving into a more genuine *chaos*.

What, then, shall Samson teach Israel about surviving amid such unique and total forms of systemic disintegration? How, precisely, could regional nuclear proliferation influence Jerusalem's calculations on how best to proceed with various and contemplated deterrence, preemption, or nuclear war-fighting options? The cumulative answer to these questions must always account for assorted and antecedent assessments of enemy rationality; plausible expectations of mechanical accident, computer hacks, or errors in information; and prospects for any newly hardening bipolarity between Russia and the United States.

Any tangible emergence of "Cold War II" could directly impact the risks and harms of nuclear proliferation in the Middle East. Further, Israel must remain wary about concluding prematurely that any expansions of inter-Arab or inter-Islamic regional violence would necessarily be to the strategic advantage of the Jewish State. After all, in the Middle East, history suggests that the "enemy of my enemy" may sometimes still remain "my enemy." For Israel, this somewhat counterintuitive warning could have special relevance to the apparently hardening enmities between Iran and Syria on the one hand and Egypt and Saudi Arabia on the other. In addition, there should be little reassurance that formal compacts with enemy states would necessarily bring any corresponding measures of safety to Israel.[4]

Even long before anyone could have imagined nuclear weapons and the "dreadful equality" of individuals in nature being replicated at the global level, Thomas Hobbes had already identified the basic perils of ordinary anarchy. In such circumstances, said the philosopher, humankind would be dominated by a "continuall feare, and danger of violent death." And what of individual human life in this fearful condition of war: "The nature of War, consisteth not in actuall fighting; but in the known disposition thereto, during all the time there is no assurance to the contrary." It must plainly be the "worst of all." Here, in the famous Hobbesian phrase that is now even more portentous than it was back in the seventeenth century, "[T]he life of man is solitary, poore, nasty, brutish, and short."[5]

ENEMY ATTITUDES TOWARD ISRAEL: ATTRITION VERSUS ANNIHILATION

With regard to the particular concerns of our discussion of Samson, there is one final conceptual issue for Israeli strategists to explore. This is the distinction, more or less meaningful, between planned enemy wars of annihilation and wars of attrition. Although it is manifestly unclear that any of Israel's enemies has focused very deliberately or self-consciously on one polar orientation or the other, it would still make strategic sense for Jerusalem to ascertain relevant enemy intentions as best it can. Among other things, the strategic utility of Samson for Israel could depend at least in part on what these attrition/annihilation intentions actually appear to be.

Traditionally, a war of attrition represents a condition designed to wear down an enemy by constant pressure to weaken, exhaust, or destroy that enemy's military forces. The word "attrition" derives from the Latin *attere* (to weaken), which derives in turn from *terrere* (to rub). In the particular sense of ongoing Arab/Islamic wars against Israel, these wars' objective of exhausting or destroying Israel's armed forces and military infrastructures is likely only an intermediate goal. The overriding objective of all these enemy-generated conflicts could still be Israel's "liquidation" (the term long favored by many Arab or Iranian officials and propagandists).[6]

In the traditional military sense, the term "annihilation" is not necessarily synonymous with complete destruction. Rather it means "to take action that causes an enemy force to be totally incapable of further resistance."[7] In the special context of protracted Arab/Islamic war against Israel, however, annihilation is convincingly synonymous with the traditional meaning—that is, with complete and utter devastation.

Going forward, any Israeli assessments of a useful Samson Option will need to factor in appropriate estimates of enemy orientations to attrition/annihilation warfare, always taking careful account of pertinent obscurities, overlaps, and policy intersections. Regarding corollary judgments on whether particular threats are genuinely existential, it will be helpful to consult *Israel's Strategic Future: The Final Report of Project Daniel* (2004). There, the *Project Daniel Group* had warned "the idea of an existential threat implies harms that portend complete annihilation or the disappearance of the state. The *Group* feels, however, that certain forms of both conventional and unconventional attack against large Israeli civilian concentrations would constitute an existential threat."[8]

In other words, we had argued at the time that because Israel is such a very small and vulnerable state, suffering certain large and consequential harms short of complete annihilation could still be *effectively existential.*[9]

The *Project Daniel Group* had also looked at a particular scenario in which an enemy state or combination of enemy states—with or without substate surrogates[10] —might be entirely rational but because of correctly perceived demographic and territorial advantages over Israel, still be willing to accept huge losses, because Israel's own expected losses would be much higher. If, for example, the calculating enemy state or various state combinations thereof were to figure that it could afford a 1-to-1 exchange with Israel, it/they could literally compel Israel's losses to fall into the high existential range. Of course, the actual likelihood of Israel's most determined adversaries thinking along such expressly exterminatory lines would be impacted more or less substantially by the felt importance of certain antecedent religious/Islamic doctrine.

In any event, the plausible prospect of any such enemy calculations could underscore Israel's ultrasensitivity to enemy weapons of mass destruction and the Jewish State's relentless imperative to prepare a policy of preemption, at least whenever possible and still cost effective. Here, too, Samson could play a useful or even decisive role in offering critical support to such a core security policy.

To the extent that certain Arab/Islamic states might be allowed to develop WMD capabilities (at the time of *Project Daniel*, the Iranian nuclear threat was just beginning to appear on Israel's strategic planning radars), the *Project Daniel Group* had identified a little-discussed peril—one that would also need to be addressed by any reasonably conceptualized Samson Option. This was an *anonymous attack scenario*, a specially fearful narrative wherein the state attacking Israel, and/or the state proxy concurrently attacking Israel, did not identify itself, and any subsequent Israeli identification of the perpetrator(s) might then become more or less problematic. Regarding effective deterrence in such confusing but altogether possible situations, we felt that Israel should declare explicitly, and very early on, that all expressly Arab enemy states and/or Iran be rendered subject to "massive" Israeli reprisal in the event of certain indecipherable biological/nuclear attacks on Israel.[11]

UNDERSTANDING SAMSON'S POWER

Second, Israel can learn from Samson the mortal dangers of exploited vulnerabilities. Like Samson, the Jewish State possesses great tangible strength. And, like Samson, this strength can be blunted or even "cut off" altogether. Israel's national power, of course, does not lie in any one single part of its "anatomy," but its constituent elements are vulnerable nonetheless. In certain circumstances, Israel could "lose its hair;" that is, these vital elements could be rendered inoperable.

What, then, is the appropriate "power lesson" from Samson? More than anything else, it must be that Israel draws at least some of its prospective power from the *land*, from the limited but still indispensable strategic depth provided by Judea, Samaria, and the Golan, and from the territorial imperative to secure conventional and unconventional retaliatory forces from enemy first strikes. Ultimately, in the absence of secure retaliatory forces, Israel's deterrence posture could quickly be eroded to fully intolerable limits.

Israel's Oslo/Roadmap trajectory of incremental territorial concessions, a policy that has always flowed directly from the so-called peace process, is a path that could weaken or destroy Israel's power. By eliminating strategic depth and preventing or jeopardizing secure retaliatory forces, this policy could encourage large-scale enemy aggressions against Israel, both conventional and unconventional, both state and substate. It is a policy, therefore, that still ignores an overwhelmingly important lesson from Samson.

The most plausible narratives here should be easy to acknowledge. Within hours of any formal declaration of Palestinian independence, Israeli Arabs would begin to transform their initially benign celebrations (at least, relative to what would still be planned) into full-scale riots and chaos, thereby indicating a now conspicuously overriding loyalty to "Palestine." To be sure, the rioters wouldn't feel any corresponding need to actually move to this new and twenty-third Arab state themselves, because they would be understandably convinced that in a matter of weeks or months, all of Israel would itself be absorbed into Palestine. Such an irredentist belief, moreover, would be entirely consistent with currently official PA and Hamas maps of Palestine, unhidden exterminatory cartographies which already include all of Israel.

For Israel, the resultant security costs would be multiple and interpenetrating, involving substantial intranational civil disturbance and terror attacks but also more or less simultaneous border incursions from the new State of Palestine. In the shorter term, the principal security dangers to Israel would likely center on domestic security and safety from both internal and external (from Palestine) rockets.

In the longer term, Israel would expectedly face a steadily deteriorating "correlation of forces," a devolution which in turn could heighten the probability of a conventional war with other Arab states. In the still-longer term, there could be new risks of escalation from conventional war to unconventional war, including nuclear war, especially if (1) Iran should be allowed to continue unimpeded to an independent nuclear posture and (2) ISIS should continue to progress with its ongoing and merciless takeovers in large parts of Iraq and Syria.

ISIS AND PALESTINE

Looking ahead further, a Palestinian state would present an attractive takeover target for ISIS. In this regard, there already exists a tangible pro-ISIS fifth column in Jordan. This suggests an additional reason for Israel to oppose any creation of a Palestinian state, another reason deriving from its unchallengeable obligation to "stay alive" as a nation.

Likely risks to Israel from ISIS in Palestine would have little or nothing to do with any authentic Palestinian sympathies for ISIS or vice versa. Even if PA and Hamas were to strenuously oppose any ISIS infiltration of the new Arab state, there is essentially nothing they could do to effectively stop them. Ironically, perhaps, this threat would almost certainly be enlarged by any prior Palestinian compliance with Israeli demands for "demilitarization."

Credo quia absurdum (I believe because it is absurd). Here, geostrategic hazards to Israel would actually stem from too much law-enforcing compliance by Palestine.

In the final analysis, an as-yet unanticipated consequence of Palestinian statehood would turn out to be the enlarged threat to Israel of both nuclear war and nuclear terror, an ominous prospect that should immediately elicit enlarged efforts in Jerusalem to strengthen Israel's core nuclear deterrent. With this in mind, certain related issues of credible intersection or synergy must be raised once again. Some of these issues concern "connecting the dots" between a disintegrating Syria, an enlarging Hezbollah (in part, as the result of increased Iranian support made possible by the Joint Comprehensive Plan of Action, or JCPOS, Vienna, July 14, 2015), another Palestinian *intifada,* and even a still likely Third Lebanon War. Hezbollah prepares to hurt Israel during an always planned "next conflict"—exactly like Hamas in Gaza.[12] More specifically, in response to such preparations, Israeli planners must continue to deal with three main problems: (1) Hezbollah firing of high-trajectory projectiles, targeting civilians, military facilities, and essential human services throughout Israel;[13] (2) Hezbollah special forces' efforts to cross over into Israeli territory, conquer certain towns, kidnap hostages, and block major transportation arteries in the north;[14] and (3) Hezbollah barrages of mortar shells and short-range rockets launched against Israel's adjacent-border communities. Here, in the fashion of Hamas toward the end of Israel's Operation Protective Edge, the Shiite militia's objectives would include the intentional maximization of civilian casualties,[15] qualifying as criminal expressions of "perfidy," and as corollary, the incremental demoralization and/or mass evacuation of Israelis from these imperiled communities.[16]

Should Israel choose to *learn from* Samson about the best ways to respond to a Palestinian state, and simultaneously to pertinent prospective enemy synergies, it would even more strenuously guard its essential sources of power. Instead of accepting further excisions of its already attenuated land mass, an acceptance that could impair strategic depth to an unmanageable degree and also encourage enemy preemptive strikes, it would insist on no additional territorial concessions. Recognizing again that international law is not a suicide pact,[17] its leaders will acknowledge forthrightly that Israel has a primary obligation to survive,[18] an obligation owed both to its current citizens and to those earlier generations of Jewish victims who must now sleep in the dust.

Israel should never be ashamed of its own power, nor should it continue to project only reasonable intentions on enemy leaderships. Recalling from Samson the terribly conclusive consequences of powerlessness—consequences brought on not by irresistible external forces but by Samson's own misjudgments—leaders of the Jewish State must now preserve and prepare to use all vital elements of their national power. Of course, optimal Israeli *use* of nuclear forces would be accomplished through certain deterrence-centered plans for *nonuse*.

In purely military terms, these elements of national power must inevitably include an intact and inviolable land mass and certain appropriate forms of nuclear weaponry.

ADDITIONAL CORE SYNERGIES AND PATHS TO REGIONAL NUCLEAR WAR FIGHTING

Should Israel's Oslo/Roadmap-based surrender of land mass lead to the creation of a Palestinian state,[19] a corollary loss of geostrategic capacity would be exacerbated by a less tangible, but no less important, power reduction. This is a loss attendant on the probable Arab and Iranian *perception* of an incessant and now unstoppable momentum against the Jewish State, a jihad-centered perception of military inevitability that might not represent a measurable loss of power but could nonetheless reinforce and magnify enemy advantages. Recognizing such perceptions, Israel could then decide to take its bomb out of the basement as a prudent deterrence-enhancing measure and/or it could accept a greater willingness to launch preemptive strikes against selected enemy hard targets.

Made aware of such Israeli reactions, reactions that would stem from both Israel's territorial vulnerabilities and its awareness of changed enemy perceptions spawned by the creation of Palestine, Arab states and/or Iran could respond in more or less parallel fashion, preparing more openly for nuclearization and first-strike attacks. Significantly, such generally unexpected results of a peace process would almost certainly increase Israel's overall dependence on nuclear weapons and nuclear strategy.

This dependence, among other things, could focus on the multiple and interpenetrating requirements of nuclear war fighting. This is because the peace process would incrementally enlarge Israel's need for nuclear weapons to fulfill particular deterrence and preemption options and these options might still not be fulfilled successfully. That is, deterrence and preemption strategies could fail even though they had originally been supported by nuclear weapons. Here, Israel's continued survival could then require the weapons and tactics needed for actual nuclear war exchanges, a "mixed blessing" requirement that by definition could represent a stark and possibly irrecoverable diminution of Israel's power.

Among the most probable paths to nuclear war fighting in the Middle East are the following: (1) enemy nuclear first strikes against Israel (not a present possibility, unless one were to include Pakistan as an enemy[20]), (2) enemy nonnuclear WMD first strikes against Israel that elicit Israeli nuclear reprisals, either promptly or as a consequence of escalation processes, (3) Israeli nuclear preemptions against hard targets in enemy states with nuclear assets (not a present possibility unless, again, we were to include Pakistan as an enemy state), (4) Israeli nonnuclear preemptions against hard targets in enemy states with nuclear assets that elicit enemy nuclear reprisals, either promptly or via incremental escalation processes (not a present possibility, excluding Pakistan), and (5) Israeli nonnuclear preemptions against hard targets in enemy states without nuclear assets that elicit substantial enemy biological warfare reprisals and, reciprocally, Israeli nuclear counterretaliations.

Some other plausible paths to nuclear war fighting in the region could include accidental/unintentional/inadvertent/unauthorized nuclear attacks between Israel and enemy states. Here, we must also consider the potentially threatening prospect of escalation arising from instances of WMD terrorism directed against Israel.

As long as it may be assumed that Israel is absolutely determined to survive, there do exist certain identifiable conditions wherein the Jewish State might become involved in actual nuclear war fighting. For example,

Israel has been facing prospective chaos on the Golan Heights for several years. To date, it has tried to manage this area of consequential instability by outsourcing its specific area security to such Syrian rebel factions as the Revolutionary Command Council in Quneitra and Golan, which has been led by a high-ranking Free Syrian Army commander. But this arrangement has already become problematic because rebels sometimes advance on Druze positions (these Druze are loyal to Assad), causing "friction" (recall Clausewitz) with the Druze actually living in the Golan.

A variety of enemy elements live across the Golan area, including Shiite militia Hezbollah and Palestinian Islamic Jihad, which too is supported by Iran. Both Hezbollah and Islamic Jihad are apt to prosper going forward vis-à-vis rivals as a result of terms codified at the Joint Comprehensive Plan of Action (JCPOA), Vienna, July 14, 2015.

There can be little doubt that Israel will still have to face this prospective chaos for decades, if not forever. Hezbollah, with its existing Lebanese border with Israel, plainly represents a continuing threat, one with even potentially existential capabilities—at least in tandem with certain simultaneous Iranian threats. Iran can already directly impact Israeli security on the Golan if the Syrian rebels are successfully pushed farther back and/or the Nusra Front is ultimately able to emerge as the strongest rebel faction. In all likelihood, there will be recurrent and more or less substantial flare-ups with Hezbollah; some of these eruptions may begin on the Golan.

All of these conspicuously unstable circumstances and threats could conceivably lead to instances of actual nuclear war fighting at some point or another.

To maintain a viable power position in the Middle East, an obligation that may also benefit from Samson, Israel must maintain some form of a preemption option[21] at all times. But as this critical option would be undermined by remnants of the Oslo/Roadmap peace process (Israel, after all, would be generally identified as the aggressor should it ever preempt while "peace" was in the process of being negotiated), that process effectively impairs such maintenance. It follows that Israel, still learning from Samson, should hold on insistently to its essential sources of power by firmly rejecting any asymmetrical kind of peace process and also simultaneously protecting the nuclear weapons that it requires for supporting any residual preemption option.

Why are nuclear weapons needed for such support? Three general and compelling answers come to mind.

As indicated earlier, Israel needs its nuclear weapons, *inter alia*, for possible preemption of enemy nuclear attacks.

Both Israeli nuclear and nonnuclear preemptions of enemy unconventional attacks could, at some time in the future, produce a nuclear exchange. This would depend, in part, on the effectiveness and breadth of Israeli targeting, the surviving number of enemy nuclear weapons, and the willingness of enemy leaders to risk Israeli nuclear counterretaliations. The likelihood of a nuclear exchange would appear to be greatest where pertinent enemy states (now primarily Iran) were allowed to deploy increasing numbers of weapons of mass destruction without interference from still-timely Israeli preemptions.

Should such a deployment ever take place, Israel could effectively forfeit the nonnuclear preemption option and thus be forced to choose between (1) an inherently catastrophic nuclear preemption and (2) relying on its nuclear deterrence posture together with its multilayered system of active defenses. Inevitably, the reasonableness of any such reliance would depend in part on the expected rationality or irrationality of the enemy leadership. In the event of a presumably irrational Iranian enemy—that is, one that no longer values Iranian national survival more highly than any other preference or combination of preferences—deterrence could become far more difficult but not necessarily impossible. This is because even an irrational nuclear Iran could display a consistent and transitive ordering of preferences.

Irrationality, once again, is not the same as madness. If the Iranian national leadership were presumably mad, an altogether different scenario, then the only real Israeli alternative to a preemption option would be to wait for the enemy to attack first.

The considerable risks of an Israeli nuclear preemption, nuclear exchanges with an enemy state, and enemy nuclear first strikes could all have been reduced by once-timely Israeli nonnuclear preemptions. These preemptions would have been directed at critical hard targets (counterforce attacks). This conclusion contradicts the conventional wisdom that might have associated any prospective Israeli preemptive strikes with aggression and/or expanded noncombatant harms—that is, with alleged violations of humanitarian international law. In principle at least, any earlier preemption could have been fully compatible with pertinent jurisprudential criteria for anticipatory self-defense.

Of course, the optimal and distinctly preferable solution to any Arab/Iranian/Israeli conflict must always seem to lie in comprehensive political settlements, but there is simply no reason to believe that such a solution could ever be deemed acceptable on the Islamic side. To recall Thomas Hobbes in *Leviathan*: "And Covenants without the Sword are but Words, and of no strength to secure a man at all."[22]

Today, a still-purposeful nonnuclear Israeli preemption against Iran is not entirely inconceivable, but it is highly unlikely. In this connection, at least in principle, Israel needs its nuclear weapons to support prospective conventional preemptions against enemy nuclear assets. With such weapons, Israel could maintain, explicitly or implicitly, a threat of nuclear counterretaliation. Without such weapons, Israel, having to rely entirely on nonnuclear forces, might not be able to effectively deter enemy retaliations for any Israeli preemptive strike.

In 2003, the *Project Daniel Group* had recommended that Israel not begin to take its bomb out of the basement until Iran first became fully nuclear. Nonetheless, if Israel should still leave open a viable preemption option against Iran, there could then be good reason for Jerusalem to modify or end its policy of deliberate nuclear ambiguity sooner rather than later. This could mean terminating ambiguity *before* actually witnessing Iran's entry into the nuclear club. Any Israeli preemption against a prenuclear Iran would certainly be nonnuclear and would certainly have to be accompanied by appropriate threats of counterreprisal.

More precisely, following any such preemption, Israel, in order to prevent an overwhelmingly destructive Iranian retaliation, would then have to make clear to Iran the following clarification of risk: Be on notice! Any "significant" conventional or chemical or biological missile reprisals launched against Israel will *certainly* be met with an unacceptably destructive Israeli counterretaliation. Moreover, be warned that such a counterretaliation may be nuclear.

But before such a postpreemption counterretaliatory threat could ever be sufficiently persuasive, Iran's leaders would first have to believe, among other things, that Israel's threatened nuclear weapons were in fact operationally usable. It is this critical belief that could be rendered more likely by a very partial and selective Israeli nuclear disclosure.[23] Ironically, one key objective of such disclosure would be to convince Iran's leaders that Israel's nuclear weapons were not "too large" or "too destructive."

ALL THINGS STRATEGIC MOVE IN THE MIDST OF DEATH

Israel can learn from Samson that all world politics and global strategy move in the midst of death. To truly understand calculations of war, deterrence, preemption, and defense, therefore, Israel's leaders will need to better understand (1) enemy orientations to death, both individual and collective, and (2) Israeli orientations to death, both individual and collective. Faced with enemies for whom personal death could sometimes be not only acceptable but entirely welcome, Israel could discover only too late that its deterrent had been immobilized or neutralized and that national survival was now dependent on some more or less feasible configuration of preemption and active defense strategies.

With regard to the latter, it has already been indicated that no system of ballistic missile defense can ever be "leakproof" and that failing to intercept even a single incoming missile armed with biological or nuclear warheads could sometime be irreversibly catastrophic.

Samson, we recall, ultimately faced death with resignation and a presumed equanimity, but it was likely never his *preferred* option. Like Samson, Israel could potentially reach a point when it would become actually willing to "die with the Philistines," but such a futile point, quite naturally, should be scrupulously avoided. Indeed, although the Jewish State must now do everything within its power to prepare for a Samson Option as part of broader strategic preparations, it must also try to avoid ever having to actually implement any such option. There is no contradiction here, because proper preparation could substantially enhance the Jewish State's core security posture.

For Israel, unlike certain of its Jihadi foes, there can never be any intrinsic satisfactions in death, whether individual or collective.

Some of Israel's enemies, we should note, may operate with very different preference orderings concerning life and death. If, for example, an apocalyptic Iranian jihad were contemplated against Israel, such a Shia holy war could reflect fundamentally different orientations to personal and collective sacrifice. It is not even out of the question that a strongly fundamentalist leadership in Tehran, ordering such a jihad, could sometime regard certain Israeli nuclear reprisals as tolerable or even desirable. Recognizing this particular and peculiar prospect, Israel, possibly with the help of Samson, could better learn the effective limits of its indispensable nuclear deterrent before it is too late.

To a significant extent, the existential problems facing the State of Israel stem from human inclinations in enemy states to rebel against an unbearable truth. Desperate to live perpetually, various portions of humankind embrace a cornucopia of faiths that promise life everlasting but only in exchange for an undying loyalty. In the end, such loyalty could yet again be transferred from faith to state, which would then battle with other states in what political scientists and strategists would doubtlessly and mistakenly describe as a "struggle for power." This, of course, would be a thoroughly superficial and sorely inadequate description.

Heinrich von Treitschke, in his published lectures in *Politics*, cites approvingly to Fichte: "Individual man sees in his country the realization of his earthly immortality." Any such "seeing" among Israel's current Jihadist enemies could represent a source of particular or even existential danger. This danger, moreover, could be exacerbated by a lack of symmetry with the "individual man" in Israel. After all, this person generally witnesses such realization much less frequently as an Israeli than does a Jihadist.

ENCOURAGING INTIMATIONS OF STRATEGIC DISASTER

Israel can learn from Samson that there are strategic advantages to concrete imaginings of catastrophe. For now, the Jewish State, it seems, can contemplate the end of the Jewish Commonwealth every day and yet still persevere quite calmly in conducting its most routine and mundane affairs. This iconic stance would not be evident if Israel could somehow begin to contemplate the actual *moment* of its disappearance. Israel, therefore, should begin immediately to replace any reassuringly abstract conceptualizations of end times with unbearably precise images of horror. At first, this would appear to represent very strange strategic counsel, but on further reflection, its net effect could assuredly prove gainful.

Sapere aude! (Dare to know!) This motto for the Enlightenment once offered by the philosopher Immanuel Kant can acquire special meaning in Israel's ongoing struggle to simply endure. Just as repression of the fear of death by individuals can sometimes occasion activities that impair the forces of self-preservation, so can Israel imperil its opportunities for collective survival by denying the very *real* possibility of national destruction.

In purely geostrategic terms (certain orthodox Jewish and Christian positions would offer a very different and religiously based view), there are no convincing assurances that Israel is forever. On the contrary, the State of Israel has likely never been as vulnerable to disappearance as it is at the present moment. Soon faced with an altogether unique combination of enemy capabilities and intentions, Jerusalem could face an even far more *immediate* genocidal danger than that confronted many years earlier by millions of individual and effectively stateless European Jews.

Let Israel take prompt heed, however painful or disorienting. The Nazis were never capable of destroying several hundred thousand lives in a fraction of a second, wreaking mega-death, without first having to acquire actual bodily custody of their prospective victim populations. With the plausible spread of nuclear weapons options in the Middle East, however, Israel's current and future foes could in fact acquire such a final capability.

In what surely must be the most unendurable irony of all, Israel, as a solution to what Herzl called "the Jewish question," has effectively made millions of Jews *more vulnerable* to genocidal assault. Incontestably, by being concentrated into a tiny area, these Jews, as well as many non-Jews also living within the green lines, are increasingly subject to an Islamic faith-based mass murder. Once targeted by enemy ballistic missiles with unconventional warheads, these Jews could then become subject to more or less prompt annihilation and in a manner that would be unprecedented and distressingly sui generis.

This is certainly not to suggest, in any way, that the Zionist solution to the "Jewish problem" was a mistake. Quite the contrary. The establishment of the State of Israel was unambiguously correct and historically imperative.

Today, decent people everywhere, not just Jews, should do whatever is needed to ensure Israel's continued durability. This obligation is hardly contestable or subject to any reasonable diplomatic debate. It is, moreover, deducible from certain utterly peremptory legal principles concerning "offices of humanity," obligatory acts of assistance that each nation always owes to all other nations.

In the expressed and oft-cited judgment of Emmerich de Vattel's *The Law of Nations, or the Principles of Natural Law* (1758): "The first general law, which is to be found in the very end of the society of Nations, is that each Nation should contribute as far as it can to the happiness and advancement of other Nations. . . . Such is the foundation of those common duties, those offices of humanity, which Nations mutually owe one another."[24]

From Israel's own strategic standpoint, the persistently imperiled nation must begin to *feel itself aware* of the dimensions of the existential threat and the consequent steps needed to ensure its physical survival. There are steps that can be taken, steps that could best vindicate Israel's raison d'être, but these steps must not be taken lightly. This brings us back to the original point "made" by Samson, the utterly core obligation to go beyond analytically abstract and anesthetized conceptions of national disaster toward fully fashioned, concrete, flesh-and-blood images.

For Israel, more than for any other state on Earth, the time for allegedly learned intellectual games is over.[25] Learning from Samson, residents of the Jewish State must now *feel*, not merely *know*, that agony is more productive than syllogism, that despair can be just as revealing as the most subtle elucidations of strategic thought, and that tears may have deeper explanatory benefits than ready diplomatic smiles.

STEPPING INTO DEATH TO PROLONG LIFE

Conceptually, Israel must learn to "step into death" to prevent its own actual death. To be sure, such an ironic movement would not mean to draw a last collective breath but instead to discover in the immanent abyss of contemplated national disappearance the optimal course of direction toward protected life. Drawing from the revelation of death's immanence in the mortality of every nation, the people of Israel could then nurture the deeply felt agony that must somehow become prerequisite to long-term national survival.

"Normal" states can never experience such a "felt agony." These states take national survival as something altogether given, as something existing independently of "death." Objectifying death as a reality transcending national life, these states can easily forget that all life is inevitably death's prisoner. Although any such forgetting has obvious short-term benefits, it can also interfere with prudential forms of long-term collective life support.

Israel cannot afford to be a normal state. It must instead feel that national survival is problematic, that collective extinction represents the end point of the same continuum that contains collective vitality, and that survival as a state cannot be detached from informed premonitions of disappearance. As a practical matter, Israel's essential presentiments of death are apt to appear only when life in the Jewish State is shaken to its very foundations. This means, in another ironic turn of reasoning, that Israel's required nurturance of unbearably precise images of national life may be contingent on coming even closer to assorted forms of national destruction.

Always, however, there is tangible danger that Israel will wait too long, that it will come so close to the edge of the cliff that it will no longer be capable of pulling itself back to safety.

To best understand and predict far-reaching global responses to Israeli military actions, Israel's leaders must never lose sight that their country is always the individual Jew in macrocosm—that is, the single Jew *writ large*. For the world, macrocosm and microcosm are always one and the same. Therefore, for Israeli planners to expect charitable global responses to indispensable Israeli military operations—that is, to expect such responses to somehow be detached from literally millennia of prejudicial hatreds—is foolhardy and potentially even irrational.

Israel must understand that it can never be just another state in world politics. Rather it must remain unique, sui generis, not in any sense that it should somehow warrant greater justice than other states—a post-Holocaust conclusion that could actually make sense in a world dominated by authentic Reason—but in the counterintuitive and retrograde meaning still offered by others that it deserves only less, always less. To wit, an exploded bus full of Israeli women and children will never elicit aptly far-reaching compassion abroad or even civilized concern from the so-called international community. On the other hand, a building of Syrian or Lebanese or Gaza civilians, blown up mistakenly by the IDF in concern with operations of essential self-defense or blown up unwittingly after Jihadist insurgents had deliberately moved Arab civilians into known hard-target areas (aka "human shields") will predictably occasion nearly worldwide grief.

What sort of one-sided justice is this?

For some reason, however monstrous or grotesque, a mountain of Jewish corpses is usually judged to be smaller and more easily excused than virtually any other group's similarly tragic assemblage of dead persons. An example would be the September 2015 image of the dead Syrian child who had drowned, as a cruelly victimized migrant, in the waters off of Italy. Although every sane or decent person would plainly regard such an image as deeply painful and abundantly sad, it is also sobering to note that, over a period of many years, no images of burned and murdered Israeli children in buses torched by Hamas had ever elicited any remotely comparable global sympathies.

Throughout the various Palestinian intifadas, when Hamas, Fatah, and Islamic Jihad took observably great pleasure in the incineration of unprotected Israeli civilians (sometimes in the attacked Jerusalem or Tel Aviv buses, including Arabs who had also happened to be on the targeted bus), comparable "civilizational" outrage was entirely absent.[26]

Israeli decision makers must take heed. Although not seemingly a straightforwardly strategic issue, there are vital intersections between worldwide attitudes toward the Jewish State and Israel's operational military posture. Israel must finally understand, therefore, that Israel and justice can never be uttered in the same breath, for the very same reason that Jews and justice can never be uttered in the same breath. Israel, always the Jew in macrocosm, will likely continue to be despised in the Arab/Islamic world, no matter how great its reluctance to use military force, and no matter how great and disproportionate may be its scientific, intellectual, technological, and medical contributions to the much wider society of nations.

Like it or not, those who fashion Israel's nuclear strategy must always plan accordingly.

THE PERILS OF TOO MUCH HOPE

Israel can learn from Samson that there are serious dangers in hoping, in always hoping too much. Mistakes can bring death, both individual and collective. Writing of the Jews as a "people of solitaries," E. M. Cioran, possibly one of the most dazzling French philosophical voices since Paul Valery, observed of the Jewish "nation" (not just the State of Israel) that this people, "unsuited to the complacencies of despair, bypassing its age-old fatigue and the conclusions imposed by fate, lives in the delirium of expectation, determined not to learn a lesson from its humiliations."

Such an injurious determination must somehow come to an end. To learn from its "humiliations," and therefore from Samson, Israel must acknowledge, quickly and forthrightly, that its most dangerous enemies are religiously and doctrinally committed to destruction of the Jewish Commonwealth. Although in Muslim parlance, all war dictated by the *sharia* is necessarily "holy," the Arabic word *jihad,* which has the literal meaning of "effort," "striving," or "struggle," should never be taken lightly.

A basic commandment of Islam, jihad is an obligation imposed on all Muslims by God and is—vis-à-vis Israel—unambiguously military in intent. Derived from the universality of Muslim revelation, jihad calls on all those who have accepted God's message and God's word to strive (*jahada*) relentlessly to convert or, at a minimum, to subjugate those who have not been converted. Significantly, for the State of Israel, this obligation is not bounded by any limits of time or space. It must continue until the whole world has accepted Islam or has at least submitted to the power of Islamic rules.

What is the prevailing Islamic worldview in the interim? According to Bernard Lewis:

> Until that happens, the world is divided into two: the House of Islam (*dar al-Islam*), where Muslims rule and the law of Islam prevails; and the House of War (*dar al-Harb*), comprising the rest of the world. Between the two there is a morally necessary, legally and religiously obligatory state of war, until the final and inevitable triumph of Islam over unbelief. According to the law books, this state of war could be interrupted, when expedient, by an armistice or truce of limited duration. It could not be terminated by a peace, but only by a final victory.[27]

Throughout the Islamic world, Israel's regular and sustained pleas for peace agreements are exploited eagerly by Israel's recalcitrant enemies. While Jerusalem may still entertain stubbornly residual hopes that these incrementally negotiated agreements could somehow point toward authentic and long-term solutions, the Arab frontline states and their substate proxies, and Iran, together with its own surrogates, regard them as a merely temporary expedient, as a welcome gift of those cursed and profane "unbelievers" who will now unwittingly help bring about their own divinely ordained destruction.[28]

It is arguable, of course, that current Islamic states and terrorist[29] movements are not genuinely animated by religious doctrine and that the obligations of jihad are thus extraneous to any serious strategic calculation. Although it is certainly correct that these states and movements are concurrently motivated as well by thoroughly pragmatic considerations, any such argumentation would be lacking in necessary nuance.

For Islamists, the unsubjugated unbeliever, in our present concerns, the Jew is *by definition* the enemy. A part of the *Dar al-Harb*, "the House of War," he is differentiated sharply from the *dhimmi*, the unbeliever who submits to Muslim rule. As for a Jewish State, one that actually rules over Muslims and "occupies" Muslim lands, it can be nothing less than the very incarnation of unbelief, an intolerable source of contamination, and a falsely codified inversion of God's will.

When Haj Amin al Husseini, the Grand Mufti of Jerusalem, spoke together with Hitler on Berlin radio in 1942, he cried out: "Kill the Jews—kill them with your hands, kill them with your teeth—this is well pleasing to Allah." Today, the Covenant of the Islamic Resistance Movement (Hamas) still calls for the "realization of Allah's promise, no matter how long that should take. The Prophet, Allah bless him and grant him salvation, has said: 'The Day of Judgment will not come until Moslems fight the Jews, killing them.'"

Here, significantly, Israel is despised not because of its land or "settlers" but solely because it is a Jewish State. Unless this deepest core of Islamist hatred is finally understood and overcome, Israel could continue to hope too much, to waste critical time in plainly vain endeavors. Samson, once again, can help Israel to better understand what is required.

AVOIDING SELF-DELUSION

Israel can learn from Samson the dangers of self-delusion. Samson was blind *before* his eyes were put out by the Philistines. Enchanted by Delilah, he refused to see what was happening before his eyes. He believed only what he wanted to believe.

For Israel, such "blindness" is not confined to the Book of Judges. It was also evident on October 5, 1973, with the start of the Yom Kippur War. Until then, the country had been committed to an idea known generally as "the concept," the *kontzeptziya,* the contrived idea that the Arabs were unwilling and incapable of renewing hostilities against the Jewish State.

IDF Military Intelligence's overall assessment of enemy designs, lasting until October 5, 1973, was that war was "highly improbable" or "improbable." It was this fundamentally incorrect assumption that created a monumental intelligence blunder. This blunder, and its corollary failure to preempt,[30] could be repeated at far greater cost in the future, primarily because of both expected and unexpected aggression consequences of a plainly moribund peace process.[31]

The dangers of self-delusion revealed by Samson can also be understood at another more fundamental level. The seventeenth-century-created Westphalian[32] state system, within which Israel and every other state must always "reside," is now in a process of continual transformation. If, however, Israel should somehow delude itself about the precise nature and momentum of this transformation, it could then pay dearly for its mistake.

The obligation to use armed force for self-defense and survival amid Westphalian anarchy[33] forms the central argument of political realism, or *Realpolitik,* from the *Melian Dialogue* of Thucydides, and later Cicero, to Machiavelli, Locke, Spykman, and Kissinger. "For what can be done against force, without force?" inquires Cicero prophetically in one of his *Letters.*[34] Later, in the 20th century, Nicholas Spykman replies: "In a world of international anarchy, foreign policy must aim above all at the improvement or at least the preservation, of the relative power position of the state."

Such arguments are not incorrect, but at one level at least, they have become trivial. This is because the anarchy that we confront today in world politics is vastly different from its predecessors. It is generally more far reaching, extending not only between individual states but also within them. Sometimes it is almost primordial, the sort of barbarous disorder suggested by William Golding's *Lord of the Flies.* Thus it is effectively and quite ominously sui generis.

Today, in the world generally and the Middle East particularly, the state also speaks more and more with various unhidden forms of *religious* authority. In many instances, the state itself is becoming more and more *sacred.* With states sometimes regarded as the proper abode of God on Earth, the profane often becomes not only permissible but even "official" doctrine. Regarding ISIS, now a common enemy of the United States, Israel, Iran, Syria, and Russia—not to mention all of the major Sunni Arab states, especially Egypt and Saudi Arabia—this Jihadist group seeks to become much more than another sovereign state or even the command center for a configuration of existing states. It seeks instead to become the nucleus of a genuinely universal *caliphate.* For Israel, dealing effectively with such an unprecedented enemy ambition could well involve drawing on Samson, preferably for initiating appropriate deterrence and/or preemption options.

A final word here about the *Jewish* State, its uniqueness, and its vital place in Jewish thought, especially in reference to traditional views on the coming of the Messiah. The question has often arisen on whether a Jewish State can be consistent with the expectations of messianic redemption. If redemption should depend on "the experience of exile" or "homelessness," the State of Israel, a state that some Jews argue would *block* the coming of the Messiah, could be productive to Jews only where it would actually cease to exist.

Now that Israel is a fait accompli, however, it is impossible to imagine a respectable Jewish position that would willingly go this far to meet any such particularistic messianic preconditions. Yet a debate did once rage on the underlying issues before 1948, when Martin Buber and Hermann Cohen argued fiercely about Zionism and messianism. Buber had advanced the view of exile as a tragic situation, while Cohen denied that the Diaspora was truly exilic. In seeking an end to diaspora, Cohen maintained, Zionists were negating the essential vision of messianism. Buber had countered that Zionism furthers the realization of messianism:

> Zionism opposes not the messianic idea, but rather the misrepresentation and distortion of this idea found in a considerable part of Liberal-Jewish, anti-Zionist literature. This misrepresentation and distortion glorifies, in the name of messianism, the dispersion, debasement and homelessness of the Jewish people, as something unconditionally valuable and fortunate, as something that must be preserved because it prepares humanity for the messianic age.

How different was Hermann Cohen's assessment, which proclaimed: "The ghetto mentality is not the ghost, but the true spirit of Judaism and Jewish reality." Recalling Micha ("And the remnant of Jacob shall be in the midst of many peoples, like dew from the Lord" [5:6, 7]), Cohen expressed his "proud conviction" that Jews must "continue to live as 'divine dew' in the midst of the peoples, and to remain fruitful among them and for them. All of the prophets place us in the midst of the peoples, and their common perspective is the world mission of the remnant of Israel."

But the role of "divine dew" must certainly be reevaluated after the Holocaust. Could Hermann Cohen affirm today that Judaism, because of its messianic core, "is thoroughly a world religion"? Could he claim purposefully more than seventy years after the greatest tragedy of Diaspora Jewry that this messianic core "cannot be impaired by historical reality, by misfortune, or even by the auspicious granting of equal rights"?

Are "hope and trust" truly the correct path to Jewish survival? "Happy is he that waiteth," (Dan. 12:12), cautioned Cohen, but how much longer shall be the wait? And who shall bear responsibility for any immeasurable strategic harms suffered in the interim?

Israel's only real option for the future as the Jewish State in the current system of states is to *endure*. Whatever the relative merits of the Zionism-messianism debate earlier on in history, Jewish redemption today positively requires survival of the Jewish State. So we may now return to Samson and to the important strategic lessons to be learned for such survival.

SAMSON SUMMARIZED

In John Milton's *Samson Agonistes*, the Chorus intones of Samson: "The glory late of Israel, now the grief." When this power of Israel had been overcome by the Philistines, when that great strength had been subjugated and humiliated, hopes for victory were supplanted by resignation and defeat. Although "divinely call'd" to "begin Israel's Deliverance," Samson's work was prevented by Delilah, that "specious Monster." Yet of his calamity, "She was not the prime cause, but I my self."

I myself. In this acceptance of direct personal responsibility lies an overriding lesson of Samson for modern Israel. Taken alone, enemy deception, which can always be taken as given, will not overcome the Jewish State.

This misfortune can happen only where Israel would willingly yield to deception, surrendering its essential sources of strength and power on behalf of persistent lies and illusions. Wherever it would strive to see clearly, Israel will not be blinded. Instead, aware that states, like individuals, are decidedly mortal, and that *unreason* can govern even the "political" world, Jerusalem can draw *wisdom* from both Israel's historical losses and Samson's exploited vulnerabilities.

If need be, Israel, following Samson, can even choose to "die with the Philistines," but it is rather the *preparations* for such a dying (preparations, as we have seen, that could helpfully *preclude* this option) with which Jerusalem should now solely be concerned.

"Eyeless in Gaza," Samson labored at the mill with slaves, lamenting that "to me, strength is my bane, and proves the source of all my miseries." But here Samson was truly mistaken. It was certainly not his too-great strength that brought about an unhappy fate but rather his needless and willful abandonment of this strength.

Had he held on to prowess and resisted the wiles and enchantments of enemy seductions, Samson would not have been reduced "[t]o live a life half dead, a living death" until choosing to "die with the Philistines." He would have prevailed.

For David Ben-Gurion, the country's first prime minister, nuclear weapons were something to be held genuinely sacred by Israel. By extrapolation, although we may have no direct evidence of this, Ben-Gurion would certainly have regarded the specific language of Israeli nuclear strategy as a sacred and divine vocabulary, or a *lingua sacra* in the more classical Latin syntax. In those places where this special language also involved one or another of Judaism's core historical or prophetic episodes, the sacredness of nuclear strategy could be magnified even further.

It follows that Samson Option lessons for Israeli nuclear strategy derive from the most conspicuously important Jewish images, and may thus warrant very special and more detailed attention in Jerusalem. At the same time, it will be important for Israeli military planners not to draw the wrong or narrowly martyrdom-centered lessons from Samson and instead work out those suitably dialectical refinements from which Israel's latent potential for inflicting maximum retaliatory destruction could be most usefully extracted. To some extent, of course, this dialectical responsibility must also involve calculated expectations of US support and assistance. Here, Jerusalem should proceed with greater caution than usual and adopt a well-founded skepticism. In the final analysis, preventing another Jewish genocide can be only a Jewish (and more specifically, Israeli) responsibility. As a suitable warning and example of prior US failures in such broadly humanitarian matters, Jerusalem would do well to recall the Reagan and first Bush administrations' indifference to extermination of the Kurds. Iraqi documents that were seized during the Kurdish uprising in March and April 1991 detail mass slayings of civilians, including authoritative videotapes of executions, beatings, and torture. American authorities, for several years at least, had openly encouraged the Kurdish revolt, only then to betray this trusting people to expressly genocidal destruction.

During the late 1980s, the US stood by silently as Saddam Hussein's regime very systematically demolished entire Kurdish villages and towns and then forcibly transferred a half million or more Kurds into specially created concentration camps. In March 1991, after urging the Kurds to rise up against the Baghdad regime, the first Bush administration did nothing to prevent inflicting new genocidal blows against the Kurds by the Iraqi army. Much more recently, US President Barack Obama announced his intent to "annihilate ISIS/ISIL," but he never matched any purposeful policies to this now plainly shallow declaration. Nor did President Obama ever follow through on his openly declared intent to rescue the then-imperiled and now-destroyed Syrian nation from President Bashar al-Assad's genocidal war.

NOTES

1. See Yehoshafat Harkabi, *The Bar Kokhba Syndrome: Risk and Realism in International Politics* (Chappaqua, New York: Rossel Books, 1983), p. 132.

2. Jurisprudentially, of course, there is always a proper place for retribution. At the Nuremberg Trials, the precise words used by the Court, "So far from it being unjust to punish him, it would be unjust if his wrong were allowed to go unpunished," represented an authoritative reaffirmation of the peremptory principle of law known as *nullum crimen sine poena* (no crime without a punishment). The earliest statement of *nullum crimen sine poena* can be found in the Code of Hammurabi (c. 1728–1686 BCE), the Law of Eshnunna (c. 2000 BCE), the even-earlier Code of Ur-Nammu (c. 2100 BCE), and—most significantly for Israel—the *lex talionis*, or law of exact retaliation, which is presented in three separate passages of the Torah. For the ancient Hebrews, moreover, when a crime involved the shedding of blood, not only punishment but also a punishment that involved a reciprocal bloodletting was demanded. For the early Hebrew nation, shedding of blood was an abomination that must be expiated in kind: "For blood pollutes the land, and no expiation can be made for the land, for the blood that is shed in it, except by the blood of him who shed it" (Numbers 35:33).

3. See Thomas Hobbes, *Leviathan*, Chapter XIII, "Of the Naturall Condition of Mankind, as concerning their Felicity, and Misery."

4. The same point can be made about pacts between Israel and assorted substate or insurgent organizations. Jurisprudentially, international law does recognize that in certain circumstances these organizations may sometimes enter into valid agreements with states, but it need not automatically follow that they would be any more likely than enemy states to actually comply. On the purely legal aspects of such pacts, see H. Lauterpacht, *International Law: Collected Papers*, Vol. 1, 1975, pp. 494–495; and I. Brownlie, *Principles of Public International Law*, 4th ed., 1990, Part II, pp. 65–66.

5. Chapter XIII, id.

6. For more specialized treatment of the concept, *War of Attrition*, see Dermot Bradley, "War of Attrition," in 6 *International Military and Defense Encyclopedia*, 2902–2906, Trevor N. Dupuy, ed., 1993. On the longstanding Arab reference to Israel's "liquidation," see Yehoshafat Harkabi, *Arab Attitudes to Israel*, Jerusalem, Keter Publishers, 1972, especially Chapters 1 and 2.

7. Id., "War of Attrition," at 2902.

8. See *Israel's Strategic Future*, p. 12.

9. The *Project Daniel Group* noted three distinct but also interrelated existential threats to Israel: (1) biological/nuclear threats from states, (2) biological/nuclear threats from terror groups, and (3) biological/nuclear threats from combined efforts of state and terror group adversaries.

10. Regarding antecedent legal obligations of substate or insurgent surrogates, Israel should remain wary about signing pacts resembling the Oslo Agreements, among other things, because such agreements can impose unequal obligations. In this connection, several US federal court decisions affirm that legal agreements between substate and state parties may even impose asymmetrical compliance expectations. More pre-

cisely, in the prominent case of *Tel-Oren v. Libyan Arab Republic*, a 1981 civil suit in US federal court wherein the plaintiffs were Israeli survivors and representatives of persons murdered in a terrorist bus attack in Israel in 1978, Circuit Judge Harry T. Edwards opined: "I do not believe the law of nations imposes the same responsibility or liability on non-state actors, such as the PLO, as it does on states and persons acting under color of state law."

11. See *Israel's Strategic Future*, p. 13.

12. For authoritative assessments of both Hamas and Hezbollah short-range rockets and missiles that threaten Israel—and that come largely from Iran—see Anthony H. Cordesman, *Iran's Rocket Missile Forces and Strategic Options* (New York: Rowman and Littlefield, December 2014), especially the author's "Executive Summary."

13. The extent of damage from any such Hezbollah attacks could depend in part on whether David's Sling, designed to intercept missiles with a longer range than Iron Dome, had already become operational.

14. Hezbollah's Hassan Nasrallah has implied, since 2011, that Hezbollah plans to "conquer the Galilee." See, Ron Ben-Yishai, "What the Third Lebanon War Will Look Like," YNetNews.com, *Magazine*, September 13, 2015.

15. It needs to be underscored in this connection that the search for any such maximization represents, prima facie, an egregious violation of humanitarian international law or the law of war. The explicit and unambiguous application of the law of war to insurgents dates to the four Geneva Conventions of 1949. Moreover, as more than codified treaties and conventions must comprise the law of war, it is plain that the obligations of *jus in bello* (justice in war) are part of "the general principles of law recognized by civilized nations" (from Art. 38 of the Statute of the International Court of Justice) and thereby bind *all categories* of belligerents. Further, Hague Convention IV of 1907 declares that even in the absence of a precisely published set of guidelines regarding "unforeseen cases," the operative preconventional sources of humanitarian international law obtain and must still govern all belligerency.

16. Id.

17. See Louis René Beres, "After Osama Bin Laden: Assassination, Terrorism, War, and International Law," *Case Western Reserve Journal of International Law*, Vol. 44, Nos. 1 & 2, 2011, pp. 93–147.

18. Interestingly, Thomas Jefferson, third president of the United States, wrote about this obligation as being generic for all nations. Writing in his *Opinion on the French Treaties* (April 28, 1793), Jefferson opined: "The nation itself, bound necessarily to whatever its preservation and safety require, cannot enter into engagements contrary to its indispensable obligations." See Merrill D. Peterson, *The Political Writings of Thomas Jefferson*, Monticello Monograph Series, Thomas Jefferson Memorial Foundation, 1993, p. 115.

19. For much earlier and original writings by this author on the prospective impact of a Palestinian state on Israeli nuclear deterrence and Israeli nuclear strategy, see Louis René Beres, "Security Threats and Effective Remedies: Israel's Strategic, Tactical and Legal Options," Ariel Center for Policy Research (Israel), ACPR Policy Paper No. 102, April 2000, 110 pp; Louis René Beres, "After the 'Peace Process': Israel, Palestine, and Regional Nuclear War," *Dickinson Journal of International Law*, Vol. 15, No. 2, Winter 1997, pp. 301–335; Louis René Beres, "Limits of Nuclear Deterrence: The Strategic Risks and Dangers to Israel of False Hope," *Armed Forces and Society*, Vol. 23, No. 4, Summer 1997, pp. 539–568; Louis René Beres, "Getting Beyond Nuclear Deterrence: Israel, Intelligence and False Hope," *International Journal of Intelligence and Counterintelligence*, Vol. 10, No. 1, Spring 1997, pp. 75–90; Louis René Beres, "On Living in a Bad Neighborhood: The Informed Argument for Israeli Nuclear Weapons," *Political Crossroads*, Vol. 5, Nos. 1/2, 1997, pp. 143–157; Louis René Beres, "Facing the Apocalypse: Israel and the 'Peace Process,'" *B'tzedek: The Journal of Responsible Jewish Commentary* (Israel), Vol. 1, No. 3, Fall/Winter 1997, pp. 32–35; Louis René Beres and (Ambassador) Zalman Shoval, "Why Golan Demilitarization Would Not Work," *Strategic Review*, Vol. XXIV, No. 1, Winter 1996, pp. 75–76; Louis René Beres, "Implications of a Pales-

tinian State for Israeli Security and Nuclear War: A Jurisprudential Assessment," *Dickinson Journal of International Law*, Vol. 17, No. 2, 1999, pp. 229–286; Louis René Beres, "A Palestinian State and Israel's Nuclear Strategy," *Crossroads: An International Socio-Political Journal*, No. 31, 1991, pp. 97–104; Louis René Beres, "The Question of Palestine and Israel's Nuclear Strategy," *The Political Quarterly*, Vol. 62, No. 4, October–December 1991, pp. 451–460; Louis René Beres, "Israel, Palestine and Regional Nuclear War," *Bulletin of Peace Proposals*, Vol. 22, No. 2, June 1991, pp. 227–234; Louis René Beres, "A Palestinian State: Implications for Israel's Security and the Possibility of Nuclear War," *Bulletin of the Jerusalem Institute for Western Defence* (Israel), Vol. 4, Bulletin No. 3, October 1991, pp. 3–10; Louis René Beres, *Israeli Security and Nuclear Weapons*, PSIS Occasional Papers, No. 1/1990, Graduate Institute of International Studies, Geneva, Switzerland, 40 pp; and Louis René Beres, "After the Gulf War: Israel, Palestine and the Risk of Nuclear War in the Middle East," *Strategic Review*, Vol. XIX, No. 4, Fall 1991, pp. 48–55.

20. Significantly, toward the end of 2015, Pakistan's nuclearization had been accelerating and was causing new worries in Washington as well as in Delhi. Going forward, should Saudi Arabia respond to the evident failure of international diplomacy to stop the Iranian bomb, Riyadh could then turn to Islamabad for specifically nuclear assistance. In this connection, the substantial diplomatic failure signified by the 2015 Vienna Iran Nuclear Agreement could spark a new wave of region-wide nuclear proliferation, including especially Saudi Arabia and plausibly Egypt.

21. It should now be understood from our earlier chapters that such a preemption option could be entirely permissible under international law. Known jurisprudentially as *anticipatory self-defense*, this permissible option can be found not in conventional law (art. 51 of the UN Charter supports only postattack expressions of individual or collective self-defense) but rather in customary international law. The precise origins of *anticipatory self-defense* in customary law lie in *The Caroline*, a case that concerned the unsuccessful rebellion of 1837 in Upper Canada against British rule. Following this case, the serious threat of armed attack has generally justified certain militarily defensive actions. In an exchange of diplomatic notes between the governments of the United States and Great Britain, then US Secretary of State Daniel Webster outlined a framework for self-defense that did not require an antecedent attack. Here, the jurisprudential framework permitted a military response to a *threat* so long as the danger posed was "instant, overwhelming, leaving no choice of means, and no moment for deliberation." See Beth M. Polebaum, "National Self-Defense in International Law: An Emerging Standard for a Nuclear Age," 59 *NYU Law Review* 187, 190–191 (1984) (noting that the *Caroline* case had transformed the right of self-defense from an excuse for armed intervention into a legal doctrine). Still earlier, see Hugo Grotius, *Of the Causes of War, and First of Self-Defense, and Defense of Our Property*, reprinted in 2 *Classics of International Law*, 168–175 (Carnegie Endowment Trust, 1925 [1625]); and Emmerich de Vattel, *The Right of Self-Protection and the Effects of the Sovereignty and Independence of Nations*, reprinted in 3 *Classics of International Law*, 130 (Carnegie Endowment Trust, 1916 [1758]). Also, Samuel Pufendorf, *The Two Books on the Duty of Man and Citizen According to Natural Law*, 32 (Frank Gardner Moore, tr., 1927 [1682].

22. Chapter XVII, "Of the Causes, Generation, and Definition of a Commonwealth."

23. The actual security benefits to Israel of any explicit reductions in nuclear ambiguity would remain dependent more or less on Clausewitzian "friction." This refers to the inherently unpredictable effects of errors in knowledge and information concerning intra-Israel (IDF/MOD) strategic uncertainties, Israeli and Iranian underestimations or overestimations of relative power position, and the unalterably vast and largely irremediable differences between theories of deterrence and enemy intent "as it actually is." See Carl von Clausewitz, "Uber das Leben und den Charakter von Scharnhorst," *Historisch-politische Zeitschrift*, 1 (1832), cited in Barry D. Watts, *Clausewitzian Friction and Future War*, McNair Paper No. 52, October 1996, Institute for National Strategic Studies, National Defense University, Washington, DC, p. 9.

24. See Vattel's Introduction and also Book II, Section 2.

25. The *reductio ad absurdum* of these games can be found in the current writings of those Israeli strategists who argue that Israel should surrender its nuclear option and prepare for regional coexistence in a nuclear weapon free zone. See, for example, Zeev Maoz, "The Mixed Blessing of Israel's Nuclear Policy," *International Security*, Vol. 28, No. 2 (Fall 2003), pp. 44–77. For my response to Maoz in the same journal, see Louis René Beres and Zeev Maoz, "Israel and the Bomb: A Dialogue," *International Security* (Harvard), Vol. 29, No. 1, Summer 2004, pp. 1–4.

26. Historically, perhaps especially for Jews, a history of hatred and victimization has not elicited parallel degrees of sympathy or concern. In this connection, Eugene Ionesco relates the following poignant passage from Andre Gide's *Journal*, dated January 29, 1932: "The idea that so much suffering can be in vain is intolerable to me; it kept me awake all night." As a "good Westerner," continues Ionesco, "Andre Gide couldn't help but think that suffering was the price of happiness, that suffering has to be rewarded." Israeli military planners should never forget that the world generally fails to pity those who suffer, all the more so those who suffer greatly. Indeed, Jews should already have observed post-Holocaust that the most unimaginable suffering can sometimes create *scorn*.

27. See Bernard Lewis, *The Political Language of Islam* (Chicago and London: The University of Chicago Press, 1988), p. 73.

28. For example, it is generally believed that the 1979 peace treaty in force between Israel and Egypt constrains the latter from joining with other Arab states or forces against Israel. But an authoritative minute to Article VI, paragraph 5, of the Israel-Egypt Peace Treaty provides that it is agreed on by the parties that there can be no assertion that the peace treaty prevails over other treaties or agreements or that other treaties or agreements prevail over the peace treaty. See Treaty of Peace, March 26, 1979, Egypt-Israel, Minute to Art. VI (5), 18 ILM, 362, 392. Geopolitics, of course, are another matter entirely, and presently at least, there does exist a clear and (for Israel) reassuring congruence of strategic interest between Cairo/President al-Sisi and Jerusalem.

29. Under international law, terrorist movements are always *Hostes humani generis*, or "Common enemies of mankind." See *Research in International Law: Draft Convention on Jurisdiction with Respect to Crime*, 29 *American Journal of International Law* (Supp. 1935) 435, 566, quoting *King v. Marsh* (1615), 3 Bulstr. 27, 81 Eng. Rep 23 (1615) ("*a pirate est Hostes humani generis*").

30. Regarding the historic and legal right of preemption, Israel's planners could now recall the early jurisprudential argument of Hugo Grotius, in his classic *Commentary on the Law of Prize and Booty*: "Now, as Cicero explains, the [justification of preemption] exists whenever he who chooses to wait [for a formal declaration of war] will be obliged to pay an unjust penalty before he can expect a just penalty; and, in a general sense, it exists whenever matters do not admit of delay. Thus, it is obvious that a just war can be waged in return, without recourse to judicial procedure, against an opponent who has begun an unjust war; nor will any declaration of that just war be required. . . . For, as Aelian says, citing Plato as his authority, any war undertaken for the necessary repulsion of injury, is proclaimed not by a crier nor by a herald, but by the voice of Nature herself."

31. As of the end of September 2015, a reliable poll conducted by the Palestinian Center for Policy and Survey Research, the leading research organization in the Palestinian territories, concluded that more than half of Palestinians no longer support a two-state solution. Nearly two-thirds of Palestinians (65 percent) want Mahmoud Abbas, the "moderate" PA president, to resign. See Ali Sawafta, "Most Palestinians No Longer Support Two-State Solution," Reuters, *Yahoo News*, September 21, 2015.

32. The reference, of course, per earlier chapters, is to the Peace of Westphalia (1648), which concluded the Thirty Years War and created the still-existing state system. See Treaty of Peace of Munster, Oct. 1648, 1 Consol. T.S. 271; and Treaty of Peace of Osnabruck, Oct. 1648, 1, Consol. T.S. 119. Together these two treaties comprise the Peace of Westphalia.

33. This *de facto* condition of Westphalian anarchy, within which Israel must necessarily make its strategic judgments, stands in very stark contrast to the jurisprudential assumption of solidarity between states. This idealized assumption concerns a presumptively common struggle against both aggression and terrorism. Such a "peremptory" expectation, known formally in law as a *jus cogens* assumption, was already mentioned in Justinian, *Corpus Juris Civilis* (533 CE); Hugo Grotius, 2 *De Jure Belli ac Pacis Libri Tres*, Ch. 20 (Francis W. Kesey., tr, Clarendon Press, 1925)(1690); and Emmerich de Vattel, 1 *Le Droit Des Gens*, Ch. 19 (1758).

34. See *Cicero: Letters to His Friends*, 78, D. R. Shackleton Bailey, tr., Scholars Press, 1988).

FIVE

Convergences of Law and Strategy

"For what can be done against force without force?"
—Cicero, *The Letters to His Friends*

As we have just seen, the core issues surrounding Israel's nuclear doctrine are abundantly strategic and not narrowly jurisprudential. Nonetheless, should Israel ever decide that it has no reasonable alternative to launching a preemptive attack against certain suitable enemy military or industrial targets, a defensive first strike would then need to be carefully justified under authoritative international law. With this in mind, it is now time to examine more closely the specifically jurisprudential correlates of Israel's nuclear doctrine. Optimally, of course, Israel would never actually allow itself to reach such an expressly final stage of existential peril.

LAW AND STRATEGY: FROM CICERO TO ANTICIPATORY SELF-DEFENSE

Long ago, Cicero, Roman philosopher and statesman, already understood the stark dilemma of maintaining kindly and peaceful intentions in a world perpetually driven by violence. Israel, now facing a steadily nuclearizing Iran amid growing chaos and "Cold War II,"[1] also understands this dilemma. Aware that the state could at some time become unacceptably vulnerable to overwhelming enemy force, its leaders may sometime have no choice[2] but to maintain consideration of all still-feasible preemption options.

Significantly, any such last resorts to self-defensive force could still be lawful or even actively law enforcing. The First Temple and Jewish Commonwealth was destroyed by the Babylonians in 586 BCE. The Second

Temple and Jewish Commonwealth ended catastrophically with Roman victory in the year 70 CE.[3] In its present political and jurisprudentially recognized form, which began in 1948,[4] Israel will last only as long as its leaders remain aptly attentive to Cicero's primal warning about force and, correspondingly, act preemptively if need be.

Such attentiveness and preparation, necessary but also plausibly insufficient, could still be consistent with the expectations of international law. In this regard, it must be borne in mind that international law is at least partially deducible from an always-valid natural law. According to Blackstone, this is the reason that the "law of nations" (international law) is always binding on all individuals and states. Each state is expected, *perpetually*, "to aid and enforce the law of nations, as part of the common law, by inflicting an adequate punishment upon the offenses against that universal law."[5]

International law, we have seen, is not a suicide pact. Israel's increasingly complex security problems[6] with Arab states and Iran could compel Jerusalem to decide once again either to wait for its enemies to strike first[7] or to strike first itself. Judged from a strategic and tactical perspective, the choice of preemption might sometime appear rational and suitably cost-effective.[8]

Once again, strategic and jurisprudential considerations may converge. "Defensive warfare . . . does not consist of waiting idly for things to happen," cautions Clausewitz in *On War*. "We must wait only if it brings us visible and decisive advantages. That calm before the storm, when the aggressor is gathering new forces for a great blow, is most dangerous for the defender."[9]

For Israel, key questions present themselves. Is it now the "calm before the storm"? If so, Jerusalem will have already examined pertinent strategic challenges and imperatives. But what about the corresponding legal ones? At what point, if any, would the danger posed to Israel by a particular enemy or combination of enemies be presumptively substantial enough to justify some still-accessible forms of anticipatory self-defense? And when such a point is actually thought to have been reached, what specific constraints would be binding on Israel in its intended applications of military force—that is, in its correct adherence to core expectations of both *jus in bello* and *jus ad bellum*?

In recent nuclear-age history, questions of threat "imminence" under customary international law have been taken with appropriate relevance and seriousness by scholars.[10] Exactly how imminent must a threat determinedly be before Israeli preemptive strikes could qualify as anticipatory self-defense? How precisely should such an inherently subjective judgment be rendered and then subsequently assessed?

In essence, we are inquiring, what does the expected convergence of strategic and jurisprudential assessments of preemption suggest about Israel's prospective calculations of striking first? One response, among others, is that Israel need not necessarily be deterred from appropriate forms of preemption out of any reasonable fear that its actions could then be correctly described as criminal.[11] Although quite predictably a substantial number of states would invariably condemn Israel for "aggression"[12] under any circumstances, this charge—so long as Israel's preemptive strikes would still meet the joint expectations of *jus ad bellum* (justice of war) and *jus in bello* (justice in war)—could be countered more or less effectively by certain appropriate references to governing international law.

The right of self-defense by forestalling an attack appears in Hugo Grotius's Book II of *The Law of War and Peace*.[13] Recognizing the need for "present danger" and threatening behavior that is "imminent in a point of time," Grotius indicates that self-defense is to be permitted not only after an attack has already been suffered but also in advance where "the deed may be anticipated."[14] Or as he says a bit further on in the same chapter, "It be lawful to kill him who is preparing to kill."

Grotius's terminology here raises an interesting and related question: Under what conditions, if any, might assassination or targeted killing be identified as a permissible form of anticipatory self-defense? Understood as tyrannicide, assassination has often been accepted as lawful. Examples would include Aristotle's *Politics*, Plutarch's *Lives*, and Cicero's *De Officiis*.

The argument that tyrannicide may even qualify as a peremptory, or *jus cogens*, rule derives from several sources of international law, enumerated at Article 38 of the UN Statute of the International Court of Justice, especially the "general principles of law recognized by civilized nations," the "teachings of the most highly-qualified publicists of the various nations," and—by extrapolation—the underlying decentralized and state-centric, or Westphalian, system of international law.[15]

Any such extrapolation leading to additional support for the peremptory right to tyrannicide would stem from the fact that international law has created a binding human rights regime without also providing, as necessary corollary, any effective and centralized enforcement mechanisms.[16] In consequence, support for this regime must, at least on occasion, require the exertion of regulatory force by individual leaders within the separate states. In the absence of this particular form of "self-help," the ambitious expectations established by the international law of human rights could have no genuinely meaningful chance of satisfaction.

A position on preemptive self-defense, similar to that taken by Grotius, is offered by Emmerich de Vattel. In Book II of *The Law of Nations* (1758), Vattel argues: "The safest plan is to prevent evil, where that is possible. A Nation has the right to resist the injury another seeks to inflict upon it, and to use force and every other just means of resistance against the aggressor. It may even anticipate the other's design, being careful, however, not to act upon vague and doubtful suspicions, lest it should run the risk of becoming itself the aggressor."[17]

Appropriately it seems, at least in the focused view of present concerns, both Grotius[18] and Vattel parallel the Jewish interpreters, although the latter speak more generally of interpersonal relations than of international relations. The Torah contains a provision exonerating from guilt a potential victim of robbery with possible violence if, in self defense, he struck down and if necessary, even killed the attacker *before he committed any crime* (Ex 22:1). In the words of the rabbis, "If a man comes to slay you, forestall by slaying him!" (Rashi, Sanhedrin 72a).

Grotius and Vattel both caution against abusing the right of anticipatory self-defense as a pretext for aggression, but this is an abuse that Israel, in its current configuration of formal ties to parts of the Arab world and Iran, cannot conceivably commit. As virtually the entire Arab world, except Egypt and Jordan, still considers itself in a formal condition of war with the Jewish state,[19] any Israeli preemption against other Arab state enemies would, in the strict legal sense, not be an act of anticipatory self-defense but rather only one more military operation in an ongoing and protracted war. It follows that any such operation's legality[20] would have to be appraised exclusively in terms of its conformance with the laws of war of international law (*jus in bello*).

Jurisprudentially, to identify such an operation as an act of aggression against another state that has already declared itself at war with Israel would be nonsense.

NUCLEAR WEAPONS, ASSASSINATION, AND ANTICIPATORY SELF-DEFENSE

Even if the state enemies of Israel were not in a declared condition of belligerence with the Jewish state, a condition often amplified by open calls for Israel's destruction,[21] Israel's preemptive action could be entirely law-enforcing. Israel, in the fashion of every state in the world legal system, is *peremptorily* entitled to self-defense. Especially in an age of uniquely destructive weaponry, international law does not require it to expose its citizens to annihilation by capitulation and/or with impunity.

The right of self-defense, as we learn from Vattel, gives rise to the "right to resist injustice." According to the writer's argument in Chapter V of *The Law of Nations, or the Principles of Natural Law* (1758), on "The Observance of Justice Between Nations":

> Justice is the foundation of all social life and the secure bond of all civil intercourse. Human society, instead of being an interchange of friendly assistance, would be no more than a vast system of robbery if no respect were shown for the virtue which gives to each his own. Its observance is even more necessary between Nations than between individu-

> als, because injustice between Nations may be followed by the terrible consequences involved in an affray between powerful political bodies, and because it is more difficult to obtain redress. . . . An intentional act of injustice is certainly an *injury*. A Nation has, therefore, the right to punish it. . . . The right to resist injustice is derived from the right of self-protection.[22]

In certain limited and distinctly residual circumstances, permissible forms of anticipatory self-defense could be expressed via assassination/targeted killing (although classical philosophical and jurisprudential arguments supporting assassination are usually cast more narrowly in terms of the tyrannicide motif). Representing an alternative or addition to standard military forms of preemption, such killing,[23] to be consistent with appropriate international legal expectations, would need to be undertaken when the danger posed to Israel actually meets the specific test of *The Caroline*. Thus, if the targeted killing were undertaken only to destroy the *potential* threat of an enemy (i.e., as a *preventive* action), it could not properly qualify as permissible. If, however, the assassination were undertaken in anticipation of an immediate or "imminent" enemy aggression (i.e., as a *preemptive* action), it could still qualify as an allowable instance of anticipatory self-defense.

Assessments of the lawfulness of assassination or targeted killing as expressive of anticipatory self-defense should always include proper comparisons with alternative forms of accessible preemption. If the perceived alternative to assassination were seen as large-scale resorts to force taking the form of defensive military strikes, a utilitarian or "balance-of-harms" standard could readily favor assassination.

Going forward, Israel may feel especially pressured by the convergence of ongoing enemy nuclearization with violent eruptions on behalf of a Palestinian state. Here, about to be deprived of altogether indispensable strategic depth,[24] Jerusalem could calculate that it had only three remaining options: (1) do nothing, rely entirely on long-term deterrence, and hope that enemy states (and also aspiring enemy states) remain dissuaded from striking first; (2) strike preemptively with military force against selected hard targets in pertinent enemy states or aspiring states and hope that any substantial reprisals are prevented by persuasive intrawar deterrence (that is, by compelling threats of an Israeli counterretaliation—by maintaining "escalation dominance"); or (3) strike preemptively by assassination (possibly "regime targeting") and hope that this more selective response will reduce the overall strategic threat to Israel without eliciting any further damaging escalations.

Although impossible to determine in the abstract, option 3 could prove to be the most reasonably cost-effective choice, at least in certain circumstances.

There are several relevant problems here. First, in the real world, judgments concerning the immediacy of anticipated aggression are exceedingly difficult to make. Second, even where such judgments are ventured, it can never be altogether clear whether the degree of immediacy is sufficient to invoke preemption rather than prevention. Third, in meeting the legal requirements of defensive *intent*, a state may have to act preventively rather than preemptively because waiting to allow a threat to become more imminent could have decisively or even intolerably negative strategic/tactical consequences. And fourth, the actual state-preserving benefits that might accrue from the assassination of enemy leaders are apt to be contingent on *not waiting* until the danger posed is already "instant, overwhelming, leaving no choice of means and no moment for deliberation."

Today, some scholars argue that the customary right of anticipatory self-defense articulated by the *Caroline* case has been overridden by the specific language of Article 51 of the UN Charter.[25] In this view, Article 51 fashions a new and far more restrictive statement of self-defense, one that relies on the literal qualification contained in Article 51: "if an armed attack occurs." Still, this interpretation ignores that international law cannot compel a state to wait until it absorbs a devastating or even lethal first strike before acting to protect itself.

The argument against the restrictive view of self-defense is reinforced, among other things, by the recurring weaknesses of the UN Security Council in offering collective security against an aggressor. Both the Security Council and the General Assembly had correctly refused to censure Israel for its 1967 preemptive attack against three Arab states. This refusal, odd in light of the world organization's longstanding double standard favoring Israel's Arab enemies, signified implicit approval by the UN of the Jewish state's resort to anticipatory self-defense.[26]

Before Israel could persuasively argue any future instances of anticipatory self-defense under international law, a strong case would have to be made that it had first sought to exhaust all available means of peaceful settlement. Even a broad view of the doctrine of anticipatory self-defense can never relieve a state of the peremptory obligations codified at Article 1 and Article 2(3) of the UN Charter.[27] Strictly speaking, these obligations should not necessarily be binding on Israel because of the condition of belligerency maintained de jure by certain of its Arab enemies and at least de facto, by Iran,[28] but—as a practical matter—the global community seems generally to have ignored this condition. It follows that Israel, should it ever decide to exercise future instances of preemption, would be well advised to demonstrate its consistent and comprehensive prior efforts at reaching a peaceful settlement.

ANCIENT ISRAEL AND CONTEMPORARY ISRAEL

The origins of such unassailable advice would have discernible roots in ancient Israel. According to Grotius, citing to Deuteronomy in *The Law of*

Prize and Booty, the Israelites were exempted from the issuance of warning announcements when dealing with previous enemies (what we might call today ongoing or protracted war, precisely the condition that currently obtains between Israel and Iran and with all Arab states, excluding Egypt and Jordan). The Israelites, recounts Grotius, had been commanded by God to "refrain from making an armed attack against any people without first inviting that people, by formal notification, to establish peaceful relations. . . ." "Yet," he continues, "the Israelites":

> Thought that this prohibition was inapplicable to many of the Canaanite tribes, inasmuch as they themselves had previously been attacked in war by the Canaanites.

"Hence," says Grotius, "we arrive at the following deduction":

> Once the formality of *rerum repetitio* has been observed, and a decree on the case in question has been issued, no further proclamation or sentence is required for the establishment of that right which arises in the actual process of execution. For [and this is especially relevant to *modern* Israel] in such circumstances, one is not undertaking a new war but merely carrying forward a war already undertaken. Thus the fact that justice has once been demanded and not obtained, suffices to justify a return to natural law.[29]

Looking back over the many years of conflict between Israel and certain Arab states, Israel has generally defended its resorts to military force as *measures of self-help short of war*. For the most part, such defense has had the effect of shifting the burden of jurisprudential responsibility for lawful behavior from the Arab states to Israel—arguably an unfortunate shift because it narrowly and incorrectly focuses blame on the Jewish State. Furthermore, earlier in its history, Israel had sometimes identified its uses of military force as "reprisals," thereby choosing a conspicuously problematic concept under international law, one that had compounded one expressly legal mistake with another.[30]

Because, under the current *Charter* system of international law, the right of reprisal is contingent on self-defense, it would be wise for Israel, so long as it chooses to ignore or downplay the declared condition of war announced by certain of its enemies as sufficient grounds for very different legal justifications for any resort to armed force, to always confine its legal rationale for needed military operations to *self-defense*. This advice would be unreasonable to challenge, especially as Israel now faces the threat not only of war but also of literal genocide.[31]

If Israel were to assume that a formal condition of belligerency already obtains with the Islamic Republic of Iran, it would then have every legal right to identify certain exertions of defensive force against that threatening state as part of an already ongoing state of war. Here, Israel's only legal obligations with respect to armed force would then be confined to considerations of *jus in bello*, or the law of armed conflict. In fact, however, despite Iran's insistent support of terror against Israel—Tehran has steadily supplied rockets and missiles to both Palestinian Hamas and Shiite Hezbollah and has also made unhidden threats to annihilate the Jewish State—such patently impermissible behavior has never been taken in Jerusalem as meaningfully tantamount to a formal declaration of war.

Genocide, of course, can take various forms. Its victims can be transported to the gas, or alternatively the gas can be brought to the victims. Either way, the jurisprudential effect is the same. It is the intentional mass murder of more or less defenseless civilian populations.

Today, Iran continues to prepare, at least residually and doctrinally, for an ultimate war with Israel. This is likely much more than a matter of a conspicuously overheated rhetoric. Rather, current preparations are expressly designed with an "intent to destroy" Israel, once and for all.[32]

Such murderous intent is much more than a matter of perceived geopolitical necessity. It is in essence a profoundly *religious* expectation. In Islam, the Prophet is said to have called for a Final Battle to annihilate the Jews. "The Hour" [salvation], Mohammed is reported to have said, "will not come until you fight against the Jews; and the stone would say, 'O Muslim! There is a Jew behind me; come and kill him.'"[33]

Outside of Iran, active support in the Arab world for genocide against the Jews is "merely" a matter of incontestable historical record. Even before creation of the State of Israel, such support had been displayed enthusiastically and openly during the Holocaust. On November 28, 1941, the Grand Mufti of Jerusalem, Haj Amin, met in Berlin with Adolph Hitler. The purpose of this meeting, which followed Haj Amin's organization of SS troops in Bosnia, was to ensure cooperation on "The Jewish Question."

It was essential, Haj Amin had insisted, that all Jews be sent to countries "where they would find themselves under active control, for example, in Poland, in order thereby to protect oneself from their menace, and avoid the consequent damage."[34]

Noteworthy also is that Palestinians and other Arabs have never publicly criticized the Mufti's complicity in the Holocaust. During the 1950s and 1960s, Hitler remained an enormously popular figure in the Arab world, a laudatory view that has changed little since then. Responses in this Arab world to the Eichmann trial in Jerusalem (1961) had widely treated the Nazi mass murderer as a "martyr" and congratulated him often for having "conferred a real blessing on humanity" by enacting a welcome "final solution."[35]

Overall, the current security situation is fraught not only with great danger but also with considerable irony. Before Israel could begin to move seriously toward Palestinian independence as part of any two-state solution,[36] an Iranian regime still preparing for a genocidal war against the Jewish State would have to recognizably reverse such preparations. This is because Israel could not afford to confront the risks of another hostile Arab state on its borders[37] unless its principal extant enemies moved toward (genuine) regional arms control.

In the absence of such movement, the creation of Palestine could affect Israel's inclination to preempt. Because of Israel's diminished size, its inclination to strike first at enemy hard targets would then be especially high. Once deprived of indispensable strategic depth, it could not hold out for as long as was possible when Palestine was still merely an "authority."

It is likely, as was discussed earlier in this volume, that a shift in nuclear strategy from deliberate ambiguity to disclosure after Palestine came into existence could reduce Israel's incentive to preempt but only if Jerusalem were first made to believe that its nuclear deterrent threat, as a result of this shift, was now being taken with sufficient seriousness by Iran.

EXTRACTING THE BOMB FROM THE BASEMENT: ANALYTIC ISSUES AND ISRAEL'S ORDER OF BATTLE

Several corollary problems must now be considered. First, how would Israel's leadership *know* that taking the bomb out of the basement had actually improved its deterrence posture? To a certain extent, the credibility of Jerusalem's nuclear threats would be contingent on the severity of different provocations. For example, it might be believable if Israel were to threaten nuclear reprisals for provocations that would endanger the very survival of the Jewish state, but it would almost certainly be unbelievable to threaten such reprisals for relatively minor territorial infringements or terrorist incursions.

There are other problems. To function successfully, Israel's deterrent, even after being removed from the basement, would have to be secure from enemy preemptive strikes. Moreover, Israel must also remain wary of "decapitation," of losing the "head" of its military command and control system because of enemy first strikes. Should Israel's enemies not be persuaded by Jerusalem's move away from deliberate ambiguity, they might then initiate such strikes as could effectively immobilize Israel's critical *order of battle.*

A contrary argument about the effects of Palestine on Israel's inclination to preempt suggests that because of Israel's newly expanded vulnerability, its nuclear deterrent could be *more credible* than ever before. As a result, Jerusalem could now better afford not to strike first than when it still had to deal with administered territories. In this situation, the principal benefit of shifting from ambiguity to disclosure would seem to lie in an explicitly identified "escalation ladder," a hierarchy of responses revealing a graduated array of intended Israeli reprisals ranging from limited conventional attacks to correspondingly measured nuclear strikes.

In weighing the different arguments concerning the effect of Palestine on Israeli preemption, particular attention must be directed toward Israel's presumptions about the inevitability of war and also the long-term expectations for Arab and Iranian vulnerability. Should Israel's leaders conclude that the creation of Palestine could make another major war more or less inevitable and that over time enemy vulnerability to Israel would diminish, Jerusalem's inclination to strike first would be increased. To a certain extent, Israel's *tactical* judgments on preemption will be affected by antecedent decisions on nuclear strategy, namely decisions concerning countervalue vs. counterforce objectives. Should it opt for nuclear deterrence based on assured destruction or countervalue, Jerusalem would likely choose a relatively small number of weapons that might be less accurate.

A counterforce strategy, on the other hand, would require a larger number of more accurate weapons, ones that could destroy even the most hardened targets. To a certain extent, "going for counterforce" could make Israeli nuclear threats more credible. This is based on the assumption that because the effects of such war-fighting weapons would be more precise and controlled, they would be more amenable to any actual use.

Yet on balance, war-fighting postures are apt to encourage preemption. And if counterforce-targeted nuclear weapons were ever fired, especially in a proliferated regional setting, the resultant escalation could still produce extensive countervalue exchanges. Indeed, even if such escalation were averted, the so-called collateral effects of counterforce detonations could still be devastating.

In making its nuclear choices, Israel will have to confront a paradox. Credible nuclear deterrence, essential to security and survival in a world made more dangerous by the creation of Palestine, would require *usable* nuclear weapons. If, after all, these weapons were obviously inappropriate for any reasonable objective, they would likely not deter.

At the same time, the more usable the weapons become to enhance nuclear deterrence, the more likely it is, at one time or another, that they will actually be fired. While this paradox would seem to suggest the rationality of deploying the least-harmful forms of usable nuclear weapons, the fact that there could be no coordinated agreements with enemy states on deployable nuclear weapons points to a very different conclusion, namely that unless Israel calculates that the more harmful weapons would produce greater hazards for *its own* population, as well as for target countries, there would exist no tactical benefit to opting for the least injurious usable weapons.

PALESTINE AND REGIONAL ENEMY NUCLEAR PROLIFERATION

All things considered, Israel, if confronted by a new state of Palestine, would be well advised to do everything possible to prevent the appearance of Arab and/or Iranian nuclear powers, including pertinent nonnuclear preemptions. Bringing its own bomb out of the basement is unlikely to serve any remediating purpose at that point unless Jerusalem were first to conclude that Arab/Iranian intractability toward the Jewish State had already become overt and overwhelming and that preparations for nuclearization in particular enemy states could no longer be stopped, even by Israeli preemptive strikes. Under these very portentous conditions, Israel would require a very believable nuclear deterrent, one that could be employed without igniting Armageddon for all regional belligerents and one that could also serve some damage-limiting military purpose (whatever the collateral effects) against Iranian weapons (nuclear and nonnuclear) should deterrence fail.[38]

A fully codified creation of Palestine, therefore, could have a dramatic effect on Israel's decision concerning anticipatory self-defense. And Israel's nuclear weapons status and strategy would likely influence this decision. More precisely, should Jerusalem determine that Israel's nuclear weapons would support preemption by deterring hostile target states from retaliating, this status could encourage Israeli first strikes. If, on the other hand, Jerusalem were to calculate that these target states would be unimpressed by threats of Israeli nuclear counterretaliation, this status would likely not encourage any Israeli defensive first strikes.

Could the precise form of Israel's nuclear strategy make a difference in these circumstances? Relying on nuclear weapons not to deter enemy first strikes but rather to support its own preemptive attacks, Israel would have to choose between continued ambiguity (implicit threats) and disclosure (explicit threats). How should it then decide?

More than anything else, the correct answer lies in Jerusalem's confidence that its adversaries already *acknowledge* Israel's nuclear capability, and in all of its prospectively usable forms. Should this confidence be high, there might be little valid reason for Jerusalem to abruptly take the bomb out of the basement. If, however, such confidence were low, the move to disclosure would plausibly be rational, especially because the provocation occasioned by the end of deliberate ambiguity would be unimportant after the onset of any Israeli first strikes. As for a predictably critical reaction by the United States, this could be significant for Israel, especially in the ever-changing "Cold War II" strategic environment. Now more than ever, perhaps Jerusalem must inquire thoughtfully about any of its still-contemplated nuclear policy initiatives: "What will the Russians think?"

In view of what is now generally believed throughout the Middle East, and indeed all over the world, there is plainly every good reason to assume that Israel's nuclear arsenal does exist. The most critical and residual question about Israel's nuclear deterrent, however, is not about *capability* but about *willingness*. How likely is it that Israel, after launching nonnuclear preemptive strikes against enemy hard targets, would respond to certain expected enemy reprisals with a nuclear counterretaliation?

To answer this core question, Israel's decision makers will first have to put themselves into the shoes of various enemy leaders. Will these leaders calculate that they can afford to retaliate against Israel (i.e., that such retaliation would not produce a nuclear counterretaliation)? In asking this question, they will assume, of course, a nonnuclear retaliation against Israel. A nuclear retaliation, should it become technically possible, would much more plainly invite a nuclear counterretaliatory blow.

What will they conclude? This depends in turn on their view of reciprocal enemy judgments about Israel's leaders. Do these judgments suggest a leadership that believes it can gain the upper hand with nuclear counterretaliation? Or do they suggest a leadership that believes such counterretaliation would bring upon Israel various intolerable levels of harm and destruction?

Depending on the way in which enemy decision makers may interpret Israel's authoritative perceptions, they would accept or reject the cost effectiveness of any nonnuclear retaliation against Israel. This means that it is in Israel's best interest to communicate the following strategic assumption to its enemies: Israel would be acting rationally by responding to certain enemy nonnuclear reprisals to Israeli preemptive attacks with a nuclear counterretaliation. The plausibility of this assumption could be enhanced considerably, of course, if enemy reprisals were also to involve chemical and/or biological weapons.

SYNERGIES AND PRINCIPAL STRATEGIC INTERSECTIONS: ANOTHER LOOK

In rendering any decisions on principal strategic imperatives, both communicational and operational, Israel's leaders should never lose sight of plausible interactions (1) between discrete threats, (2) between these separate threats and considered counterthreats (anticipated remediations), and (3) between likely remediations and more or less predictable enemy counterremediation measures. Further, before this complex advice can actually be followed, Jerusalem will have to construct its relevant theory on certain explicit assumptions concerning ascertainable characteristics and differences among Israel's foreseeable adversaries. In other words, Israel's strategic theory will need to accommodate a meaningful variety of conceivable adversaries. Israel might expect, for example, very different calculations and responses from Baghdad, Beirut, or Ramallah than from Damascus or Tehran.

How to accomplish this accommodation without neglecting either the growing complexity of Cold War II[39] or the incessant and recalcitrant chaos already immobilizing the Middle East will present Jerusalem with a very tall order. In any event, there can be no reasonable alternative for Israel to fashioning a carefully worked out and disciplined framework of policy inquiry (an antecedent theory); otherwise Israel would be compelled to deal with each emerging threat issue in a visceral seat-of-its-pants reaction, on a mistakenly compartmentalized ad hoc basis, disjointedly, unsystematically, *in media res*. For a set of problems as many sided and complicated as the security conundrum that will continue to confront and confound the Jewish State, any such default option could quickly prove catastrophic.

Particular strategic risks facing Israel are apt to form an intricately interconnected network. The more that is known in advance about any such network, the better that Jerusalem will be able to understand expectedly threatening crisis situations. In more technical terms, Israeli planners will soon need to look at the deteriorating situations in Syria, Iraq, Lebanon, Palestine, and so on with a view to identifying such high-risk properties as *contagion potential, persistence,* and *cascades of failures*. Although it would generally be difficult to actually measure adverse effects of assorted risk interdependencies, even nonquantified assessments could prove gainful to security policy formulations and to further enhancements of system stability in the region.

Returning to Israel's nuclear doctrine and pertinent synergies, *cascades of failures* represent one particular iteration of threat intersection. Here, Israeli planners must be attentive to any accumulating torrent of diverse security threats still being materialized. Not all vital synergies, however, even when they "couple" between systems in diverse domains, should be expected to "cascade."

Whether or not an interesting strategic synergy is expected to cascade, Israeli analysts must acquaint themselves with the related concept of "skipping." This concept comes into play when one or more events or issues interact surreptitiously with several others, but only where some of them actually react. Moreover, these surreptitious reactions would be nonlinear and intermittent.

For Israel, at least in the best of all possible planning worlds, it could be entirely practical to meaningfully quantify the dynamics of all large-scale risk materializations now lying latent within the broad regional tapestry of strategic synergies. Whether or not such Israeli efforts are already under way is not the role of independent scholars to discover—and is, therefore, a question far beyond the boundaries of this current inquiry. But it still remains well worth mentioning that the overall adequacy of Israel's nuclear doctrine should always rely on much more than traditional strategic-balance or "order-of-battle investigations."

In essence, armed with a suitably complex strategic model that is aptly attentive to regional synergistic effects, Israeli leaders could better learn how to decouple the most potentially severe risks of harm from the much larger network and also to better reduce their initial materialization prospects. A timely example of this obligation will likely continue to concern Russian and American strategic divergences in the Middle East and the particular intersections of these significant divergences with Israel's own pertinent security policies.

RATIONALITY AND IRRATIONALITY: ANOTHER LOOK

Such difficult matters of intersecting regional risks notwithstanding, Israeli policy assessments of enemy decisional calculations must normally assume rationality. In the absence of calculations that would compare the costs and benefits of available strategic alternatives, what could happen in the Middle East must remain only a matter of conjecture. Significantly, as was discussed earlier, the prospect of nonrational judgments in the region is always distinctly plausible, especially as the influence of Islamist/Jihadist ideologies remains potentially determinative among certain significant enemy elites.

To the extent that Israel might one day believe itself confronted with nonrational enemies, particularly ones with highly destructive weapons in their arsenals, its incentive to preempt could then become overwhelming. In fact, should such enemies be believed to hold nuclear weapons, Israel could conceivably decide, quite rationally, to launch a *nuclear* preemption. This would appear to be the only calculable circumstance in which a rational Israeli preemptive strike could ever be nuclear and would require an additional assumption that the pertinent enemy or enemies were actively planning an expressly nuclear attack.

Israel's enemies should understand from all this that there are conditions wherein Jerusalem might decide to actually use its nuclear weapons. These conditions concern the intolerable prospect of total defeat. Faced with any imminent destruction of the state, Israel's leaders would almost certainly do whatever is needed to survive, including a resort to nuclear retaliation, nuclear counterretaliation, nuclear preemption, or nuclear war fighting.

NUCLEAR RETALIATION

Should an enemy state launch a nuclear first strike against Israel, Jerusalem would certainly respond, to the extent possible, with a nuclear retaliatory strike. If enemy first strikes were to involve other forms of unconventional weapons (i.e., chemical and/or biological weapons), Israel *might* launch a nuclear reprisal depending in large measure on Jerusalem's expectations of follow-on aggression and its associated calculations of comparative damage limitation. If Israel absorbed a massive conventional attack, a nuclear retaliation could not be ruled out, especially if (a) the aggressors were perceived to hold nuclear and/or other unconventional weapons in reserve, and/or (b) Israel's leaders were to believe that nonnuclear retaliations could not prevent destruction of the state. A nuclear retaliation by Israel could be ruled out only in circumstances where enemy aggression were clearly conventional, typical (i.e., consistent with previous instances of enemy attack, in both degree and intent), and exclusively hard-target directed.

NUCLEAR COUNTERRETALIATION

Should Israel feel compelled to preempt enemy aggression with conventional weapons, the enemy response would largely determine Jerusalem's next moves. If this response were in any way nuclear, Israel would assuredly resort to some form of nuclear counterretaliation. If this retaliation were to involve chemical and/or biological weapons, Israel might also feel pressed to take the escalatory initiative—again depending on Jerusalem's judgments of enemy intent and on its sober calculations of essential damage limitation.

Should the enemy response to Israel's preemption be limited to hard-target conventional strikes, it is unlikely that the Jewish State would then move on to nuclear counterretaliations. If, however, the enemy conventional retaliation were all out and directed toward civilian populations as well as to military targets, an Israeli nuclear counterretaliation could not be ruled out. It would appear that such a counterretaliation could be ruled out only if the enemy conventional retaliation were entirely proportionate[40] to Israel's preemption, confined exclusively to Israeli hard targets, circumscribed by the jurisprudential limits of "military necessity,"[41] and accompanied by verifiably explicit assurances of nonescalatory intent.

NUCLEAR PREEMPTION

To note once again, it is extremely unlikely that Israel would ever decide to launch a preemptive nuclear strike. Although circumstances might arise wherein such a strike would be perfectly *rational* (i.e., the calculated prospective benefits of the strike would outweigh the prospective costs), it is implausible that Israel would allow itself to reach these "end-of-the-line" circumstances. Moreover, unless the nuclear weapons involved were used in a fashion consistent with the authoritative expectations of the laws of war—the limits of discrimination, proportionality, and military necessity—this unambiguously ultimate form of preemption would represent an egregious violation of international law.

Even if such consistency were possible, the psychological/political impact on the wider world community would be negative and far reaching. It follows that an Israeli nuclear preemption could be expected only (a) where certain of Israel's enemies had acquired nuclear and/or other unconventional weapons judged capable of destroying the "Third Temple Commonwealth," (b) where these enemies had made clear that their intentions paralleled their capabilities, (c) where these enemies were believed ready to begin a countdown to launch, and (d) where Jerusalem believed that Israeli nonnuclear preemptions could not achieve needed minimum levels of damage limitation (i.e., levels consistent with preservation of the Jewish State).

NUCLEAR WAR FIGHTING

Should nuclear weapons be introduced into conflict involving Israel either by the Jewish State or by an identifiable foe, nuclear war fighting at one level or another would ensue. This would hold true as long as (a) enemy first strikes against Israel would not destroy Jerusalem's second-strike nuclear capability, (b) enemy retaliations for Israeli conventional preemption would not destroy Jerusalem's nuclear counterretaliatory capability, (c) Israeli preemptive strikes involving nuclear weapons would not destroy Arab or Iranian second-strike nuclear capabilities, and (d) Israeli retaliation for enemy conventional first strikes would not destroy Arab or Iranian nuclear counterretaliatory capability.

None of this is meant to suggest that an Israeli defensive first strike would necessarily give rise to a nuclear war. Quite the contrary; Israel's resort to nonnuclear preemption might in fact represent the optimal way to *prevent* nuclear war.

Unless Jerusalem's regional adversaries, especially Iran, begin to end their persistent threats to Israel's existence, such resort could at some time become the Jewish State's only reasonable alternative to suffering possible annihilation.

Plus ca change, plus c'est la même chose (The more things change, the more they remain the same). Despite extraordinary steps to preserve the Commonwealth, the State of Israel remains subject to indisputably grave threats of harm. In the fashion of the First and Second Jewish Temple Commonwealths, this current state, notwithstanding international law's formal presumption of juridical solidarity between states,[42] could at some time face annihilation and disappearance.

To prevent such a fate, permissibly, Israel could resort to the jurisprudential protections afforded by anticipatory self-defense under international law. Mediating between survival and chaos, these protections could offer the Jewish State an essential opportunity to confront force with force, not to initiate war but to prevent oblivion. Although in the best of all possible worlds, preemption would be unnecessary, and therefore illegal, this is not yet such a world.

As long as Israel's expression of anticipatory self-defense had been prompted by imminent dangers of considerable magnitude and was executed in full conformance with authoritative expectations of discrimination, proportionality, and military necessity, accepting the preemption option could be manifestly lawful.[43] Of course, such lawfulness would not necessarily imply any corresponding strategic benefit. Always, pertinent judgments of *legality* and *expected efficacy* should remain discrete and analytically distinct. This point cannot be overstated.

There is a passage in the *Odyssey* that speaks of two gates, one of horn and the other of ivory. Through the ivory gate, false dreams pass to humankind, and through the gate of horn go only the true and prophetic dreams. At this moment in its always precarious history, Israel may be tempted by the ivory gate, choosing to base Israel's preservation on various fanciful visions of regional solidarity and good intentions (a temptation encouraged, to be sure, by the so-called global community as a whole).

It would be better for Israel to pass instead through the gate of horn, preparing if need be to use its military force selectively and preemptively in order to endure but also alternatively to employ such force as a presumptively more suitable means of deterrence. Occasioning more or less pain in the short run, any such passage would base preservation of the Jewish State on appropriately sober assessments of *Realpolitik*[44] and would simultaneously affirm, rather than reject, the peremptory obligations of international law.

In principle, realistic defensive actions by Israel against Iran may not necessarily require any actual resort to anticipatory self-defense. Following the 2015 Joint Comprehensive Plan of Action (JCPOA), there is increasing faith, at least in certain circles, that Iran can still be turned away from its nuclear weapons program. Whether or not such faith is justifiable,[45] Jerusalem will still need to clarify and enhance its nuclear deterrence policy, with special attention to codifying and maintaining a recognizably *survivable* and *penetration-capable* strategic retaliatory force.

Such clarification and enhancement will also need to be conceptualized with regard to other still-conceivable regional nuclear adversaries.

It will also be important to enhance Israel's ballistic missile defenses, namely the Arrow, and to convincingly communicate to Tehran that Israeli nuclear forces are (1) usable and (2) would be used as a complement (not as an alternative) to expected ballistic missile defense interceptions. Among other things, this communication should include a very selective and partial end to Israel's deliberate nuclear ambiguity, or bomb in the basement. As for Cicero's warning of the existential obligations to use national force in a world of endlessly primal rancor and violence, Israeli strategists would be well advised to shape their final recommendations in line with a substantially capable and antecedent *scholarship*.

In the final analysis, each state's basic right to self-protection—including at times to anticipatory self-defense—is the discernible reciprocal of every national leader's core obligation to protect national populations. Always, in the history of political philosophy, even in predemocratic or nondemocratic states, sovereign authority must ultimately be based upon an assurance of such protection. According to Thomas Hobbes, the seventeenth-century English philosopher, whose views on chaos and the "state of nature"[46] have already figured prominently in this book: "The obligation of subjects to the sovereign is understood to last as long, and no longer, than the power lasteth by which he is able to protect them."[47] Similarly, sixteenth-century French thinker Jean Bodin argued that citizen or subject obligation to the government must derive incontestably from the sovereign's capacity to provide enduring safety:

> The word of protection in generall extendeth unto all subjects which are under the obeysance of one soveraigne prince or seignorie: As we have said, that the prince is bound by force of armes; and of his lawes, to maintaine his subjects in suretie of their persons, their goods, and families, for which the subjects by a reciprocall obligation owe unto their prince faith, subjection, obeysance, aid, and succour.[48]

To survive amid growing chaos, Israel's leaders will need to draw on a broad variety of strategies and resources. Following Cicero, they cannot afford to ignore all possible resorts to armed force, but they will also need to ensure that wherever practicable any such resorts are tempered or supported by suitable nonmilitary alternatives. As for nuclear strategy and doctrine, this security "template" will become altogether central and even indispensable, but only if it is first fashioned very capably and conscientiously in Jerusalem. Always, recalling both Sun Tzu and *Project Daniel*, Israel must remain aware that its nuclear weapons can truly succeed only through their calculated nonuse.

Long before the nuclear age, the philosopher Niccolo Machiavelli distinguished between using "violence to spoil things" and "violence . . . to mend them."[49] Such a subtle distinction is still meaningful, especially on the urgent subject of the present volume. To "mend" rather than "spoil," Israel's nuclear weapons must become part of an antecedent and coherent nuclear doctrine. This doctrine, in turn, must represent the product of a relentless strategic struggle of mind over mind, not merely one of mind over matter. Always, especially in bewilderingly arcane matters of nuclear strategy, the most critical battlefield will be conceptual and intellectual, not geographic.

Finally, it must be asked yet again: What about international *law*? This chapter, after all, has sought to place key questions of Israel's nuclear doctrine within a jurisprudential as well as strategic framework of inquiry. Moreover, the obligations of international law would seem to be both obvious and incontestable. To wit, in a now-famous 1837 lecture on "The Dignity of the Law as a Profession," Timothy Walker underscored the "high moral sublimity" of international law. Inquired Walker: "Who, then, will question the dignity of this branch (international law) of legal study? Next to religion, I know not that the human mind can employ itself in contemplations more interesting or sublime; and if the law of nations be not as practical, as the branches which follow, it certainly makes up in grandeur, what it lacks in every day utility."[50]

"Grandeur," of course, is woefully extraneous to any primary meaningful considerations of Israel's nuclear doctrine. Rather, in this prevailing weapons technology context, it is best to understand that world legal order can never be improved by rules alone and that the persistently sorrowful record of human civilization suggests very little that has changed in human destructiveness over several thousands of years. Now, in fact, historically consistent inclinations to form warring human communities, including states, is being joined with an expanding human access to nuclear weapons technologies.

Could there be any more insidious or less promising "synergy"? This is a question that needs to be raised everywhere, but especially in Israel.

Despite glaring evidence of newly impending harms in world politics—harms nurtured or at least impacted by both expanding chaos and Cold War II—Israel can still discover, within the indissoluble core of international law, a usable template for survival. This template, standing above all narrowly technical rules that might otherwise cloud imperative strategic judgments for national security, goes back to the beginning, back to the ancient Hebrew view of a "Higher Law" and to the conceptually complementary Roman formulations of "Natural Law." This immutable template overrides all narrowly regulatory norms that might be invoked by friends and foes alike and inherently reaffirms the always overriding right to remain "alive."

"True law," says Cicero, in *De Republica*—in what is arguably the most famous passage written about law in the past two thousand years—"is right reason, harmonious with nature, diffused among all, constant, eternal; a law which calls to duty by its commands, and restrains from evil by its prohibitions. . . . It is a sacred obligation not to attempt to legislate in contradiction to this law; nor may it be derogated from nor abrogated. . . . [I]t is one eternal and unchangeable law, binding all nations through all time."[51]

It is not too difficult to understand that Israel's nuclear doctrine can be somehow rendered consistent with this "eternal and unchangeable" law. International law, we should recall, fully incorporates the complementary notions of Higher Law and national survival.[52] Israel's strategic needs and corresponding legal expectations are fully compatible, especially if Jerusalem continues to bear in mind the very basic maxim expressed in *Israel's Strategic Future: The Final Report of Project Daniel*: "The overriding priority of Israel's nuclear deterrent force must always be that it preserves the country's security without ever having to be fired against any target. The primary point of Israel's nuclear forces must always be deterrence *ex ante*, not revenge *ex post*."[53]

NOTES

1. In essence, hypothesizing the emergence of Cold War II means expecting that the world system is becoming increasingly *bipolar*. For early writings by this author on the global security implications of such an expanding bipolarity, see Louis René Beres, "Bipolarity, Multipolarity, and the Reliability of Alliance Commitments," *Western Political Quarterly*, Vol. 25, No. 4, December 1972, pp. 702–710; Louis René Beres, "Bipolarity, Multipolarity, and the Tragedy of the Commons," *Western Political Quarterly*, Vol. 26, No. 4, December 1973, pp. 649–658; and Louis René Beres, "Guerillas, Terrorists, and Polarity: New Structural Models of World Politics," *Western Political Quarterly*, Vol. 27, No. 4, December 1974, pp. 624–636.

2. Current Israeli security concerns center on the conspicuous threat from Iran, but in the future, existential nuclear perils could also originate elsewhere. Regarding Iran, Professor Beres's earliest published warnings on this particular enemy nuclearization go back many years. See for example, "Israel, Force and International Law: Assessing Anticipatory Self-Defense," *The Jerusalem Journal of International Relations*, Vol. 13, No. 2, June 1991, pp. 1–14; "After the Gulf War: Israel, 'Palestine' and the Risk of Nuclear War in the Middle East," *Strategic Review*, Vol. XIX, No. 4, Fall 1991, pp. 48–55; "Israel, Iran and Prospects for Nuclear War in the Middle East," *Strategic Review*, Vol. XXI, No. 2, Spring 1993, pp. 52–60; "Israel, Iran and Nuclear War: A Tactical and Legal Assessment," *Jerusalem Letter*, Jerusalem Center for Public Affairs, Jerusalem, Israel, November 1993, pp. 1–7; "North Korea Today, Iran Tomorrow," *Midstream*, June/July 1994, pp. 5–7, coauthored with Col. (IDF/res.) Yoash Tsiddon-Chatto; "The Security and Future of Israel: An Exchange," *Midstream*, Vol. XXXXI, No. 5, June/July 1995, pp. 15–23 (an oft-reprinted debate between Professor Beres and Maj. General [IDF/Res.] Shlomo Gazit, a former Chief of the IDF Intelligence Branch [AMAN] and later Military Advisor to Prime Minister Shimon Peres); "Israel, Iran and Preemption: Choosing the Least Unattractive Option Under International Law," *Dickinson Journal of International Law*, Vol. 14, No. 2, Winter 1996, pp. 187–206; "Israel, Iran and Nuclear War: A Jurisprudential Assessment," *UCLA Journal of International Law and Foreign Affairs*, Spring 1996, Vol. 1, No. 1, pp. 65–97; "The Iranian Threat to Israel: Capabilities and Intentions," *International Journal of Intelligence and Counterintelligence*, Vol. 9, No. 1, Spring 1996, pp. 51–62; "The Iranian Threat to Israel," *Midstream*, Vol. 44, No. 6, September/October 1998, pp. 8–11; *Security Threats and Effective Remedies: Israel's Strategic, Tactical and Legal Options: A Comprehensive Master Plan for the Jewish State in the Third Millennium*, The Ariel Center for Policy Research (Israel), ACPR Policy Paper No. 102, April 2000, 110 pp.; "Iran's Growing Threat to Israel," *Midstream*, Vol. XXXXVI, No. 7, November 2000, pp. 2–4; and "Israel and the Bomb: A Dialogue with Professor Zeev Maoz," *International Security* (Harvard), Vol. 29, No. 1, Summer 2004, pp. 175–180.

3. The so-called Great Revolt of the Jews against Rome lasted from 66–70 CE. The fall of Masada is dated 73 CE.

4. The declaration of the State of Israel was made on May 14, 1948, by the members of the People's Council—the parliamentary body of the "state in process."

5. See William Blackstone, *Commentaries on the Laws of England*, Book 4, "Of Public Wrongs."

6. For much earlier analyses of these problems by this author, see "Israeli Security and Self-Reliance After the Cold War: Geopolitical Imperatives, Strategic Considerations and Tactical Options," delivered at the international scholarly conference Security Regimes—Israel and Its Neighbors, Bar-Ilan Center for Strategic Studies, June 3, 1992; "The Real Bases of Middle East Instability," *Midstream*, Vol. XXXVIII, No. 5, June–July 1992, pp. 9–10; "After the Scud Attacks: Israel, 'Palestine,' and Anticipatory Self-Defense," *Emory International Law Review*, Vol. 6, No. 1, Spring 1992, pp. 71–104; "After the Gulf War: Israel, Palestine, and the Risk of Nuclear War in the Middle East," *Strategic Review*, Vol. XIX, No. 4, Fall 1991, pp. 48–55; "Israeli Security in a Changing World," *Strategic Review*, Vol. XVIII, No. 4, Fall 1990, pp. 11–22; "The Growing Threat of Nuclear War in the Middle East," *The Jerusalem Journal of International Relations*, Vol. 12, No. 1, 1990, pp. 1–27; and *Israeli Security and Nuclear Weapons*, The Graduate Institute of International Studies, Programme for Strategic and International Security Studies, Geneva, Switzerland, Occasional Paper No. 1/1990.

7. Should Israel decide to wait for its Iranian enemies to strike first, the Jewish State could choose to respond with disproportionately severe reactions to aggression, reactions that would then represent an ironic inversion of the Jewish *lex talionis*.

8. Preemption has figured importantly in previous Israeli strategic calculations. This was most glaringly apparent in the wars of 1956 and 1967, the destruction of the Iraqi Osiraq nuclear reactor in 1981, and Operation Orchard, Israel's defensive strike on Syria's suspected nuclear reactor on September 6, 2007. Significantly, it was essentially the failure to preempt in October 1973 that contributed to heavy Israeli losses on the Egyptian and Syrian fronts during the Yom Kippur War and almost brought about an Israeli defeat. During January, May, and October 2013, Israel, understandably apprehensive about Damascus's supply of military materials to Syria's Hezbollah surrogates in Lebanon, preemptively struck pertinent hard targets within Syria itself. For a jurisprudential assessment of these undeclared but still-appropriate expressions of anticipatory self-defense by this author, see Louis René Beres, "Striking Hezbollah-Bound Weapons in Syria: Israel's Actions Under International Law," *Harvard National Security Journal*, Harvard Law School, posted online August 26, 2013.

9. See Carl von Clausewitz, *Principles of War*, Hans W. Gatzke, tr., New York, Dover Publications, 2003, p. 54, from III, "Strategy."

10. See, for example, M. McDougal, "The Soviet-Cuban Quarantine and Self-Defense," *American Journal of International Law*, 57, pp. 597, 598–600 (1963) (acknowledging that prior to the UN Charter, the right of anticipatory self-defense was customary international law); P. Jessup, *A Modern Law of Nations* 166 (1948) (noting that the right of self-defense under customary international law included anticipatory actions against "imminent threats").

11. Nonetheless, Israel might also be constrained by strategic rather than narrowly jurisprudential considerations. In this connection, see Amos Yadlin and Avner Golov, "If Attacked, How Would Iran Respond?" *INSS Strategic Assessment*, Vol. 16, No. 3, October 2013, pp. 7–21. See also *The Iran Project: Weighing Benefits and Costs of Military Action Against Iran*, Woodrow Wilson Center, 2012. Maj. Gen. (IAF ret.) Amos Yadlin is a former Head of Israel's Military Intelligence Directorate (Aman).

12. See especially Resolution on the Definition of Aggression, Dec. 14, 1974, UNGA Res. 3314 (XXIX), 29 UN GAOR, (Supp. No. 31) 142, UN Doc. A/9631, 1975, reprinted in 13 ILM 710, 1974; and Charter of the United Nations, Art. 51. Done at San Francisco, June 26, 1945. Entered into force for the United States, Oct. 24, 1945, 59 Stat. 1031, T.S. No. 993, Bevans 1153, 1976, YBUN 1043.

13. Chapter I "Of the Causes of War; and first of Self-Defense, and Defense of our Property," (1625), Book II, reprinted in *Classics of International Law*, Vol. 2, 168–175, Carnegie Endowment tr. 1925.

14. Id. at 173–174.

15. For an early study of the effects of expanding global centralization by this writer, see Louis René Beres, "Examining the Logic of World Federal Government," *Publius: The Journal of Federalism*, Vol. 4, No. 3, Summer 1974, pp. 75–87.

16. In this connection, noted Sigmund Freud: "Wars will only be prevented with certainty if mankind unites in setting up a central authority to which the right of giving judgment upon all shall be handed over. There are clearly two separate requirements involved in this: the creation of a supreme agency, and its endowment with the necessary power. One without the other would be useless." See Sigmund Freud, *Collected Papers*, cited in Louis René Beres, *The Management of World Power: A Theoretical Analysis*, University of Denver, Monograph Series in World Affairs, Vol. 10 (1972–1973), p. 27.

17. See Chapter IV, "The Right of Self-Protection and the Effects of the Sovereignty and Independence of Nations," (1758), Book II, reprinted in *Classics of International Law*, Vol. 3, 130 Carnegie Endowment, tr., 1916.

18. Grotius cites to Cicero's observation (from the latter's *Defense of Milo*) that "the act [of homicide] is not only just, but even necessary, when it represents the repulsion of violence by means of violence." See *Commentary on the Law of Prize and Booty*, a translation of the manuscript of 1604 by G. L. Williams, New York, Oceana Publications, Inc., 1964, p. 67.

19. The agreements that put an end to the first Arab-Israeli War (1947–1949) were general armistice agreements negotiated bilaterally between Israel and Egypt on February 24, 1949 (42 UNTS 251-70, 1949); Israel and Lebanon on March 23, 1949 (42 UNTS 287-98, 1949); Israel and Jordan on April 3, 1949 (42 UNTS 303-20, 1949); and Israel and Syria on July 20, 1949 (42 UNTS 327-40, 1949).

20. Regarding such legality in an ongoing war begun by another state, we may recall the opinion of Grotius in his *Commentary on the Law of Prize and Booty*: "[I]t is obvious that a just war can be waged in return, without recourse to judicial procedure, against an opponent who has begun an unjust war; nor will any declaration of that just war be required. . . . For as Aelian says, citing Plato as his authority—any war undertaken for the necessary repulsion of injury, is proclaimed not by a crier nor by a herald, but by the voice of Nature herself." See H. Grotius, *De Iure Praedae Commentarius*, ed. by James Brown Scott, a translation of the original manuscript of 1604 by Gladys L. Williams, with the collaboration of Walter H. Zeydel, New York, Oceana Publications, Inc., 1964, p. 96.

21. There is nothing new about such calls concerning Israel's very existence. From the first, Arab states, and more recently Iran, have regarded Israel as the institutionalized manifestation of multiple crimes, particularly colonialism, imperialism, and aggression. Indeed, often denounced as "an instrument of evil," constructed "on a foundation of evil," Israel is taken to be immutably criminal, irremediable, fit only for liquidation/extermination. See, for example, the discussion of "The External Aspect: Aggression, Intrigues, Exploitation," in Yehoshafat Harkabi, *Arab Attitudes to Israel*, Jerusalem, Keter Publishing House Ltd., 1972, pp. 307–310.

22. See Vol. 3, translated by Charles G. Fenwick, Washington, DC, The Carnegie Institution of Washington, 1916, p. 135.

23. For important distinctions between assassination and targeted killing, see Amos N. Guiora, *Legitimate Target: A Criteria-Based Approach to Targeted Killing* (New York and Oxford: Oxford University Press, 2013), 107 pp.

24. Even long before the nuclear age, ancient Chinese strategist Sun-Tzu had recognized the importance of strategic depth. Although he did not, of course, use such a precisely modern term, Sun-Tzu did note as follows: "If there is no place to go, it is fatal terrain." See Sun-Tzu, *The Art of War*, Chapter 11, "Nine Terrains."

25. See Ian Brownlie, *International Law and the Use of Force by States*, 272–273 (1963) (asserting that the United Nations Charter modified the international custom of anticipatory self-defense and that self-defense is justified only in response to an actual armed attack); Quincy Wright, "The Cuban Quarantine," *American Journal of International Law*, 57, pp. 546, 559–563 (1963) (interpreting Article 51 in conjunction with

Article 33 to allow only a "peaceful means" of dispute resolution and a prohibition on the use of unilateral force until an actual armed conflict occurred); L. Henkin, *How Nations Behave*, pp. 141–144 (2d ed. 1979) (arguing that the Charter restricts the traditional right of self-defense to those situations where an armed attack has occurred); L. Goodrich, E. Hambro, and A. Simons, *Charter of the United Nations: Commentary and Documents*, p. 178 (1946) (advocating a restrictive interpretation of Article 51 under which self-defense is justified only in response to an actual armed attack).

26. International law remains a "vigilante" system, or in other words, "Westphalian." This latter reference is to the Peace of Westphalia (1648), which concluded the Thirty Years War and created the now still-existing decentralized, or self-help, state system. See Treaty of Peace of Munster, Oct. 1648, 1 Consol. T.S. 271; and Treaty of Peace of Osnabruck, Oct. 1648, 1, Consol. T.S. 119. Together these two treaties comprise the Peace of Westphalia.

27. A similar imperative can be found in Jewish religious law: "When thou comest near to a city to fight against it," proclaims Deuteronomy 20:10, "then proclaim peace to it." Maimonides also calls for diplomatic solutions before hostilities begin to *milhemet mitzvah* (a war commanded by the Torah or Pentateuch): "No war is declared against any nation before peace offers are made to it." The biblical commentator Abrabanel (1437–1508) argues not to *hurry* to go to war. For more complete examinations of war in the Jewish tradition, consult Efraim Inbar, "War in Jewish Tradition," *The Jerusalem Journal of International Relations*, Vol. 9, No. 2, June 1987, pp. 83–99.

28. The formal Iranian position on a state of war with Israel is unclear. If, however, Tehran did start to make it clear that it does regard its bilateral relationship with Israel as one of belligerency, a state of war would then legally obtain in spite of the fact that Israel itself would still consider itself to be in a "state of peace."

29. See *Commentary on the Law of Prize and Booty*, *supra* note 20, p. 102. The idea of natural law is based on the acceptance of certain principles of right and justice that prevail because of their own intrinsic merit. Eternal and immutable, they are external to all acts of human will and interpenetrate all human reason. This idea and its attendant tradition of human civility runs continually from Mosaic Law and the ancient Greeks and Romans to the present day. For a comprehensive and far-reaching assessment of the natural law origins of international law, see Louis René Beres, "Justice and Realpolitik: International Law and the Prevention of Genocide," *The American Journal of Jurisprudence*, Vol. 33, 1988, pp. 123–159. This article was adapted from Professor Beres's earlier presentation at the International Conference on the Holocaust and Genocide, Tel Aviv, Israel, June 1982.

30. The problem of reprisal as a rationale for the permissible use of force by states is identified explicitly and categorically in the UN Declaration of Principles of International Law Concerning Friendly Relations and Co-operation among States. Additionally, the prohibition of reprisals is deducible from the broad regulation of force in Article 2(4), the obligation to settle disputes peacefully in Article 2(3) and the general limiting of permissible force by states to self-defense.

31. On the faith-based genocidal threat from Iran, see especially Andrew Bostom, "Iran's Final Solution for Israel," *National Review Online*, February 10, 2012.

32. From the standpoint of international law, these preparations constitute planned *aggression* as well as genocide.

33. See D. F. Green, ed., *Arab Theologians On Jews And Israel: Extracts from the Proceedings of the Fourth Conference of the Academy of Islamic Research* (Geneva: 1976), p. 51; see also Robert S. Wistrich, *Antisemitism: The Longest Hatred* (New York: Pantheon Books, 1991), p. 230.

34. See Joan Peters, *From Time Immemorial: The Origins of the Arab-Jewish Conflict over Palestine* (London: 1984), pp. 436–437, which reproduces the Mufti's own account of his meeting with Hitler.

35. See Wistrich, *supra* note 33, p. 247; see also Y. Harkabi, *Arab Attitudes to Israel* (Jerusalem, 1971), p. 279.

36. It is important to recognize the jurisprudential fallacy of describing the disputed territories as "occupied." On this matter, see Louis René Beres and Paul Eidelberg, *Preserving the Land and People of Israel in the Face of "Disengagement": Obligations of Higher Law, International Law, and Torah Law*, Ariel Center for Policy Research, ACPR Policy Paper No. 158 (Israel, March 2005), 71 pp. See also Howard Grief, "Legal Rights and Title of Sovereignty of the Jewish People to the Land of Israel and Palestine under International Law," *Nativ Online*, a journal of politics and the arts, Israel, Vol. 2, 2004.

37. Palestinian hostility to Israel is ultimately oriented to removal of the Jewish State by both attrition and annihilation. This orientation has its doctrinal foundations in the PLO's "Phased Plan" of June 9, 1974. On this author's early opposition to the Oslo Accords, which were openly repudiated by the president of the Palestinian Authority in late September 2015, see Louis René Beres, "Why the Oslo Accords Should Be Abrogated by Israel," *American University Journal of International Law and Policy*, Vol. 12, No. 2, 1997, pp. 267–284.

38. These complex and nuanced expectations bring to mind Sun Tzu's well-known suggestion (in military matters) to embrace the "unorthodox." For a recent and specific application to Israel of Sun Tzu's ancient wisdom by this author, see Louis René Beres, "Lessons for Israel from Ancient Chinese Military Thought: Facing Iranian Nuclearization with Sun-Tzu," *Harvard National Security Journal*, Harvard Law School, posted online October 24, 2013.

39. Toward the end of 2015, much of this complexity concerned then-recent Russian air attacks in Syria, designed to protect the regime of Bashar al-Assad (actions, therefore, consistent with Iranian strategic preference in the Syrian civil war). During that period, Israeli Defense Minister Moshe Ya'alon had made it clear to Russia's President Vladimir Putin that Israel would continue to act in Syria to protect its own particular strategic interests and would not coordinate activities such as Syrian cross-border fire with Moscow. See Ya'alon, "We made it clear to Russia that Israel Will Continue to Protect Its Interests," *Unity Coalition for Israel*, October 1, 2015.

40. The law of armed conflict is largely concerned with the principle of *proportionality*, which has its jurisprudential and philosophic origins in the biblical *lex talionis*, the law of exact retaliation. The "eye for eye, tooth for tooth" can be found in three separate passages of the Jewish Torah and the Biblical Pentateuch.

41. The principle of military necessity has been defined authoritatively as follows: "Only that degree and kind of force, not otherwise prohibited by the law of armed conflict, required for the partial or complete submission of the enemy with a minimum expenditure of time, life, and physical resources may be applied." See US Navy, US Marine Corps, and US Coast Guard, *The Commander's Handbook on the Law of Naval Operations*, NWP 1-14M, Norfolk, Virginia, October 1995, p. 5-1.

42. The presumption of solidarity between states in the fight against crime gives rise to the increasingly important principle of *universal jurisdiction*. It is mentioned in the *Corpus Juris Civilis*; Grotius, *The Law of War and Peace* (1625), Book II, Chapter 20; and E. Vattel, *Le Droit Des Gens*, Book I, Chapter 19 (1758). The case for universal jurisdiction, which is strengthened whenever extradition is difficult or impossible to obtain, is also built into the four Geneva Conventions of August 12, 1949, which unambiguously impose on the High Contracting Parties the obligation to punish certain grave breaches of their rules regardless of where the infraction was committed or the nationality of the authors of the crimes.

43. This point had already been understood by Israeli strategist and IDF Military Intelligence Head, Yehoshafat Harkabi, in the mid-1960s. Writing in *Nuclear War and Nuclear Peace*, Harkabi indicated: "It must be emphasized that the impulse to act first, the competition to preempt, is not a result of aggressive tendencies or bloodlust on either side. It is a defensive action inherent in the very instability of an unfortunate situation, in which survival depends upon opening fire first, or, in other words, upon initiating a *surprise attack*." See Y. Harkabi, *Nuclear War and Nuclear Peace*, translated from the Hebrew, Israel Program for Scientific Translations, 1966, p. 42.

44. See, in this connection, classical observations by John Locke and Nicholas John Spykman. According to Locke: "In all states and conditions, the true remedy of force without authority, is to oppose force to it" (John Locke, *The Second Treatise of Civil Government*, Chapter XIII, Section 155); and quite similarly according to Nicholas John Spykman: "In a world of international anarchy, foreign policy must aim above all at the improvement or at least the preservation of the relative power position of the state" (Nicholas John Spykman, *America's Strategy in World Politics*. New York: Harcourt, Brace & Co., 1942, p. 41.

45. Under terms of the JCPOA, Iran can, among other things, (1) pursue the development of a nuclear device and key nuclear technologies, (2) prevent the inspection of military sites, and (3) maintain Arak as a heavy water and hence plutonium-capable facility. See Yigal Carmon, "What Iran Is Permitted to Do Under the JCPOA," *Mideast Outpost*, *MEMRI Daily Brief*, No. 57, September 17, 2015.

46. Apropos of Hobbes's argument that the state of nature is worse among individuals than among states, the philosopher Spinoza also suggested that "a commonwealth can guard itself against being subjugated by another, as a man in the state of nature cannot do." See A. G. Wernham, ed., *The Political Works, Tractatus Politicus*, iii, II, Clarendon Press, 1958, p. 295.

47. See Thomas Hobbes, *Leviathan* (1651), C.B. Macpherson, ed., Penguin Books, Middlesex, England (Viking, New York, 1968) Chapter XXI, p. 272.

48. See Jean Bodin, *The Six Bookes of a Commonweale*, ed., K. D. McRae (Cambridge, MA: Harvard University Press, 1962), p. 69.

49. "For it is the man who uses violence to spoil things, not the man who uses it to mend them, that is blameworthy." See *Discourses*, I, ix, (2).

50. See Timothy Walker's lecture, delivered at the Cincinnati College, November 4, 1837, in Perry Miller, ed., *The Legal Mind in America* (New York: Doubleday and Co., 1962), p. 243. Walker was a noted jurist and American legal scholar.

51. In the specifically Jewish tradition, God is unambiguously the source of all law. In this tradition, law is thus an aspect of the divine order of the cosmos. The Torah reflects both God's transcendence and His immanence.The ultimate basis of obligation to this law lies in its plainly timeless and overriding character.

52. Under international law, the idea of a Higher Law—drawn originally from the ancient Greeks and ancient Hebrews—is contained within the principle of *jus cogens* or peremptory norms. In the language of pertinent Article 53 of the Vienna Convention on the Law of Treaties (1969): "A peremptory norm of general international law . . . is a norm accepted and recognized by the international community of States as a whole, as a norm from which no derogation is permitted, and which can be modified only by a subsequent norm of general international law having the same character."

53. See *Israel's Strategic Future: The Final Report of Project Daniel*, Louis René Beres, Chair, Ariel Center for Policy Research, ACPR Policy Paper no. 155, ACPR, Israel,May 2004, p. 11. This final report of *Project Daniel* was delivered by hand to then Prime Minister Ariel Sharon on January 16, 2003.

SIX

Conclusion

Intellectual Daring and Strategic Wisdom

"In a dark time, the eye begins to see."

—Theodore Roethke

When the sculptor Auguste Rodin began the most ambitious project of his career in 1880—a pair of doors, deriving its theme from Dante's allegorical journey through hell—he was determined to create a distinctly personal vision of the underworld. Significantly, the artist's vision was intended to be far more complex than the one originally represented in the *Inferno.* Ultimately, Rodin's plaster composition developed to display an agonizing body of humanity, writhing desperately against an ever-changing background. The solitary tranquil form in this work is "The Thinker," who, from his notably lofty position in the lintel, broods sorrowfully but also contemplatively on the dreadful swarm below.

Rodin must have felt that *The Thinker* is both reviewing and reimagining the fate of our imperiled species.[1]

Then, as now, the background of the world, always in flux, was highlighted by an immeasurable vastness of man-made harms.[2]

Then, as now, it was up to The Thinker to seek and then identify suitable global alternatives.

In so doing, it is only the focused human mind, contemplative in its most capable and creative forms, that can point the way toward "salvation." For Israel, a tiny state living amid palpable chaos, the cumulative challenge of "mind over mind" is far more than a narrowly military or strategic issue,[3] but it still remains at the core a physical life or death challenge.

Nuclear strategy is a "game" that Israel's leaders can and must play. As we have just seen in substantial detail, this strategy and its underlying doctrine must remain an indispensable equalizer for such a perpetually beleaguered mini-state. Those who would suggest otherwise and merely prescribe business as usual in fashioning Jerusalem's pertinent security policies most resemble contemporary occupants of Plato's cave. Somehow deprived of a more genuinely illuminating vision of regional strategic reality, these unwitting dreamers are destined to live (or die) in a world of ever-twisting illusion. In any such patently misleading world, their particular notions of strategic truth must always remain little more than a deceiving shadow of images.

WHAT IS TO BE DONE?

Is it already too late for Israel? Is the Jewish State already destined to continue to seek safety in only a "shadow world"? There are, of course, those who would answer viscerally and in the affirmative. For them, both policy makers and scholars, looking at all essential matters objectively, the correct reply is obvious: "*Après nous, le déluge*," they advise.[4] Let us not think unpleasant thoughts. They are needless and would only disturb our sleep.

"We shall do what we have always done. That's all we can really do. And after all, we are still here. Isn't that proof enough for Israel?"

At the other end of this existential continuum are those who believe that it can literally never be too late for the Jewish State and that Israel need never worry. For them, as it is promised, the land and people of Israel shall be preserved forever under divine protection. Jerusalem, therefore, can proceed smugly, fearlessly, and without debilitating survival dread.

Here, consummate strategic truth is apparent and manifest: "Plainly, God Himself is Israel's supreme commander. God, of course, shall never choose to surrender or abandon His own 'chosen people.'"[5]

For Israel, however, going forward, at least in scientific analytical terms, neither polar position is ever apt to prove optimal or even adequate. For Israel, rather, the time is already at hand to think instead of new and more promising theoretical directions. "What is the good," inquires the Irish playwright Samuel Beckett, "of passing from one untenable position to another, of seeking justification always on the same plane?" Now is the time for Israel's leaders and senior military planners to look elsewhere along a variety of new dimensions and with a manifestly courageous willingness to look where they may have never even thought to look before.[6] More than anything else, as we have already observed, this means to acknowledge and operationalize the steadily expanding complexity of strategic theorizing, especially the multiple intersections and synergies of all relevant issues and concepts.

Ongoing chaos in the Middle East is creation in reverse. For Israel in particular, there are very special lessons to be learned from this growing and bewildering pattern of regional disintegration. Even chaos can have a more or less discernible geometry, and it must be Jerusalem's task to fathom what it is. In essence, for Israel, the geometry of chaos, in a strange and paradoxical symmetry, could reveal both sense and geostrategic form.

How, precisely, shall they be discovered by Israel?

Also important is that Israeli strategists begin these "geometric" inquiries with an apt awareness that, throughout history, warfare has had its many enthusiastic supporters. This observation, moreover, is manifestly pre-Islamic and antedates the specially threatening eschatologies of the Jewish State's current Arab (Sunni and Shiite) and Iranian foes. In his *The Transformation of War*, military historian Martin van Creveld is certainly correct in emphasizing humankind's seemingly irrational delight in the regular exertion of armed force. This well-documented observation from events taking place since time immemorial may be lamentable. But truth is exculpatory, and this specific truth provides a sorely needed corrective to the more widely popular and dangerous notions that no one really wants war.

THE "NOBODY WANTS WAR" FICTION: ORIGINS

Such generally erroneous presumptions may have their Western origins in the poetry of the Classical Age, the poetry of Pindar: "Sweet is war to him who knows it not, but to those who have made trial of it, it is a thing of fear." Similar sentiments may be uncovered in the less-than-exultant tone of the herald's tale of victory in the *Agamemnon*; the distinctly harsh words of Euripides for that very same victory in the *Troades*; and the poignant words of Pericles, referencing those who had perished in Samos: "It was as if the spring had been taken from the year."

Nonetheless, even before van Creveld, fellow military historian Michael Howard had correctly opined: "In Western Europe, until the first part of the seventeenth century, warfare was a way of life for a considerable section of society, its termination was for them a catastrophe, and its prolongation, official or unofficial, was the legitimate objective of every man of spirit." And in the eighteenth century, war was accepted by a great many as an essential and indispensable element of all social life, one that was needed to combat what the German philosopher Immanuel Kant had then called a "mere commercial spirit, and with it, a debasing self-interest."

Today, well into the Nuclear Age, it is unlikely that anyone could readily find similar levels of enthusiasm for war, but even now there do remain certain substantial and far-reaching eschatologies that contain distinctly welcoming ideas of "final battle," or "apocalypse."[7] This means, among other things, that ongoing nuclearization across the world is not likely to diminish simply because of the far greater destructiveness of modern warfare. While the expected spread of nuclear weapons need not necessarily correlate with any expanded interest in war making—after all, the core rationale for acquiring such weapons must be the creation of a credible national *deterrent*[8] —there could still be some meaningful and unpredictable exceptions. Moreover, as we have already discovered in this volume, even a world of well-intentioned nuclear weapons states could still make a variety of judgment errors and miscalculations, these "slips" leading perhaps inexorably to an unwitting nuclear exchange.

Now, nearly half a century after the five declared nuclear weapons states pledged "to pursue negotiations in good faith on effective measures relating to the cessation of the nuclear arms race at an early date, and to nuclear disarmament,"[9] all of the planet's nuclear-weapon states are busily modernizing their respective arsenals.[10] Not a single one of them seems remotely interested in eliminating its nuclear weapons, including the United States, led until January 2017 by a president who literally favors a "world free of nuclear weapons." Historically, in fact, only one state, South Africa, has ever actually chosen to denuclearize.

Analytically at least, the problem of reaching any sort of genuine nuclear disarmament agreements is a variant of the "tragedy of the commons." In this metaphor, no single state can ever accept the presumed "gainfulness" of disarming because (1) the calculated benefits of its own nuclear disarmament would require expectations of more or less general compliance, and (2) no single state could ever be sure that its own willingness to comply would be generally enough reciprocated. In essence, disarming one's own state must always be contingent on the (presumptively implausible) expectation that all states or perhaps just some critical number of other states will also comply.

THE COMPLEXITY OF ISRAEL'S NUCLEAR CHALLENGE AND STRATEGY

Israel, of course, is uniquely dependent on its nuclear weapons and strategy and could not even begin to rationally consider any prospects for regional nuclear arms control or disarmament. For the foreseeable future, Israel's plans for simple physical survival will need to be made contingent on properly maintaining these indispensable weapons and strategy. In this connection, the most urgent operational task for the country's senior military planners will concern deciphering the overwhelming complexity of all key decisional factors.

More than anything else, these planners will have to figure out multiple and intersecting scenarios of enemy intentions and capabilities, calculations that must take into account an ever-changing correlation of forces in the Middle East and also multiple variants of a presumptively optimal order of battle. Moreover, such determinations will need to consider both state and substate adversaries, often in assorted forms of alignment or adversarial competition with each other and, among other things, the prospective rationality or irrationality of all conceivable adversaries. To add yet another layer of complexity to the relevant equations, Jerusalem will need to ascertain a large and steadily growing number of possible synergies and/or cascades of synergies between (1) enemy threats, (2) possible Israeli responses to enemy threats, and (3) enemy threats and Israeli responses. The second listed obligation is sometimes described in more narrowly military parlance as a required search for "force multipliers."

About rendering careful assessments of a regional correlation of forces, IDF strategists and planners have likely begun to use this operational planning paradigm in certain creative and promising ways. Historically, a correlation of forces approach has been more or less usefully applied as a tangible measure of competitive armed forces, ranging from quantitative considerations at the subunit level and extending all the way up to major formations. It has also likely been used to compare resources and capabilities at both the operational levels of day-to-day strategy and the higher levels of "grand strategy." On occasion, this particular application has been plausibly related to the similar but less far-reaching military notion of "force ratios."

Looking ahead, Israel, now facing a broader and considerably more ominous variety of existential security threats originating from both state and substate adversaries, must undertake still broader and even more complex "correlation of forces" assessments. Strategic planners must in this newer and wider search obligation seek more than a traditionally *objective* yardstick for measuring all relevant enemy forces. Although IDF planners routinely compare all available data that concern both numerical and qualitative characteristics of enemy units, including personnel, weaponry, and equipment, field commanders will now also need to cultivate some more expressly *subjective* kinds of understanding. Such an unorthodox recommendation may appear to fly in the face of the usual military science emphasis on *facts*, but in war as well as in peace, these facts are often the result of purely personal and particular interpretations.

In exploiting a suitably improved concept of correlation of forces, Israel's senior planners will seemingly have to reject a basic axiom of mathematics. From now on, they will need to recognize that some truly critical force measurements must always remain imprecise but that the unavoidable imprecision may still itself include certain important forms of military insight and understanding. A good example of this phenomenon is what has been discussed throughout this book. A particular enemy's consuming dedication to certain presumed religious expectations—that is, his theologically inspired strength of will, which may be utterly uncompromising—could resist all traditional forms of measurement but still remain determinative. In Israeli military assessments, as in human psychology generally, there exist certain variables that are stubbornly refractory to all measurement but are still of very great importance.

CHAOS, RATIONALITY, AND PALESTINE

Several developing hazards to Israel's national security will be shaped at least in part by a discernible geometry of chaos. Within this delicately balanced and largely unprecedented set of more or less precise calculations, the whole may turn out to be more or less than the arithmetic sum of its parts. This means, among many things, that purposeful military planning, including even deterrence, must sometimes take account of enemy irrationality and should also allow meaningful distinctions to be made between irrationality and pretended irrationality.

The very same questions of rationality and irrationality will need to be asked with reference to Israel's own declarations of security policy. On occasion, therefore, IDF planners will need to decide whether Israel could be better served in both its deterrence and war-fighting needs by deliberately projecting the image of limited or partial irrationality. However counterintuitive, Israel could sometimes benefit from having its enemies believe that Jerusalem would be willing to act more or less irrationally.

From the time of the Second Lebanon War (2006), a US Air Force Effects-Based Approach to Operations (EBAO) has likely been employed by the Israel Air Force. Usually, EBAO is described as a new and more audacious paradigm for secure military operations—that is, as an alternative to more traditional destruction-based targeting and corollary target-based operations. With this paradigm, instead of focusing on destruction and enemy attrition per se, a state's military forces are consciously and conspicuously deployed to wage "parallel warfare."

Such an orientation seeks, above all, to motivate enemies to act according to one's own (here, *Israel's* own) overriding strategic interests. Ideally, EBAO could permit Israel's own forces to achieve their objectives without combat of any kind, thereby fulfilling Sun Tzu's ancient dictum in *The Art of War*: "Supreme excellence consists of breaking the enemy's resistance without fighting."

Applied to air operations, an EBAO strategy could encourage Israel to supplant more standard forms of series warfare, hence to no longer prepare to necessarily attack enemy target sets in a prescriptively linear sequence.

By its willingness to consider such seemingly eccentric kinds of advice, Israel could be better positioned to seize every available opportunity for greater security. This would include assorted intelligence and counterintelligence functions. Inevitably, these specialized functions will be needed to complement more expressly military and strategic moves.

Once again, Israeli strategists and planners will need to keep in mind the intersection of Palestinian statehood issues and the country's nuclear doctrine. Considered by itself, of course, a Palestinian state would seem to have no bearing on Israel's nuclear strategy. Yet, as we have already seen, Palestine—though foreseeably nonnuclear itself—could still substantially diminish the Jewish State's capacity to wage most usable forms of conventional war. In turn, this consequential diminution of escalation dominance could progressively enlarge Israel's incentive to rely on nuclear weapons and doctrine in assorted circumstances.

Any future Palestinian state, even one that somehow was able to avoid takeover by more expressly Jihadist insurgents (e.g., ISIS), would nonetheless remain committed to elimination of Israel. On exactly the same day that he signed the 1993 Declaration of Principles (Oslo l), Yasser Arafat addressed the Palestinian people on Jordanian television. There, he assured his listeners that the new agreement was nothing more than a tactically codified implementation of the prior (1974) PLO "Plan of Phases"—that is, a ten-point program designed for the purposefully incremental annihilation of the State of Israel.

The first stage, said Arafat, was "the establishment of a national authority on any part of Palestinian soil that is liberated or from which the Israelis withdraw."[11] The very same assertion was repeated by Chairman Arafat after the signing of Oslo II. These openly belligerent assertions, especially when considered together with Israel's unambiguous legal right to survive, its corollary obligation to punish terrorist crimes, and the PLO's persistent breach of all extant agreements with the Jewish State,[12] clarify beyond a reasonable doubt that Palestine could become an integral and enthusiastic part of the overall existential threat facing Israel.

Regarding this threat, there are other more specifically Jewish and Israeli factors to consider. An historic *halachic* (Jewish law) opinion, issued in 1995 by prominent rabbis in Israel, is meaningfully consistent with antecedent natural law and international law. The ruling in this particular matter stipulated, "It is forbidden, under any circumstances, to hand over parts of *Eretz Yisrael* (the Land of Israel) to Arabs."[13] This position was linked to the *halachic* principle of *Pikuach Nefesh*, which emphasizes the broader and overriding Jewish obligation to save Jewish lives. Under no circumstances, says *Pikuach Nefesh*, can Israel knowingly place its civilian citizens in a position of "life or death."[14]

Significantly too, the rabbinic argument here recalls (first prime minister) David Ben-Gurion's warning at the Twenty-First Zionist Congress in Basel, Switzerland (1937):

> No Jew has the right to relinquish the rights of the Jewish Nation in the Land of Israel. No Jew has the authority to do so. No Jewish body has such authority. Even the whole Jewish people—alive today—has no authority to relinquish any part whatsoever of the Land. This is the right of the Jewish Nation, in all its generations, a right which may not be forfeited under any condition. Even if, there would be, at some time, those who would announce that they give up this right, they have neither the power nor the authority to deprive future generations of this right. The Jewish Nation is neither obligated nor bound by any such relinquishment. Our right to the Land—to this entire land—is valid and enduring forever, and until the full and complete redemption is carried out, we shall not budge from this historic right.

Plainly, of course, those particular Israeli prime ministers who gave their blessings to the Oslo Agreements,[15] as well as several others, did seek to "budge" from this "historic right." The Palestinian response, a relentless cycle of war and terror against Jewish civilians, continues unabated to the present day. This response is part of a much broader pattern of region-wide chaos, a pattern that embraces both state and substate adversaries in a densely variegated pastiche of utterly willful violence.

ISRAEL, TERRORISTS, STRATEGY, AND THE LAW OF WAR

All too frequently complementing this chaos are various conceptual and political "confusions" among Israel's few allies, especially the United States. Again and again whenever Israel very reluctantly resorts to assorted and indispensable counterterrorist operations, the predictable response from Washington is a ritualistic and ill-informed warning not to use "excessive force." In law, of course, judgments of "proportionality" do not require tangible measures of equivalence. Rather these judgments when correct have to do with using the least amount of force that is needed to accomplish a defensibly legitimate goal. Moreover, these judgments do not automatically indict those military or police forces that must unwittingly kill or injure noncombatants if transpiring during the inherently proper obligation to supply essential national self-defense.

Whenever a terrorist adversary deliberately inserts its own civilians near its military assets or vice versa, it is committing "perfidy." Reciprocally, such a codified and customary war crime, when it is committed by a terror group and not by the state actually firing its weapons, is exculpatory for that state. During the so-called Third Intifada in the autumn of 2015, hundreds of individual Palestinians, spurred on by official PA incitement, went on stabbing sprees across Israel. When Israel understandably responded by neutralizing the criminals, the United States and others cautioned against the use of excessive force. Ironically, one such warning was issued just a week or so after US bombs struck a hospital in

Afghanistan, killing and wounding several dozen human rights and medical workers from Doctors Without Borders.

Credo quia absurdum (I believe because it is absurd). Historically, the United States, notably during the Obama years—and often while American forces were themselves unwittingly killing and wounding large numbers of noncombatants in Syria, Iraq, or Afghanistan—insistently blamed Israel for alleged violations of humanitarian international law (the law of armed conflict). As Hamas, Hezbollah, Islamic Jihad, and PA's Fatah routinely and very deliberately place Arab civilians in harm's way, any legal responsibility for harm that comes to these civilians always belongs exclusively to these substate terror organizations and not to Israel's reciprocally obligatory self-defense efforts.

For Israel, the effective operationalization of counterterrorism measures ultimately presents an even more difficult problem than the pertinent jurisprudential issues. Again, during the autumn of 2015, assorted Palestinian terror organizations, operating in the West Bank (Judea/Samaria), Gaza, and Israel proper (within the "green lines"), began a Third Intifada. In response, Israel mobilized a huge fraction of its military and police agencies, but its task was made even more difficult than usual because of the peculiarly insidious form of this newest "uprising."

Then, seemingly isolated individuals were randomly assaulting Jews on the streets—men, women, and children—indiscriminately, solely with a view to bringing pain and death to Israel. This explosion of grotesquely personal violence was not inspired by any meaningful hopes for a two-state solution (always subterfuge), as the Palestinian Authority and Hamas had earlier declared an end to any residual peace process. Rather, these assaults were motivated, as all Palestinian violence had always been animated, by the "sacred" search for a *one-state solution*. For the terrorists and their supporters, this one state, of course, could be only "Palestine."

For present analytic purposes, of course, our concern with Palestinian terrorism is oriented to the much larger picture of Israel's nuclear strategy. We have already seen that such terrorism, considered together with assorted and more or less intersecting risks of conventional war, could produce an overall weakening of Israel's security posture, especially if it results in a Palestinian state. This weakening in turn could prod various adversaries, either acting singly or in some form of collaboration with each other, to create conditions wherein Israel's nuclear deterrent could become increasingly relevant or perhaps even vital.

On the purely operational side of things—a side that would intend to keep conflict to a level wherein expressly nuclear threats would never need to be actually invoked by Israel—remedies can range from training and employing counterterrorism surrogates in different theaters of conflict, to sending IDF units to terror-basing enemy countries, to making a more systematic use of standoff weapons. The first example would include participation in the training of sympathetic and capable proxies in certain surrounding or nearby states (in principle at least, states that are either friend or foe), but this remedy can entail substantial risks, as is most plainly evident with the endlessly overwhelming US difficulties in controlling ISIS terror advances in Syria.[16]

The second example would be represented by Israel's Lebanon wars, periodic efforts intended to protect mostly the north of Israel from the Shiite militia, Hezbollah. Today, the rocket arsenals of this substate terror organization are perhaps much larger than those of enemy Arab states. At the same time, the very categorization of a state as an "enemy state of Israel," is no longer easy to determine. To wit, the greater danger to Israel from Syria is not from Bashar al-Assad's remaining army and air force but rather from ISIS and Hezbollah activities being mobilized within a rapidly disintegrating Syria.[17]

Historically, since the 1967 war, Israel has been appropriately wary of returning the Golan Heights to Syria but, for the most part, because of understandably direct concerns about the belligerent Damascus regime itself. Now, the Assad regime threat, *per se*, is less worrisome in Jerusalem than certain substate harms that could come from that same direction either from regime proxies (e.g., Hezbollah) or from regime enemies (e.g., ISIS). Operationally, this means that going forward Israel's principal security concerns in this area will have to focus even more specifically on the expanding terror threat. Should such a focus not succeed, there would be a greater chance for Israel of suffering dilution of its "escalation dominance" and, correspondingly, certain heightened probabilities of full-fledged conventional wars. Incrementally in such tangibly diminished security circumstances, Israel's nuclear strategy could at some level more likely come into play.

Regarding the use of standoff weapons for counterterrorism purposes, such measures could be of at least conceivably good use in this era of continuing asymmetrical conflicts.[18] To achieve desired "overbalance," standoff weapons could sometimes require additional elements or force-multiplying conditions, and even then could sometimes confer advantages for only a limited period of time. Historically, the prospectively limited time period to enjoy any tactical advantage exists because sometimes these weapons could also be acquired by the enemy.

Today, in confrontations with a determined terrorist adversary, that enemy is less likely to actually "catch up" with such weapons. At the same time, simply by eliciting an Israeli response where standoff weapons are employed, a terrorist enemy could consider itself the victor. From the standpoint of traditional media coverage of Palestinian terrorism and Israel counterterrorism, where all considerations of a reasonable media judgment are cast to the winds, this point should neither be difficult to understand nor should it be dismissed out of hand.

Conceptually, the way to achieve an overbalance is by utilizing increasingly effective and progressively longer firing ranges. For planned air combat encounters, Israel should continue to develop air-to-air missiles that offer superior launching ranges and performance envelopes. In urban counterterrorism settings, Israel can emphasize assorted laser and electromagnetic wave systems as a useful standoff option; these would be nonlethal but still prospectively helpful and cost effective. However, all such technical and technological requirements notwithstanding, the overall challenge faced by the Jewish State—a challenge that could at some time rise to authentically existential levels—will also have to be met at far "softer," less quantifiable, and more broadly intellectual and psychological levels.

RECONCEPTUALIZING ENEMY FORCE THREATS

In his 1988 book, *The Art of the Novel*, Czech writer Milan Kundera describes a sheer force of violence in the world that "wills to assert itself" as force. He proceeds to describe this unfocused force as "naked, as naked as in Kafka's novels. . . . The aggressivity of this force is thoroughly disinterested; unmotivated; it wills only its own will. It is *pure irrationality*." While such a diagnosis is likely not yet a plausible depiction of what is generally happening in world politics, it is not far off the mark in the Middle East. There, where already nuclear superpowers are being held at bay by medieval-style warriors harboring premedieval points of view, the entire meaning of international power may soon need to be refigured and reconceptualized.

"For it is by wise counsel," Israel may learn from *Proverbs* (24:6): "Thou shalt make thy war." But in all related efforts at strategic theorizing, one truly underlying issue cannot be disregarded. This is the always antecedent question of human nature, especially the seemingly flawed character of an entire species and its discernible connections to any actual Israeli nuclear posture. Although international relations theory and strategic theory have long been focused on a struggle for power, this focus, while basically correct, is also trivial. Ultimately, it is what underlies this visible struggle—that is, the individual human being's most private apprehensions, anxieties, needs, and terrors—that gives core direction to any global region's tangibly chaotic disintegration.

Ultimately, unless we learn how to "fix" this individual human being at the subpolitical or "molecular" level, chaos or inclinations to chaos will never quite go away.

The German philosopher Immanuel Kant once remarked: "Out of timber so crooked as that from which man is made, nothing entirely straight can be built."[19] If Kant was correct—and there is every good reason to suppose such correctness—there is still little that can actually be done about its indictment on any practical or operational level. Surely, the transformation of an enemy's individual human nature is not a proper task for Israeli nuclear planners, nor, for that matter, for any other imperiled state's strategic planning community. Nonetheless, the eternal threat of "The Other" is so generic in world politics and is now becoming so irrepressibly primary in the Middle East that it must become the critical task of all serious strategic thinkers to at least take pertinent individual human traits into some analytic account.

Moving forward, Israel's nuclear theorists must always avoid any hint of believing that Reason necessarily governs the strategic world. Although by definition, strategies of deterrence must always include certain basic assumptions of rationality, it is also clear that much of what is likely to happen regarding war and peace will lie far beyond the comforting rules of logical inference.[20] More precisely, these results are apt to stem from the universally compelling need of individuals *not to die*—that is, to welcome any reassurances of personal immortality. And where can individuals throughout the Islamic Middle East expect such seductive promises? From faith, of course, but also from various state and substate bodies that presume to represent God in His more expressly mundane planetary duties. Here, of course, Iran and ISIS should most immediately come to mind.

How do these states and terror organizations sustain the incomparable promise of immortality? One principal way, as we may readily witness daily, is through the enthusiastic legitimization of killing and murdering of "others." While not a social scientist, aptly renowned playwright and thinker Eugene Ionesco wrote in his *Journal* (1966):

> I must kill my visible enemy, the one who is determined to take my life, to prevent him from killing me. Killing gives me a feeling of relief, because I am dimly aware that in killing him, I have killed death. My enemy's death cannot be held against me, it is no longer a source of anguish, if I killed him with the approval of society: that is the purpose of war. Killing is a way of relieving one's feelings, of warding off one's own death.

There is a deeply insightful observation and complex idea in this passage. It is the notion that killing can confer an immunity from one's own mortality. This seductive idea of death as somehow a zero-sum commodity is captured best in psychologist Ernest Becker's paraphrase of Elias Canetti: "Each organism raises its head over a field of corpses, smiles into the sun, and declares life good." Similarly, in his *Will Therapy and Truth and Reality*, psychologist Otto Rank affirms: "The death fear of the ego is lessened by the killing, the Sacrifice, of the Other. Through the death of the Other, one buys oneself free from the penalty of being killed."

In the best of all possible worlds, human beings all over the planet, not only in the Islamic Middle East, could follow the Spanish philosopher

Miguel de Unamuno's vital words: "to consider our mortal destiny without flinching." But this is certainly not yet the best of all possible worlds and, expectedly, Israel's principal enemies will continue to flee from any prospect of personal death as the very prototype of evil. It follows, however reluctantly, that Israel's strategic thinkers will still have to plan accordingly.

Truth, we have seen repeatedly in this volume, can sometimes be counterintuitive. Normally, faith and reason struggle mightily against each other, and today, in the Islamic Middle East, any prospective triumph of faith must ordinarily suggest a corollary triumph of war and terror. Nonetheless, in his great modern classic, *The Decline of the West*, Oswald Spengler had already understood that religion can potentially overcome otherwise-threatening death fears and religious faith can also become part of the solution, not just the problem. Here, says Spengler, somewhat paradoxically, faith can represent "the beginning of all man's *intellectual* life."[21] These remote forms of understanding are never obvious[22] and must always remain inconspicuous and bewilderingly complex, but that does not mean that they ought necessarily to be ignored.[23]

But how not to ignore? This is a staggering task to place before Israel's political leadership and strategic planners (a task, by the way, that will also need to be assigned to national leaderships elsewhere, especially in Washington), but it is no longer arguable that deeper forms of strategic understanding should be left exclusively to the philosophers. All war, we have already noted, calls for a determined triumph of "mind over mind," not just mind over matter, and this utterly rudimentary form of triumph calls for much more than merely technical or operational kinds of understanding.

In the end, this call will require Israel to deal with its most relentlessly murderous enemies at much higher intellectual levels of planning—that is, not just to counter their most fearful weapon systems and alignments[24] but also their determinably core inclinations to do harm to others. This firm obligation will make the strategists' task much harder, but the alternatives are simply unacceptable.

Simultaneously, as we have gleaned from continually referencing Sun Tzu to von Clausewitz, and beyond, Israel must continue to fashion its nuclear strategy with an overriding commitment to use its military power purposefully and judiciously. The principal problem will be to figure out what exactly should constitute such use. For example, to a significant extent the enemies of Israel, both state and substate, will continue to take their unequivocal anti-Israel stance on a ground of a willful irrationalism. More or less disinterested in any classical definitions of "security communities" or "balances of power," these particular enemies will never be satisfied with mere transfers of land or with accepting any generous expressions of compromise. At times, these enemies will be interested far more in means than in ends, in satisfying the viscerally primal (and presumptively life-extending) passions of mass killing and wanton destruction.

Planning ahead, therefore, Israel's nuclear strategists will need to inquire: How, precisely, can Israel's nuclear assets perform optimally against these seemingly unfathomable threats? This is not to suggest that nuclear assets would in any way assume a "lead responsibility" here but rather that they can and must be used creatively and selectively to complement all other suitable strategic assets. For the most part—in a theme that has recurred pointedly throughout this book—such use should focus on deterrence *ex ante,* not revenge *ex post.*

RETURNING TO THE CORE: ISRAEL'S NUCLEAR STRATEGY AS A JEWISH PROBLEM

In the final analysis, Israel's leaders must never forget that in the eyes of its many enemies, Israel represents the individual Jew in macrocosm. With such an inherently hateful representation, ordinary policies of promise and reward and incentive and disincentive may not have ordinary results. Then, it will be of very great importance that Israel's overall strategic posture—including, especially, its residual nuclear component—be fashioned with an exquisite attention to detail and creative opportunity. Yet again it becomes apparent that this will remain for Israel a relentless struggle of "mind over mind."

Earlier, we noted Emmerich de Vattel's notion of "mutual aid" among the nations,[25] but Israel is already aware that this eighteenth-century principle has little or no connection to the twenty-first century. This means, at least in the short and intermediate term, a strategic planning model that would reflect actual principles and passions of all adversaries in the region, including the complex intersections or synergies between them. While capably rejecting all idealized visions of any "New Middle East" (crudely naive visions that have in fact been periodically incorporated into Israel's overall foreign policy), this model must reluctantly affirm that these adversaries, crouched for so long in a self-imposed and bruising darkness, are apt to remain facedown to life for *any* Jewish State—at least for the foreseeable future.

In 1882, Leo Pinsker, a Jewish physician of Odessa, horrified by the pogroms of 1881 (not very different from the assorted Arab pogroms still being launched today in Israel), concluded that anti-Semitism is an incurable psychosis. The best remedy, he adduced at that time, must be for all Jews to accept the fixed obligations of self-help. Later, Theodore Herzl, after witnessing the tragic spectacle of anti-Semitism in the affairs of Alfred Dreyfus, in France, authored *The Jewish State.* In an attempt to solve once and for all "The Jewish Question," Herzl premised his new pamphlet on the following thesis: The nations in whose midst Jews live are all either covertly or openly anti-Semitic. This meant, he proceeded, that a perfectly simple plan was needed: "Let the sovereignty be granted us over a portion of the globe large enough to satisfy the rightful requirements of a nation; the rest we shall manage for ourselves."

The necessary grant of sovereignty did eventually take place, in May 1948, but there has been nothing "simple" about Israel's short history. Although the amount of land designated for a Jewish State (a portion much smaller than what had originally been pledged by all pertinent international treaties and declarations) was smaller than the amount of land taken up by certain counties in California, the world generally continues to begrudge Israel even this miniscule portion. In the region itself, pressures continue for the creation of a twenty-third Arab state, a state of Palestine, to be carved from the still-living but markedly tiny body of Israel. In the end, such pressures could play a palpable and very tangible role in generating both nuclear terrorism and nuclear war.

Left to themselves, neither preempted nor deterred, certain Islamic enemies of Israel—especially after any further codifications of Palestinian statehood—could bring the Jewish State face to face with the torments of Dante's *Inferno*, "Into the eternal darkness, into fire, into ice." There is no systematic or scientific way to ascertain just how probable any such portent might actually be, but Israeli security at this point represents far more than an esoteric mathematical problem. Rather, it is already plainly knowable that the combination of regional nuclear proliferation with Palestinian statehood would create overwhelmingly negative force multipliers for Israel and Jerusalem must therefore prepare to deal with these intersecting threats on a coherent and unified basis.

To best satisfy such a staggering requirement, Israel's leaders must probe deeply the prospective benefits of the country's nuclear strategy and exploit these benefits in the interest of protecting the state from all manner of existential harms. One such way that will warrant much closer examination and possibly less deliberate ambiguity must concern Israel's long naval arm, especially its submarine fleet. More than likely, the INS (Israeli Navy submarine) *Tanin*, an air-independent propulsion *Dolphin*-class submarine, could destroy much of the entire Middle East with a single salvo of nuclear missiles. For the moment, of course, there can be no assurances that *Tanin*'s missiles will even be nuclear or that there could necessarily be any optimal correlation between the total destructive power of these weapons and Israeli security. Also unclear is that Israeli submarines would ever be armed with weapons other than torpedoes and surface-to-surface missiles—that is, with nuclear-capable *cruise missiles*. What is certain, however, is that the *Dolphin* submarines are the single most expensive weapon system in the IDF arsenal—more expensive than even the F-35 stealth fighter—and that the *Dolphin*-force mission will ultimately coalesce around critical issues of Israeli nuclear deterrence.[26]

Taken together with other more or less visible components of Israel's nuclear posture, the country's submarine force could provide an example of distinctly positive force multipliers. Here, of course, Israel faces the very same zero-sum budgetary constraints now facing the United States and every other nuclear or near-nuclear state. Simultaneously within Israel, the navy generally, and the submarine component in particular, must always prepare to cooperate operationally with the Israel Air Force (IAF), the IDF Intelligence Directorate, the Mossad, and also assorted IDF special operations units.[27] Again, depending on how such exceedingly complex forms of cooperation might actually materialize or "synergize," there could be generated some corollary and substantially valuable force multipliers.

"In a dark time," says the American poet Theodore Roethke, "the eye begins to see."[28] For Israel, it is most important that what is seen includes what is also lying latent, "below the surface," and can be harnessed in the perpetually overriding interest of national survival. In the end, Israel's continuance amid growing chaos will depend on the adequacy and audacity of its core nuclear strategy and the antecedent understanding that such strategy must always reflect the triumph of mind over mind.

In the end, of course, there can be no fully meaningful assurances. Even the correct linking of strategic responsibility to intellectual effort can never overcome Clausewitz's still valid concern for "friction" or the utterly critical distinction between "real war and war on paper."[29] Israeli strategists already understand, with Clausewitz, that their planning should never be reduced to any reassuringly fixed set of quantitative rules or principles, and that they should also bear in mind that a very deliberate audacity could sometimes prove indispensable.

By definition, uncertainty and lack of clarity must remain an integral part of Israeli strategizing amid chaos, but this foreseeable constant need not necessarily become an impediment to policy. Once again, Clausewitz can serve as a timeless mentor, even in the nuclear age: "In war . . . all action is aimed at probable rather than certain success. The degree of certainty that is lacking must in every case be left to fate, chance, or whatever you like to call it. . . . But we should not habitually prefer the course that involves the least uncertainty. That would be an enormous mistake. . . . There are times when the utmost daring is the height of wisdom."[30]

NOTES

1. With such feelings, Rodin would hardly have been the first to inquire about the fate of such a manifestly destructive species. Note, for example, the relevant queries of an ancient Greek tragedian: "Where will it end? When will it all be lulled back into sleep, and cease, the bloody hatred, the destruction?" (1 *The Complete Aeschylus: The Oresteia* 146, Peter Burian and Alan Shapiro, eds., 2nd ed., 2011).

2. See, on such vastness, Seneca, 1st Century CE: "We are mad, not only individuals, but nations also. We restrain manslaughter and isolated murders, but what of war, and the so-called glory of killing whole peoples? . . . Man, the gentlest of animals, is not ashamed to glory in blood-shedding, and to wage war when even the beasts are living in peace together" (*Letters*, 95).

3. Another significant part of this challenge is the special role and responsibility of Israel's intelligence community. See on this point, Louis René Beres, "Israel's Strategic Doctrine: Updating Intelligence Community Responsibilities," *International Journal of Intelligence and Counterintelligence*, Vol. 28, No. 1, Spring 2015, 89–104.

4. Such a view might be nurtured by the plausible expectation of further regional nuclear proliferation and the philosopher Thomas Hobbes's previously cited understanding of "nature" (chaos) as that condition where "the weakest has strength enough to kill the strongest." (*Leviathan*, Chapter XIII). This is because nuclear weapons spread would bring the international system into ever closer and more dreadful alignment with the condition of true anarchy suffered among individuals in nature.

5. On the promise of eternality for Israel as an expressly Jewish State, note scripture: "And I will ratify My covenant between Me and you and between your offspring after you throughout their generations, as an everlasting covenant, to be a God to you, and to your offspring after you; and I will give to you and to your offspring after you, the land of your sojourns, the whole of the land of Canaan, as an everlasting possession" (*Bereshit* 17:7, 8).

6. This statement is not meant to suggest any Israeli abandonment of scripture-based beliefs (that would, of course, be presumptuous), but only to argue more pragmatically that Israel's survival imperatives must also demand dispassionate and deeply analytic strategic calculations. "Behold," we find in Psalm 121:4, "he that keepeth Israel shall neither slumber nor sleep," but this ought not to be taken as an excuse for Israel not to prepare itself. That overriding responsibility continues always, whatever "God's promise."

7. Ironically, the very idea of an apocalypse seems to have been born in ancient Iran (Persia) with the Manichaeism of the Zoroastrians. However, similarly Manichean ideas can also be found in the Jewish Dead Sea Scroll, subsequently named "The War of the Sons of Light Against the Sons of Darkness." This elucidating document, discovered in a Qumran cave in 1947, reveals a comprehensive description of Jewish military tactics and regulations at the end of the Second Commonwealth. The Sons of Light were expected to prevail in battle against the Sons of Darkness before the "end of days," and the later fight at Masada was widely interpreted as a genuinely apocalyptic struggle between a saintly few and the wicked many.

8. This rationale, of course, is a special case of Sun Tzu's more general advice—that is, the very best way to protect oneself from an enemy is always without actually having to use one's available armed force.

9. See Nuclear Nonproliferation Treaty, 1968.

10. Rather than constraining the role of American nuclear weapons, President Barack Obama's nuclear weapons employment strategy reaffirmed the extant posture of a nuclear triad on high alert. The United States has been modernizing its nuclear arsenal primarily by upgrading existing weapon systems rather than by deploying altogether new types of such weapons. The ICBM force is in a final phase of a decade-long $8 billion modernization program. Beginning in 2017, the US Navy will start to deploy a modified version of the Trident II D-5 submarine-launched ballistic missile. The US Air Force has already begun life extension programs for its air-launched cruise missile, as well as for the B-2 and B-52 bombers. In any event, apparently US nuclear modernization efforts and plans undercut the publicly stated US goal of achieving "bold reductions" in Russian and US nonstrategic nuclear weapons in Europe and "to create the conditions for a world without nuclear weapons." For more on these complex and interpenetrating "great power" strategic issues, see Hans M. Kristensen, "Nuclear Weapons Modernization a Threat to the NPT?" *Arms Control Today*, Arms Control Association, September 2015.

11. See "Solid Paper Facts," editorial, *The Jerusalem Post*, International Edition, October 7, 1995, p. 10.

12. For earlier elucidations of this argument by this author, see Louis René Beres, "International Law Requires Prosecution, Not Celebration, of Arafat," *University of Detroit Mercy Law Review*, Vol. 71, No. 3, Spring 1994, pp. 569–580. See also Louis René Beres, "Israel's Survival Imperatives: The Oslo Agreements in International Law and National Strategy," Ariel Center for Policy Research, Israel, Policy Paper No. 102, 2000, 110 pp.; Louis René Beres, "Implications of a Palestinian State for Israeli Security and Nuclear War: A Jurisprudential Assessment," *Dickinson Journal of International Law*, Vol. 17, No. 2, Winter 1999, pp. 229–286; Louis René Beres, "Israel After Fifty: The Oslo Agreements, International Law, and National Survival," *The Connecticut Journal of International Law*, Vol. 14, No. 1, Summer 1999, pp. 27–81; Louis René Beres, "Israel's Freeing of Terrorists Violates International Law," *Journal of Counterterrorism and Security International*, Winter 1999, Vol. 5, No. 4, pp. 44–46; Louis René Beres, "The Oslo Agreements in International Law, Natural Law, and World Politics," *Arizona Journal of International and Comparative Law*, Vol. 14, No. 3, pp. 715–746; and Louis René Beres, "Why the Oslo Accords Should Be Abrogated by Israel," *American University Journal of International Law and Policy*, Vol. 12, No. 2, 1997, pp. 267–284.

13. The full text of this historic opinion, *Das Torah*, was published in the July 20, 1995, issue of *The Jerusalem Post*, p. 3.

14. Classical secular (not specifically Jewish) political theory also emphasizes every government's primary obligation to provide security for its citizens. Most famously perhaps is the statement of seventeenth-century Englishman Thomas Hobbes in Chapter XXI of *Leviathan*: "The obligation of subjects to the sovereign is understood to last so long, and no longer, than the power lasteth by which he is able to protect them." As an interesting side note, one of Israel's Dolphin-class submarines is the INS (Israeli Navy Submarine) *Leviathan*.

15. Oslo II was signed at the White House on September 28, 1995. Oslo I was signed at the same US venue on September 12, 1993. Neither accord took the form of an authentic treaty under international law—that is, under terms of the Vienna Convention on the Law of Treaties.

16. In September 2015, the US general running Central Command, the Pentagon's Middle East command, testified before the Senate Armed Services Committee that the number of Syrian anti-ISIS rebels trained under a $500 million program had managed to produce a total of *four* actual fighters. At such a cost of over $100 million per trainee, this is not apt to be an attractively cost-effective remedy for Israel.

17. It also ought to be recalled that, earlier, North Korea had helped Syria build a nuclear reactor, the same facility that was ultimately destroyed by Israel in its Operation Orchard, on September 6, 2007. Although operationally unlike earlier Operation Opera, this preemptive attack in the Deir ez-Zor region was presumptively a second expression of the so-called "Begin Doctrine." It also illustrated, because of the North Korea connection, a much wider *global* threat to Israel.

18. For an authoritative and fully informed treatment of such weapons and related measures, see David Ivry, "Stand-Off Fire: The Feasibility of Overbalance and the Deterrence Aspect," *Israel Defense*, December 24, 2014. MG Ivry (IDF/ret.) is a former Israeli Ambassador to the United States and Israel Air Force Commander. He was IAF Commander at the time of the Osiraq raid in Iraq on June 7, 1981.

19. The original German is, "Aus so krummem Holze, als woraus der Mensch gemacht ist, kann nichts ganz Gerades gezimmert warden." See Isaiah Berlin, *The Crooked Timber of Humanity*, xi (Henry Handy, ed., 1991) (quoting Immanuel Kant, *Idee Zu Einer Allgemeinen Geschichte In Weltburgerlicher Absicht* (1784).

20. "But men love abstract reasoning and neat systematization," observes Fyodor Dostoyevsky, in his *Notes from Underground*, "so much that they think nothing of distorting the truth, closing their eyes and ears to contrary evidence to preserve their logical constructions."

21. Says Spengler: "'I believe' is the great word against metaphysical fear, and at the same time it is a promising avowal of love." See *The Decline of the West*, his illuminating chapter on "Pythagoras, Mohammed, Cromwell."

22. These forms can also be encountered in the writings of the great Spanish existentialist Miguel de Unamuno, especially his discussion of "The Hunger of Immortality," in *Tragic Sense of Life* (1921). In essence, Unamuno had understood that passion need not undercut rational thought and that universal hunger for immortality can actually be turned into a universal conscience. This is not the stuff of ordinary strategic/military discourse, but it just as surely ought not continue to be ignored by strategists. In short, the time is now at hand for undertaking a quantum intellectual leap in dealing with strategic problems, most plainly in Israel.

23. "Whenever the new Muses present themselves," says that other (than Miguel de Unamuno) great Spanish existentialist philosopher, José Ortega y Gasset, "the masses bristle." See Ortega y Gasset, *The Dehumanization of Art* (1925) (Princeton: Princeton University Press, 1948, 1968), p. 7.

24. Notwithstanding formal expectations of the July 14, 2015, pact with Iran—the Joint Comprehensive Plan of Action, or JCPOA—Iran continued unabated with its seemingly irreversible nuclear ambitions. Already in mid-October 2015, the Commander of the Islamic Revolutionary Guards Aerospace Force, Brigadier General Amir Ali Hajizadeh, declared that the IRGC planned to replace its solid and liquid fuel long-range missiles with an upgraded new generation in 2016. While BG Hajizadeh underscored that "[t]oday, all surface-to-surface missiles are fully built in Iran," the Islamic Republic also continued to buy advanced military equipment from Russia, especially satellite-related equipment and assorted military aircraft. Further, according to Iranian Vice President Sorena Sattari, in late August 2015, Tehran was very interested in using Russian rocket carriers to launch satellites into orbit. On these issues, see "IRGC to Introduce New Generation Missile," *Tehran Times*, October 17, 2015, Volume 12394; and "Iran to Purchase Russian Satellite Equipment, Super jet in $21 Bln Deal," *Sputnik International News*, September 26, 2015, also Reuters, September 26, 2015.

25. Says Vattel, in his *The Law of Nations* (1758), "The first general law, which is to be found in the very end of the society of Nations, is that each Nation should contribute as far as it can to the happiness and advancement of other Nations."

26. The INS *Tanin* first sailed under the Israel flag in June 2014, reaching the port of Haifa in September. The expected arrival of a fifth submarine, INS *Rahav*, will allow Israel to continuously maintain at least one submarine at sea, a deployment that should offer conspicuous strategic benefit to Israel's overall nuclear deterrence posture depending in part on any policy relaxations of deliberate nuclear ambiguity. For more specifics on Israel's submarine fleet, see Or Heller, "Peacetime or Wartime: Israel's Long Naval Arm," *Israel Defense*, posted online August 10, 2015.

27. See Heller, *supra* note 26.

28. See Theodore Roethke, *Collected Poems* (1966).

29. See Clausewitz, *On War*, Chapter VI, "Friction in War."

30. See *supra* note 29.

Index

About the Author

Louis René Beres, emeritus professor of political science and international law at Purdue University, has long been involved with issues of Israeli security and nuclear strategy. Educated at Princeton (PhD, 1971), he is the author of many scholarly articles, monographs, and books dealing with core issues of war, peace, and terrorism. The chair of *Project Daniel* (Israel, 2003), Professor Beres has lectured widely at all of Israel's major strategic studies institutes, including the IDF National Security College. His more general writings on world politics and international law have been published in such places as *The New York Times, Chicago Tribune, The Jerusalem Post, Los Angeles Times, Christian Science Monitor, Boston Globe, Washington Times, U.S. News & World Report, The Hill, Oxford University Press Blog,* and *The Atlantic*. Professor Beres was born in Zürich, Switzerland, at the end of World War II, the only son of Austrian Holocaust refugees.

OTHER BOOKS BY THE AUTHOR

America Outside the World: The Collapse of U.S. Foreign Policy (1987)
Security or Armageddon: Israel's Nuclear Strategy (1986)
Reason and Realpolitik: U.S. Foreign Policy and World Order (1984)
Mimicking Sisyphus: America's Countervailing Nuclear Strategy (1983)
People, States and World Order (1981)
Apocalypse: Nuclear Catastrophe in World Politics (1980)
Terrorism and Global Security: The Nuclear Threat (1979, second edition 1987)
Planning Alternative World Futures: Values, Methods, and Models (coauthor, 1975)
Transforming World Politics: The National Roots of World Peace (1975)
Reordering the Planet: Constructing Alternative World Futures (coauthor, 1974)
The Management of World Power: A Theoretical Analysis (1973)